D0462898

TERROR
AND
WONDER

BLAIR KAMIN

THE UNIVERSITY OF CHICAGO PRESS

Chicago and London

TERROR AND WONDER

ARCHITECTURE IN A
TUMULTUOUS AGE

BLAIR KAMIN is the Pulitzer Prize–winning architecture critic of the *Chicago Tribune*. He is the author of the critically acclaimed *Why Architecture Matters: Lessons from Chicago* and *Tribune Tower: American Landmark*.

THE UNIVERSITY OF CHICAGO PRESS, Chicago 60637
THE UNIVERSITY OF CHICAGO PRESS, LTD., London

© 2010 by The University of Chicago
All rights reserved. Published 2010

Printed in the United States of America

18 17 16 15 14 13 12 11 10   2 3 4 5

ISBN-13: 978-0-226-42311-1 (cloth)
ISBN-10: 0-226-42311-5 (cloth)

Library of Congress Cataloging-in-Publication Data

Kamin, Blair.
  Terror and wonder: architecture in a tumultuous age / Blair Kamin.
    p. cm.
  Includes index.
  ISBN-13: 978-0-226-42311-1 (cloth: alk. paper)
  ISBN-10: 0-226-42311-5 (cloth: alk. paper) 1. Architecture—United
States—History—21st century. 2. City planning—United States—History—
21st century. 3. Architecture—Illinois—Chicago—History—21st century. 4.
City planning—Illinois—Chicago—History—21st century. I. Title.
  NA712.7.K36 2010
  724′.7—dc22   2010007665

♾ The paper used in this publication meets the minimum requirements of the American National Standard for Information Sciences—Permanence of Paper for Printed Library Materials, ANSI Z39.48-1992.

TO BARBARA, WILL, AND TEDDY, AND TO MY PARENTS

There can be no separation between our architecture and our culture. Nor any separation of either from our happiness.

FRANK LLOYD WRIGHT

CONTENTS

2 | The Building Boom   55

3 | The Age of Icons   129

5 | A New Era and New Challenges   229

INTRODUCTION

For a journalist, there is no more precious commodity than time. Deadlines once were daily. Now, if you blog, as I do, they bear down almost hourly, permitting even less chance for careful reflection than in the hoary, pre-blogging days of, say, 1999. Against that backdrop of relentless pressure, the opportunity to put together this book was the ultimate luxury, allowing me to collect my thoughts as well as my columns. The exercise has allowed me to look back on an incredible era of striking buildings and cataclysmic events, which are recent enough to remain vivid in the memory but distant enough to be seen with the sort of clarity that daily journalism rarely permits.

Inevitably, I think back to the morning of September 11, 2001, and picture an editor rushing to my desk, where I was already furiously typing a story about the attack on the World Trade Center for an extra edition of the *Chicago Tribune*. When the editor told me that the first of the twin towers had collapsed, the shock was visceral. This was no distant disaster. Growing up in the small town of Fair Haven, New Jersey, I had gazed at the big, glinting boxes of the World Trade Center from the beaches of Sandy Hook, a thin, windswept peninsula whose northern tip is less than 16 miles from Lower Manhattan. From that vantage point, the twin towers had seemed as permanent as the Pyramids. Now one was gone, and the other would soon follow—the first time that iconic skyscrapers had vanished from the sky.

But I can conjure up an equally powerful recollection of the raucous scenes that accompanied the opening of Chicago's Millennium Park on July 16, 2004. On that day, the city's children discovered the twin glass-block towers of the Crown Fountain, where human faces projected on LED screens spewed jets of water on the kids, like modern versions of medieval gargoyles. The picture was sheer delight—an instant piazza. It was as if the joy-inspiring fountain had been created to help dispel the gloom induced by the destruction of the World Trade Center. After the short-lived, post-9/11 phenomenon of "cocooning," in which terrified Americans found sanctuary in their homes, Millennium Park's debut marked a triumphant return to, and restoration of, the public realm.

This book, which assembles 51 of my columns from the *Tribune* and other publications, brings together such stories to accomplish what they cannot do by themselves: to reveal the arc of a tumultuous epoch and to shed fresh light on some of its most significant works of architecture as well as the culture that produced them. How did what we built reflect and affect how we lived? Where did we make superlative art, and where did we scar our cityscapes? Where did we overbuild, and where did we underperform in our role as stewards of the natural and built environments? And, above all, how can a better understanding of this complex and contradictory era help us to avoid repeating its worst mistakes?

The columns examine buildings and public spaces throughout the United States—from New York to Los Angeles, New Orleans to Milwaukee—with a special emphasis on Chicago, the first city of American architecture, and one detour outside the country to the debt-ridden Persian Gulf emirate of Dubai. While the places are almost exclusively American, many of the architectural players and the themes their work raises are global, reflecting the rapid internationalization of the field. In these years, even third-tier American cities imported architectural stars from abroad to design major civic buildings. Conversely, U.S. firms exported their expertise in commercial architecture, particularly the skyscraper, to booming countries like China or city-states like Dubai.

Considered chronologically, the columns are bracketed by two great thunderclaps in the sky—the destruction of the World Trade Center in 2001 and the opening of the Burj Khalifa, the world's tallest building, which rose a staggering half mile above Dubai's desert floor, in 2010. As the columns reveal, this was an era of extreme oscillation—between artistic triumph and urban disaster, teeming public spaces and repressive security measures, frugal energy-saving architecture and giddy design excess, luxury-laced McMansions and impoverished public works, great expectations for rebuilding and painfully unrealized hopes. It was a Dickensian construction zone, a time of terror and wonder, with a seemingly endless capacity to shock and surprise. And buildings were central to its narrative.

In these years, in addition to the stunning vertical plunge of the twin towers, the nation witnessed the sickening horizontal tableau of nearly an entire American city, New Orleans, under water. In response to the terrorist attacks, a new security apparatus encroached upon the mobility embodied by America's airports and the ability of its government buildings to serve as vibrant centers of community. A housing bubble grew bigger and bigger until it inevitably burst, helping bring down the economy and leaving dreams for grandiose skyscrapers, such as Santiago Calatrava's twisting Chicago Spire, as nothing more than holes in the ground.

And yet, not everything in these years ended in disarray. In addition to the exuberant landscape of Millennium Park, an extraordinary collection of cultural buildings by such architects as Frank Gehry and Renzo Piano provided new focal points for urban life. The push for an energy-saving "green architecture" moved from the fringes of American society to the mainstream, where it promised not only to reduce global warming but also to create more humane environments inside homes and workplaces. And with Barack Obama's election to the presidency, that clumsy word "infrastructure" moved decisively into the public conversation, as the nation finally began to redress its shameful lack of attention to the unheralded but essential networks of transportation, water, and power that undergird all of modern life.

Ludwig Mies van der Rohe, Chicago's master of steel-and-glass modernism, once declared, "Architecture is the will of an epoch translated into space." Yet even this cursory review of events suggests that there was no single direction to this epoch, but a series of cross-currents and counter-revolutions pulling in different directions at once. Nor was there any consensus on the right path for architects to take. Indeed, architectural culture, with its bitter divisions between aesthetic radicals and traditionalists ("the rads and the trads," as Robert Campbell, my colleague at the *Boston Globe*, cheekily calls them), was as deeply polarized as the broader culture, with its split between red-state and blue-state America.

There were, however, broad themes that characterized this period, and they provide the organization for this book. Its five parts discuss, respectively, the state of cities in the aftermath of the 9/11 and Hurricane Katrina disasters; the fevered residential and commercial building boom; the equally frenzied construction of iconic cultural and campus buildings; the changing face of historic preservation and the rise of green architecture; and the beginnings of a new era, crystallized by Obama's election, in which fresh ideas about infrastructure and other long-ignored issues came to the fore. Brief introductions situate the parts within the book's overall framework, and postscripts follow many of the columns. I have edited the columns, shortening and sharpening them, but I have changed none of the opinions. Architecture criticism, like architecture, is an act of construction. Arranging the columns—seeing where they unexpectedly snapped together like the pieces of jigsaw puzzle—has been a process of discovery.

One of the most fascinating parts of the story is what *didn't* happen after September 11, both to the culture at large and to architecture in particular. After the shock of 9/11, opinion leaders such as *Vanity Fair* editor Graydon Carter and *Time* magazine's Roger Rosenblatt portentously declared "the end of irony." Soon after, Carter backtracked and said (ironically) that he actually had been talking about "the end of ironing." Just as irony declined to die, so the skyscraper did not succumb to the terrorist threat, as some real estate developers and architecture critics had predicted it would. Instead, as the fear from the attacks ebbed and an unfounded exuberance took hold, the world experienced the greatest skyscraper building boom in history, with more towers rising to a greater height, in a wider variety of places, and with greater formal invention, than ever before.

But there was also something called the "new normalcy," and it was plainly—and painfully—evident in the security lines choking airports and in the ugly Jersey barriers that popped up in front of everything from Sears (now Willis) Tower in Chicago to the Lincoln Memorial in Washington, DC. Even the managers of the Rookery, the muscular Burnham & Root office building on Chicago's LaSalle Street, shut its gossamer-light atrium to tourists, as if an 11-story, brownstone-covered landmark was actually going to be on Al-Qaeda's hit list.

Why this overreaction? It had to do, in retrospect, with a central theme of the era: spectacle. The dictionary defines *spectacle* as a dazzling display, something remarkable to be seen or viewed. In a fiendish, twisted way, the terrorist attacks of 9/11 fit this definition precisely. They were emblems of spectacular destruction. By toppling iconic buildings—totemic symbols of American financial might and technological prowess—the terrorists succeeded in instilling deep-seated fears and destabilizing everyday life. A response was clearly needed, given the threat to the national security that the attacks posted, but the ensuing reaction was overwrought, adding self-inflicted damage to the devastation already wreaked by the terrorists. It came in a new wave of fortress architecture that disfigured public spaces, transportation hubs, and government buildings—and promised to mar the very skyscraper, the Freedom Tower (now called 1 World Trade Center), that was rising in place of the destroyed twin towers.

The new museums of these years more easily fit the conventional definition of spectacle. They were like fireworks blazing across the sky, fully intent upon knocking your eyes out. Calatrava's crowd-pleasing addition to the Milwaukee Art Museum, which flaunted a 217-foot-wide sunshade that unfurled like the wings of a giant bird, exemplified the type. This was architecture as entertainment, an urban event. Enabled by the latest computer technology, as well as advances in materials and construction methods, the spectacle buildings burst the traditional, rectilinear boundaries of architecture to make aesthetic statements that were more baroque than classical—and, above all, distinctly personal rather than anonymous. As if to underscore this phenomenon, Milwaukeeans referred to the museum addition as simply "The Calatrava."

As the world became more generic, with stores and banks in one city resembling stores and banks in every other city, the spectacle buildings were increasingly what distinguished cities from one another. At best, as in Gehry's Walt Disney Concert Hall in Los Angeles, they uplifted their environs and created interiors that were stirring expressions of democracy. Far less satisfying were designs like Daniel Libeskind's addition to the Denver Art Museum, a striking but self-indulgent structure that elevated form over function.

However they turned out, spectacular or subtle, far too many of these cultural buildings saddled their institutions with financial burdens that proved difficult to bear. Some proved unable to replicate the tourist-magnet magic of Gehry's 1997 Guggenheim Museum in Bilbao, Spain, and its so-called Bilbao effect. A little-noticed pattern repeated after architecture critics cheered each building's opening and then departed for the next extravaganza: attendance and revenues didn't match projections, and once the recession dramatically reduced the value of endowments, the sponsors of the new edifices were forced to lay off staff and cut hours as well as operating expenses. At Steven Holl's partly underground addition to the Nelson-Atkins Museum of Art in Kansas City, cost-cutting literally meant dimming the beauty of the addition's proudest feature—the glass pavilions, or lenses, that drew daylight into the galleries and shone like jewels at night—for 14 hours per week. If you built it, they didn't necessarily come.

This pattern of expansion and retrenchment was part of the much-noted phenomenon of overbuilding, symbolized by the foreclosure signs tacked onto exurban starter homes. Yet such excess was also evident in the nation's frozen-in-place skylines, most notably Chicago's. In the summer of 2007, when the stock market soared to new peaks, Chicago's builders were poised to do the same, with three mega-towers—the 2,000-foot-tall Chicago Spire, the 1,361-foot Trump International Hotel & Tower, and the 1,047-foot Waterview Tower—under construction simultaneously. A little more than a year later, amid the stock market collapse and the credit crunch, work on the Spire stopped and the building of the Waterview Tower halted at its 26th story, leaving its hulking concrete frame looming over the Chicago River. Only the Trump Tower reached completion, and it was no financial home run, with roughly of a third of the skyscraper, including its 14,260-square-foot, $30 million penthouse, empty upon opening.

The saga of the three mega-towers hints at the vast extent of the building boom and its double-edged impact on cityscapes nationwide. In the 10 years ending in 2008, Chicago's developers completed or started construction on nearly 200 high-rises—more than twice as many as in all of nearby Milwaukee. True, those high-rises created a healthy urban density, allowing more people to walk to jobs and shops. Yet far too many of them were stark slabs plopped atop blank-walled parking-garage podiums. For all the media buzz about star architects turning out "starchitect condos," the Chicago boom was, in reality, a two-track production line, in which top talents created rare successes, such as Jeanne Gang's marvelously curvaceous Aqua tower, while hacks cranked out pervasive architectural junk.

Even the tiny branch banks that financed the housing bubble were eyesores. And the boom wrought new forms of destruction on old buildings, from the demolition of mid-20th-century modernist landmarks to the "facade-ectomies" that saved nothing more than thin pieces of historic structures, like a slice of prosciutto. In London's St. Paul's Church, the epitaph for Sir Christopher Wren famously reads: "Si Monumentum Requiris, Circumspice"—"If you would seek his monument, look around you." In the post-crash America of 2010, our architectural and urban planning mistakes are all around us.

At the same time, beneath the surface of the glitter and the visual dreck, a countervailing force was gathering—a new push for *sustainability*, a word that once simply meant "capable of being sustained," but increasingly took on ecological overtones. Rooted in concern that buildings account for almost half of the greenhouse gases in the United States, the new sustainable, or green, architecture made a startling ascent. At the beginning of the decade, it was rare for architects to concern themselves with energy efficiency and environmentally friendly building materials. By the end of these years, such attentiveness to architecture's environmental consequences, while by no means universal, was happening more and more. In an unmistakable sign of green design's growing popular appeal, crafty developers flaunted their buildings' sustainable credentials as a marketing tool while in some cases environmental awareness devolved into "green sheen." My favorite example: the planted roof of a showcase McDonald's in Chicago. Putting some shrubs and grass atop such a symbol of the energy-wasting car culture was like slapping a piece of lettuce on a bacon double cheese-burger and calling it healthy.

In contrast to the spectacle buildings, which bore the branded looks of individual stars, the movement for sustainability was by its very nature a collective enterprise, focused on the environment as a whole rather than stand-alone architectural objects. Its proponents dwelled less on architec-tural form than building performance, deemphasizing the architectural dazzle of today in favor of saving the planet for tomorrow.

In the broadest sense, sustainability was not simply about being green, but about reasserting values that were missing or overlooked during the boom years—practicality rather than profligacy, modesty rather than van-ity, humility rather than hubris, enduring quality rather than evanescent bling. The infrastructure portion of Obama's $787 billion stimulus pack-age, which funded the weatherization of modest-income homes and rehabs that made federal buildings more energy efficient, reflected and began to restore those values. Yet, unexpectedly, so did a building like Gang's Aqua, which wasn't simply alluring because of its spectacularly undulating bal-conies. It was beautiful because it put 738 apartments and condominiums within minutes of workplaces, shops, and entertainment, reducing their residents' reliance on energy-wasting driving. In architecture, as in life, true beauty is more than skin-deep.

My aim, as such examples are intended to suggest, is not to construct this story as a two-dimensional morality play, in which "spectacle" is bad and "sustainable" is good. There is no simple formula for architectural creativity or building vibrant cities. An iconic building can be sustainable just as a sustainable building can be an eyesore. It is even possible for architects to make a spectacle of sustainability, transforming energy-saving features into over-the-top, formal flourishes. What counts in the end are not good intentions but good buildings. The current intellectual fashion, which has critics lumping together the masterpieces and the mediocrities of these years under the facile rubric of "The Decade of Excess," will, I suspect, prove as shortsighted as the attempts to dismiss the art deco architecture of the 1920s after the stock market crash of 1929 and the Great Depression. Art endures. And so does architectural quality; the char-acter of the work matters more than foibles of the era that produced it. The point is not to rid the world of spectacle buildings; the point is that cities and urban regions based on spectacle alone cannot sustain themselves. A new century and new circumstances demand a new architectural ethic, one that brings the opposing approaches of spectacle and sustainability into better balance.

The ultimate issue is not technical or even aesthetic but cultural. It's about how we live, not how many British thermal units a new green building saves or how many people pour through the doors of an eye-popping new museum. We are what we build. We build what we are. After a wild spree of overbuilding, and the shocks of disasters, wars, and economic collapse, the end of this tumultuous decade brought an opportunity to gaze back with keen-eyed clarity at the glories we left behind as well as our all-too-abundant failures. Amid the ugliness and the excess were gems that promised to light the way down a brighter path.

1 | THE
URBAN
DRAMA

THE MOST UNFORGETTABLE AND CONSEQUENTIAL ARCHITECTURAL STORIES OF the first decade of the 21st century were not about great feats of construction; they were about spectacular acts of destruction, both natural and man-made. The terrorist attack on the World Trade Center and the devastation wrought by Hurricane Katrina both played out on urban stages and in real time, riveting and unsettling the millions who watched them. This confluence of disasters reset the American agenda, turning the nation's gaze, if only fleetingly, toward its cities.

Before September 11, 2001, urban development concerns had taken a backseat to public fascination with the eye-popping, neo-baroque creations of such architects as Frank Gehry. But 9/11 and Katrina thrust the gritty field of city planning into America's public conversation: What should replace the tangled ruins at ground zero? Should New Orleans be abandoned or rebuilt? How should America implement the "new normalcy" of heightened security? When and how might Americans begin to reclaim their cities?

Amid the shock of disaster, the first task was to articulate the physical and emotional landscape of the moment—and what it portended for the future.

DISASTER

Raising Up a Fallen Sky

THE BEST WAY TO FILL THE CHILLING VOID IN THE LOWER
MANHATTAN SKYLINE IS WITH A GREAT NEW URBAN CENTER,
NOT A REPRODUCTION OF THE DESTROYED TWIN TOWERS

SEPTEMBER 17, 2001

Imagine if Sears Tower were suddenly, wrenchingly obliterated from the
Chicago skyline and there was nothing but blue sky where an enormous
black mass of steel and glass once stood. Then you have some idea of what
the astonishing disappearance of the World Trade Center means to the
New York skyline—and to the American mind.

In truth, almost no one loved the twin towers as they loved the Empire
State and Chrysler Buildings, the great art deco skyscrapers that exemplify New York's special brand of exuberance and arrogance. Even with the
failed flourish of their modern Gothic arches, the twin towers were bland
rather than bold, almost mute despite their chest-thumping height. Their
scale-less gigantism overwhelmed the grand collection of Lower Manhattan spires that once dazzled the eyes of huddled masses yearning to be
free.

But the towers were undeniably landmarks in the most basic sense of
that overused but under-considered word. They marked the land. The
shiny square boxes with the slice of sky in between compelled our glance

as massive minimalist sculptures, neither beautiful nor stirring, but fixed points on the map that were impossible to ignore. They gave us our bearings, a way to orient ourselves. By sheer virtue of their enormous size, they lent coherence to the chaos of modern life. So it seems all the more jarring that they should succumb to that very chaos.

One-hundred-ten-story high-rises are not supposed to turn into pillars of dust and ash, pancaking downward with apocalyptic fury. Yet that is precisely what happened last Tuesday after hijacked jetliners slammed into the towers at 8:45 a.m. and 9:03 a.m., shattering the illusion of permanence once conjured by these man-made monoliths.

When the towers were completed in 1972 and 1973, it was painful to contemplate Lower Manhattan's skyline with them. Today that same skyline seems incomplete—and incomprehensible—without them. The sky where they once stood looks hauntingly empty, a void where just a week ago, tens of thousands of people traded bonds, managed money, wrote law briefs and insurance policies. The absence of the towers speaks louder than their presence ever did.

It would be disturbing enough if an earthquake had caused last week's damage and its thousands of deaths. Yet the fact that the calamity was planned and perpetrated by human beings makes it even more unsettling. Earthquakes can only happen in certain parts of the world. This nightmare could happen anywhere there is a very tall building that symbolizes the global reach of American capitalism—and a jet, filled with fuel, that can stoke an inferno able to melt a skyscraper's structural steel and cause it to collapse.

Now some zealots argue that the best course is to rebuild the twin towers exactly as they were before the attacks to show that Americans have not been intimidated. Others make the case that the World Trade Center site should be exclusively devoted to a memorial, like the tribute in downtown Oklahoma City to the victims of the 1995 terrorist attack on the federal building there. The film critic Roger Ebert even has suggested a grassy public space, perhaps including a cornfield, where two towers of more than 1,360 feet each once rose.

None of these ideas merits a thumbs-up.

Downtown Manhattan is not downtown Oklahoma City. It is, and is almost sure to remain, the world's financial capital. Setting aside a huge plot of land solely for a memorial would permanently disrupt the flow of commerce, aggravating the damage the terrorists already have done. Ebert's dreamy suggestion of a cornfield might work in a Hollywood screenplay,

THE RUINS OF THE WORLD TRADE CENTER
Confronting the unthinkable—and the charged issue of rebuilding.

but it is sure to be a non-starter in the capital of capitalism. And it seems even more unrealistic now that Larry Silverstein, the developer who leads the group that purchased the Trade Center's 99-year lease in 1999, has signaled he is committed to rebuilding the complex.

Americans have always mixed down-to-earth practicality with the lofty idealism associated with the Puritans' desire to raise a shining city on a hill. So they should treat this site by marrying the pragmatic and the poetic: build new office towers that include a major memorial in the public plaza that surely will be placed between them. There is no need to mindlessly replicate the original twin towers. Why do that? The World Trade Center's design was terrible to begin with.

It would be far wiser to erect a new commercial center, at once less gigantic than the old one and more in keeping with the Lower Manhattan skyline. That does not mean a cluster of buildings that would literally reproduce the classic skyscrapers of the 1920s. It does mean creatively reinterpreting those forms, using the latest technologies and the latest theories of how we can make cities lively.

Amid the deep gloom of this tragedy, it is hard to remember that the core of the American character is soaringly optimistic. A new commercial and civic complex, which vigorously demonstrates that this spirit lives on, would be the most meaningful new landmark—and the best way to fill the skyline void that is among the attack's most chilling legacies.

POSTSCRIPT

In the supercharged days after 9/11, when the air was thick with fear, some real estate developers wondered whether builders would ever again commission extremely tall towers—and whether city governments would approve them. "Never before has a world's tallest building been viewed as a liability. And now it is," said Chicago developer J. Paul Beitler, who once tried unsuccessfully to build a record-shattering skyscraper, the Miglin-Beitler Skyneedle, in Chicago's Loop. "Instead of being icons representing man's finest hour and business's highest achievement, they are now being viewed as targets in fanatics' gun sights."

After the crisis passed, however, the world went on a skyscraper-building binge, with China and Dubai leading the way. Upon its completion in 2010, the Burj Khalifa skyscraper (see p. 122) rose to an unprecedented height of 2,717 feet— more than half a mile high, or taller than one of the World Trade Center towers stacked on top of the other. Americans also returned to the sky, a shift symbolized by the 2009 reopening of the crown in the Statue of Liberty, which the authorities closed after the attacks. The tall building, in other words, proved far more resilient than the doomsayers had forecast.

The redevelopment of what soon became known as ground zero would prove far more challenging. That became clear in 2002 when the Lower Manhattan Development Corporation unveiled six mediocre redevelopment proposals for the 16-acre site. All included a memorial as well as office and retail space, yet none rose to the level of creativity the occasion demanded. "Six cookie-cutter losers," the Wall Street Journal'*s architecture critic, Ada Louise Huxtable, branded them. Only in December of 2002 would Daniel Libeskind's captivating ground zero plan emerge (see p. 32), creating a brief moment of promise.*

Don't Abandon New Orleans

THE BIG EASY, AN AMERICAN MASTERPIECE, DESERVES TO
BE SAVED; ITS REBUILDING SHOULD STRESS SUBSTANCE
OVER SHOW

SEPTEMBER 14, 2005

Four words describe the New Orleans that has been socked by Hurricane Katrina: disaster, yes; apocalypse, no.

The horizontal tableau of entire neighborhoods swamped beneath stinking, sewage-infested waters is as stunning as the vertical drama of the collapsing twin towers in New York. Big cities are symbols of human achievement. We do not expect them to be humbled by nature and evacuated any more than we expected terrorists to fly jets into skyscrapers.

But the relentless focus of the media eye on New Orleans' sunken districts and the unprecedented dispersal of its residents obscure the bigger picture: the real issue is not whether to rebuild the Big Easy, but how.

Cities are collective works of art, and New Orleans is one of America's masterpieces—a delectable multicultural gumbo whose value is only more pronounced in a nation where the same stores, banks, and malls make every place feel like every other place.

For that reason alone, the much-hyped "should we rebuild New Orleans?" debate is preposterous. Of course we should save New Orleans. To abandon it would be like Italy abandoning Venice. Besides, anybody who sets foot in this town knows that the great (and not-so-great) symbols of New Orleans don't need to be rebuilt. They're still there.

You could hold a Mardi Gras parade tomorrow in the bone-dry French Quarter. The modern office towers and hotels of the central business district, graceless though they are, remain standing, poised to resume their role as hubs of commerce. Some of the city's extraordinary neighborhoods,

THE BYWATER DISTRICT OF NEW ORLEANS
A devastating flood that revealed gaping holes in America's infrastructure.

such as the Garden District and its white-columned antebellum mansions, came through the storm with little more than downed trees.

There is a difference, the surviving structures make clear, between mass evacuation and mass destruction.

Yet the debate about the future of the city's heavily flooded areas is real, prompted in part by the remarks of House Speaker J. Dennis Hastert (R-IL), who generated a brief controversy when he seemed to question whether they should be rebuilt. Hastert quickly said his remarks had been twisted, a wise move.

You don't simply discard cities that are plagued with deadly infrastructure problems. You solve those problems, as Chicago did in 1900 when it reversed the flow of the Chicago River and prevented a recurrence of the typhoid and cholera epidemics that had plagued the city.

It is already a cliché to say that the flood gives New Orleans a chance to turn disaster into opportunity and to transform itself into a truly 21st-century city. But the most progressive rebuilding plan of all may be based on a new interpretation of an old idea: building with respect for nature rather than arrogantly dismissing it.

To venture into the emptied city is to experience the strange sensation of enjoying its extraordinary collection of everyday buildings while the people who once lived and worked there are gone. It is a stage set without actors, shrouded in an eerie blanket of quiet that is interrupted only by the *chop-chop* of military helicopters, the roar of Humvees, and the pitiful barking of abandoned dogs swimming through germ-filled waters.

At Pete Fountain's Club in the French Quarter, there is no Dixieland clarinet music wafting out onto Bourbon Street. But the two-story red-brick building and its lacy black-iron railings appear to be in good condition. The same is true throughout the Quarter, which is simply the most prominent example of New Orleans' polyglot architecture. The French, who founded New Orleans in 1718, laid out the district. Then it was rebuilt by the Spanish, who took over in 1763 and put up all that fancy ironwork.

To walk the Quarter is to freshly appreciate how New Orleans prizes oldness in a way that Chicago values newness, and how its architecture is as sensual and playful as Chicago's is beautifully austere. Like San Francisco, New Orleans is not a city of great individual buildings, but a place that derives its charm from harmonious groups of buildings—*le tout ensemble*, as the French call it. And the buildings are real. The city is no theme park.

New Orleans has a higher percentage of its neighborhoods honored by inclusion on the National Register of Historic Places than any other major city in America. Some of these historic districts clearly have fared better than others, with those on the relatively high ground near the Mississippi River typically enduring far less flood damage than those in the middle of the bowl-shaped city.

Take the Garden District, which begins southwest of downtown and is as distinctly American as the French Quarter is European. Here, in the 19th century, hustling entrepreneurs built monuments to their success, with the mansions ranging in style from understated Greek revival to over-the-top Victorian.

Today the Garden District looks disheveled but not devastated. Katrina walloped some big trees, which are piled up in the boulevard where the streetcar runs. But the buildings along the street—houses, churches, synagogues, and businesses—seem to have suffered no major damage.

In other historic neighborhoods, such as Gentilly Terrace, home to early 20th-century craftsman bungalows and colonial revival homes, the picture is the one you've seen on TV: Homes remain trapped in floodwaters that reek of sewage. A slick of oil runs atop the water's surface. It's hard to imagine these homes escaping a date with the bulldozer.

"Once they've been in water a few days, it's impossible to save a house," acknowledged Patricia Gay, executive director of the Preservation Resource Center of New Orleans, a citywide nonprofit preservation advocacy group.

DIFFERENT METHODS, DIFFERENT OUTCOMES

About 80 percent of New Orleans was flooded, so it would be easy to conclude that 80 percent of the city will have to be razed. In reality, the floodwaters rose to different heights in different areas, and some houses were far better equipped to defend themselves than others.

In the post–World War II subdivision of Gentilly Woods, where the one-story tract homes on concrete slabs look like something out of northwest suburban Cook County, the floodwaters could race right in. But in the Carrollton area near the Garden District, where homes were built the old-fashioned way, with raised living areas and crawl spaces beneath, the houses were able to ride above floodwaters that reached three to four feet high, judging by the water lines on some buildings.

The contrast between the prewar and postwar neighborhoods is revealing: time moved forward, but building practices went backward. Postwar builders of subdivisions such as Gentilly Woods undoubtedly advertised their homes as the latest in modern conveniences. But Katrina revealed just how primitive they really are.

How should New Orleans be rebuilt, then? Job one should be to give priority to substance over show. It would be folly for the city's leaders to concentrate their efforts on flashy symbolic events, like holding a scaled-down Mardi Gras, rather than nuts-and-bolts matters such as building better neighborhoods and infrastructure.

New Orleans should strictly enforce its building codes, ensuring that new homes sit higher above the street than the ones they replace. The federal government should bankroll the rebuilding of the eroded coastal marshes and barrier islands that would act as shock absorbers against the jolt of future hurricanes. Without such defenses—and the construction of massive floodgates that would provide another line of defense against hurricane-spawned storm surges—New Orleans will be defenseless.

Looking at the side-by-side pictures of New Orleans—extraordinary devastation paired with miraculous survival—and considering the special place that New Orleans holds among America's cities, it is hard to take seriously the arguments of those who say that spending billions of federal dollars to rebuild the city would be throwing good money after bad. To do so would be the ultimate anti-urban snub—a loss for New Orleans but, more importantly, a loss for the nation.

This is not the time to tell New Orleans to drop dead.

POSTSCRIPT

On September 15, 2005, President George W. Bush called for rebuilding the Gulf Coast region, an area that also encompassed the hurricane-devastated Mississippi coastline. "There is no way to imagine America without New Orleans, and this great city will rise again," the president said, speaking before the brightly lit backdrop of St. Louis Cathedral in the French Quarter. By 2009, the U.S. Census Bureau reported, New Orleans' population had rebounded to 312,000, or 65 percent of its pre-storm total of 484,674. Among those returning to the city were Lower Ninth Ward residents living in single-family homes commissioned by actor Brad Pitt and designed by internationally renowned architects. Pitt optimistically called his post-Katrina rebuilding project "Make It Right."

But making all of New Orleans right turned out to be far more difficult. Some neighborhoods appeared little changed on the flood's fourth anniversary. "Much of the Lower Ninth Ward, with its concrete slabs and grassy lots, still looks like an oversize graveyard," the New York Times *reported. Even recovering neighborhoods were beset with problems. Lax enforcement of the city's building code produced an incoherent cityscape, in which old houses on slabs sat alongside new ones whose first floors were lifted 10 feet in the air. With the federal government pumping billions of dollars into the city, the Army Corps of Engineers made substantial progress bolstering levees. But some expressed concern that the continuing disappearance of Louisiana's coastal wetlands would render even the most heavily fortified levee system deficient. As Loren C. Scott, a professor emeritus of economics at Louisiana State University, told the* Times, *"It's going to take another hurricane to hit the area to demonstrate the levees will hold."*

SECURITY

ONCE THE SHOCK OF THE TWO DISASTERS HAD PASSED, THE NATION WAS LEFT TO grapple with the longer-term consequences of these events on its people and its buildings. The terrorist attacks of 2001, in particular, had repercussions for the country as a whole, forcing a culture that had long prized open public spaces and freedom of movement to come to terms with daunting new demands for security. This shift immediately made itself felt on the streets of Chicago.

Land of the Sort-of Free

IN A NERVOUS CITY, PLACES LIKE THE FEDERAL PLAZA RUN
SCARED, WHILE THE DALEY PLAZA HANGS TOUGH

OCTOBER 29, 2001

A new peril has arisen after the September 11 terrorist attacks, yet it is not a threat from the outside, as were the fanatics who hijacked planes and slammed them into the World Trade Center and the Pentagon. It is a threat from within, the danger that Americans will overreact to the destruction of the twin towers by barricading public spaces that form centers of community and symbolize American openness and optimism.

CHICAGO'S FEDERAL PLAZA
Where temporary barriers signaled the chilling effect of "the new normalcy."

A walk through downtown Chicago shows that this danger is real. Concrete "Jersey barriers" protect the three giants of the skyline—Sears Tower, the Aon Center (the former Amoco Building), and the John Hancock Center. Those barriers, ugly and forbidding, also guard the perimeter of the Chicago Federal Center and its once-vibrant outdoor plaza.

The new defensiveness does not stop there. Passageways through private buildings that used to be open to the public, like the one linking the Chicago Board of Trade Building and its neighboring 1980 addition, have been sealed off against unwanted intrusions. Even atrium lobbies that for years welcomed architectural tour groups, like the one inside the landmark Rookery Building, are shunning visitors on the questionable grounds that the buildings must be secured.

A rare exception to the new architecture of fear is the Richard J. Daley Center Plaza. There, beneath the inscrutable gaze of the Picasso sculpture, crowds mill around, drinking warm apple cider, watching jugglers and gymnasts, and walking through the temporary haunted house that celebrates Halloween.

The stark contrast between the Daley Center and the other buildings raises questions that transcend Chicago: Are Americans being prepared or paranoid? Why are some public spaces eerily quiet while others are bustling visions of normalcy? And just what is normal, anyway, after September 11?

City officials who work with Mayor Richard M. Daley are studying these questions and plan to issue design standards for security measures in no more than six months. The officials already are concerned by requests from the owners of smaller skyscrapers who want to erect even more anti-terrorist barriers in front of their buildings. "There is a hope that some of this will pass," one official said.

This is more than a beautification issue. At stake are the costs, both hard and soft, that Americans must pay for fighting terrorism. Those costs are measured not just in the salaries of the police officers and security guards who patrol the perimeters of skyscrapers. They also are calculated in more abstract ways, like the loss of the freedom of movement that is an integral part of the American way of life.

Yet due to the ill-defined nature of the undeclared war on terrorism, the issue is complex. In this war, there is not likely to be a V-E Day or V-J Day, some clearly demarcated time of celebration in which America lets down its guard and gets back to normal. Indeed, some building managers, like TrizecHahn Properties, which runs Sears Tower, assert that the nation has entered a new stage of history and that they must take permanent steps to protect their investment and their tenants.

"I don't think the threats have multiplied, but the awareness of the threats has multiplied. That will affect design," said Carol Ross Barney, the Chicago architect who shaped the low-rise office building that will replace the destroyed Alfred P. Murrah Federal Building in Oklahoma City.

No single place better illustrates these tensions than the Chicago Federal Center, the Ludwig Mies van der Rohe–designed downtown complex that includes the black steel-and-glass towers of the Dirksen courtroom building and the Kluczynski federal office building.

A NATIONAL MODEL

After the 1995 attack on the Murrah Building, the Federal Center's plaza was a national model for balancing security and openness. Discreet measures were taken to beef up security, like locking some doors around the perimeter of the high-rises to control public access. But the complex's modern architecture stayed undefiled while its airy plaza, punctuated by Alexander Calder's bright red *Flamingo* stabile, remained open, even hosting farmers' markets on Tuesdays.

All that changed on September 11, a Tuesday, when the farmers' market was shut down by midafternoon because trucks delivering produce to the farmers were thought to pose a security threat. Within days the concrete barriers were erected, and the plaza took on a whole new character—people could still walk through it, passing through small openings in the barriers, but it seemed hauntingly empty.

Federal officials defend the decision to erect the barriers, saying that after the Oklahoma City bombing, law enforcement agencies like the FBI, which has offices in the Dirksen building, were thought to be prime terrorist targets. But, the officials acknowledge, the barriers went up in part to calm those inside the building, including judges anxiously protecting themselves and their staffs.

"This is a psychological thing," said one official. "[The barriers] make people feel better—some people. You have other people saying, 'They are the ugliest things I've ever seen, and I don't think they would stop my son-in-law in his jalopy.'"

SOOTHING TENANTS

A desire to soothe jittery tenants appears to have played a part in the decision to erect concrete barriers on the Randolph Street side of the Aon Center. That flank of the skyscraper already is defended from a car or truck bomb by a moat-like plaza and big flights of stone steps. In contrast, while

CHICAGO'S DALEY PLAZA
Striking a better balance between security and openness.

the north and south flanks of the John Hancock Center are lined with Jersey barriers, the skyscraper's Michigan Avenue facade remains barrier-free, protected by its own sunken plaza.

Elsewhere, property managers are using the terrorist threat as a pretext to eliminate access to spaces within historic buildings that have long been open to the public. A case in point: the Rookery's two-story light court, a birdcage of an atrium that feels as weightless as feathers in contrast to the building's muscular masonry facade.

For decades, architecture tour groups have walked in to admire the space, which was originally designed by Daniel Burnham and John Wellborn Root and later remodeled by Frank Lloyd Wright. Now the light court is being treated as though it were on Al-Qaeda's hit list. Tenants "have expressed concern because there are visitors in the building," said Jeannine Rio, assistant general manager at Clarion Realty Services, which manages the building.

It is understandable that real estate firms would take such precautions, particularly after federal officials warned two weeks ago that more terrorist attacks were imminent. But surely there is a difference between iconic buildings like the Chicago Board of Trade or Sears Tower, where tight security measures seem prudent, and a modest 19th-century structure like the Rookery, where those same measures seem overbearing. One has to wonder if certain building managers are protecting those in their structures—or merely themselves—if something goes wrong.

City officials will need to draw the line against such unnecessary measures, if only to prevent sidewalks from turning into a gauntlet of Jersey barriers. When one building has barriers in front of it, those in charge of another building may feel they have no choice but to have barriers too, a phenomenon that former senator Daniel Moynihan of New York, an outspoken opponent of fortress architecture, once termed "the iron law of emulation."

Fortunately, the city seems to be on the right course, judging by the way it has handled Daley Plaza. Wanting to avoid the forbidding impression conveyed by the Federal Plaza barriers, city officials opted instead after September 11 to move granite benches from the center of the plaza to its perimeter, where they guard against vehicle-delivered bombs. Attractive drum-shaped metal planters also were deployed on the plaza's flanks.

HALLOWEEN GOES ON

Typically, the presence of people draws more people to public spaces, making everyone feel safer. And so it is here. Anyone crossing the plaza is likely to feel comforted by the way its seasonal rituals, like the Halloween festival, are going on despite the threat of terrorist violence.

"We are not going to eradicate Halloween," said Eileen Carey, who heads the Public Building Commission, the agency that manages the plaza. "The day that the Halloween display comes down, the Christmas tree will start going up."

To be sure, the federal government is more likely than the city government to be the target of terrorist attacks during this war. But what the city government has so far done at the plaza sets an admirable example, both for other government agencies and for skittish people in the private sector. Here is one way to balance security and openness and to keep those competing interests—and our fears—in proper perspective.

POSTSCRIPT

The temporary security barriers installed in downtown Chicago after the September 11 attacks eventually came down. Some access restrictions eased. At the Rookery, for example, tour groups were allowed into the first floor of the building's light court, though they were still not permitted to enjoy the second-floor overlook.

Nonetheless, the crisis left a permanent mark. At the Hyatt Center office building,
which opened in 2005, pedestrians were not allowed to walk through the main
lobby. It was open only to tenants and their guests. Other commercial buildings,
new and old, heightened lobby security and shut down secondary entrances. While
these steps were not ideal, Chicago was a paragon of openness and common sense
in contrast to Washington, DC. There, new perimeter defenses rose around in-
numerable government buildings, blighting—and deadening—the public realm.

Fort Washington

FROM THE HEARTLAND TO THE CAPITAL, FEDERAL BUILDINGS
PUT ON THE ARMOR OF A NATION UNDER SIEGE

SEPTEMBER 10, 2006

They are ruining Washington, ruining it in the name of saving it.

Five years after the September 11 terrorist attacks, this once-lovely city
of broad diagonal avenues and open vistas is becoming an ever more mili-
tarized zone that illustrates the profound tension convulsing government
buildings throughout the nation. Disturbing long-established patterns of
everyday life in cities big and small, that tension is between security and
openness, the imperative to fortify and the desire to beautify.

And in this struggle between armor and aesthetics, armor is invariably
emerging the victor, marring public buildings and public spaces that symbolize the ideals of democracy and help hold together a diverse, often-
fractious society.

The two-block stretch of Pennsylvania Avenue in front of the White
House, which then-president Bill Clinton closed to traffic after the Oklahoma City bombing in 1995, has been transformed into a bland pedestrian
mall. The sidewalks of the Federal Triangle, that lordly wedge of classical
office buildings between the Capitol and the White House, are cluttered by
an ever-expanding assortment of protective posts and planter pots. Even
rare success stories, like the revamped grounds of the Washington Monument, have been marred by the new demands of security.

To visit Washington now is to realize that America has entered a new
and troubling phase, in which various arms of the federal government have
started replacing the clumsy, temporary security measures installed in the
aftermath of Oklahoma City and September 11 with permanent ones.

Yet these new designs, while less obviously ugly than their makeshift
predecessors, are visually monotonous, functionally one-dimensional, in-

THE TREASURY DEPARTMENT BUILDING
A stark symbol of the high price America pays for security.

sensitive to treasured landscapes, and debilitating to city life. And they are costing taxpayers big-time, not only due to the barriers set outside federal buildings but also because of the beefed-up structures of the buildings themselves.

AMERICA THE BESIEGED

Since a yellow Ryder truck driven by Timothy McVeigh exploded outside the Alfred P. Murrah Federal Building in Oklahoma City 11 years ago, killing 168 people and injuring 850, the federal government has spent at least $1.2 billion on protection against vehicle-delivered bombs, according to *Security Planning and Design*, a 2004 primer developed by the American Institute of Architects.

Officials at the General Services Administration—the federal agency that erects, manages, and leases federal buildings in 500 cities nationwide—declined to comment on that figure. But David Winstead, the GSA's commissioner of public buildings service, acknowledged that the cost of surrounding one city block with bollards and other perimeter security measures is about $1 million. A single bollard, consisting of a high-strength post secured in a concrete foundation, costs $5,000 to $8,000, according to interviews with designers and planners.

Then there are the intangible costs, which go beyond ugliness to the locked doors and closed streets that hinder citizens' direct contact with those who govern them. When the overriding purpose of government buildings becomes warding off danger, these structures invariably lose the chance to become centers of community.

America the Beautiful becomes America the Besieged.

If you doubt that, look at the classical temple of the Treasury Department, ringed by a fence and a guardhouse, and greeting you with this sweet sign: "PASSHOLDERS AND APPOINTMENTS ONLY." If this is how we're going to treat federal buildings, then why not simply move them, like the vice president, to an undisclosed location?

Such self-inflicted damage is hardly confined to Washington. In Chicago, tombstone-like granite posts disturb the openness of the Federal Center, the South Loop complex designed by Ludwig Mies van der Rohe. In St. Louis, graceless steel bollards surround Eero Saarinen's glistening, gracefully soaring Gateway Arch. Even small cities cannot escape the scourge. Peoria's federal courthouse, a classical gem whose walls are adorned with lovely sculptures, is now ringed by concrete stumps that are completely unsympathetic to its design.

What is happening in Washington and other centers of federal power raises vexing questions, to which there are no simple answers. Because the Oklahoma City bombing was carried out by homegrown terrorists rather than foreigners, and because they struck at a nondescript federal high-rise in a medium-size heartland city, it is not easy for anyone in the government to say: "It will never happen there." It could happen anywhere. The trouble is, where do you draw the line between negligence and overreaction in confronting the specter of terrorism?

THE CITY NO LONGER BEAUTIFUL

While Washington offers some model examples for confronting that question, it reveals, on the whole, what happens when security becomes paramount: the city becomes a pallid version of its formerly robust self. A case in point is the remade, two-block stretch of Pennsylvania Avenue in front of the White House.

When Clinton shut the once-bustling area to vehicle traffic at the recommendation of the Secret Service, the reason was simple: to carve out what security experts call a "standoff distance"—in essence, a moat big

PENNSYLVANIA AVENUE IN FRONT OF THE WHITE HOUSE
Protecting the president, killing the city.

enough to prevent another vehicle-delivered bomb from doing lethal damage to the White House and its occupants. In time, makeshift guardhouses were installed on the flanks of the protected zone. So were ugly concrete barricades that marred the vista arranged by Pierre-Charles L'Enfant, the celebrated French architect who created Washington's master plan in 1791. Between the flanks was nothing but asphalt—a boon for in-line skaters, but an eyesore to everybody else.

After it dawned on people that this state of affairs was a national disgrace, the government in 2002 held a design competition. Yet the winning plan by New York City landscape architect Michael Van Valkenburgh has proved unable, in its final constructed form, to overcome the all-encompassing security mandate.

The flanks of Van Valkenburgh's redesign, at least, are well-handled, with handsome neoclassical guardhouses and oval-shaped posts that don't block the view. But the center, a vast expanse of granite pavement, is dignified but lifeless, making the redesigned zone a sterile, sealed-off compound rather than the lively, integral part of Washington it used to be. The Secret Service, which reviewed the plan and helped devise the final outcome, has won a hollow victory: this is a textbook case of how to protect the president and kill the city.

Because of its heavy concentration of government buildings, Washington offers an extreme example of the deadening impact such defensive measures can have on public spaces. In most American cities, a federal building or two might be sprinkled amid the skyscrapers. But the government presence is ubiquitous in Washington's Federal Triangle, which stretches along Pennsylvania Avenue between the Capitol and the White House. Chicago architect Edward Bennett laid out this triangular grouping in the "City Beautiful" style of grandly scaled, harmoniously assembled buildings. But what you see on the sidewalks of the Federal Triangle today is hardly beautiful.

Consider the parade of concrete planter boxes that march in front of the Commerce Department Building on 14th Street—squat, vaguely classical tubs that were installed as a temporary measure after September 11. They go on forever, like Mickey Mouse's endlessly multiplying brooms in the movie *Fantasia*. You can't sit on them, though they provide a convenient place to dump cigarette butts. And they may be providing a false sense of security.

The planters would likely fall over if a vehicle rammed them, explained Patricia Gallagher, the executive director of the National Capital Planning Commission, which reviews federal plans in the Washington region. "The appearance is oppressive, and functionally they don't do much," she said.

The planning commission has encouraged a more enlightened approach to perimeter security. It looks with favor on defense measures that are site-specific rather than generic, such as the National Museum of the American Indian's appealing combination of large rocks, low walls, and bollards. The commission also supports planter boxes that are both useful and attractive, such as those at the International Monetary Fund, which echo the building's sleek modernism and double as benches and bus shelters.

THE COSTS OF SECURITY

But can we really design our way out of this problem? Block upon block of planters and bollards are apt to look heavy and intrusive no matter how well they are designed. There's only so much that tasteful camouflage can do. Its multitude of defense precautions gives Washington a surrealistic air—a city of majestic buildings that project power and authority while conveying the impression of an Old West stockade readying for an attack by marauding Indians. Architect Allan Greenberg, a distinguished classicist, called the phenomenon "bollard acne on the face of Washington."

And while this "acne" represents the most visible aspect of costly security design, it is the less visible changes to a building—the bones, not the skin—that really wind up burning money.

After the Oklahoma City bombing, at the direction of an influential committee representing major federal departments, the General Services Administration began beefing up structures to prevent a repeat of the collapse that destroyed the Murrah Building. Since September 11, GSA officials said, the requirements have only become more stringent—and more costly. The agency stretched the required standoff distance for most new buildings to 50 feet from 20 feet. A building that once required three acres of real estate now requires four, which means the government has to buy more land.

Eight percent of the construction budget for a typical new courthouse is now devoted to security costs. With the GSA's total annual construction budget averaging $1.1 billion, a conservative estimate of security costs is at least $60 million, nearly enough to build a medium-size federal courthouse.

A BLIGHT ON THE WASHINGTON MONUMENT'S REVAMPED GROUNDS

Washington and the nation are on a steep learning curve, as the reshaping of the grounds around the Washington Monument reveals. Designed by Philadelphia landscape architect Laurie Olin and completed last year, the project replaces the twin rows of concrete Jersey barriers that were hastily installed around the monument after the 1998 bombings of U.S. embassies in Kenya and Tanzania. The barriers were more than ugly objects. They destroyed the beauty of the hill because they were set in the middle of it.

Charged with creating a barrier to block a vehicle-delivered bomb, Olin had the inspired notion of putting his wall at the bottom of the hill—400 feet from the monument rather than 200 feet away, as the Jersey barriers had been. His wall, 30 inches high and clad in granite, is in effect a curving bench—high enough to stop a vehicle laden with explosives but low enough to provide a spot for tired tourists to sit. Olin even provided a stone footrest at the base of the wall. Realizing that eagle-eyed cost-cutters would ask, "Why do we need a footrest?" he cleverly called it a curb.

The outcome is wonderfully unobtrusive, fully restoring the openness of the National Mall. When the monument is seen from the Lincoln Memorial, the wall even seems to disappear. Yet nothing is ever simple here.

The National Park Service, which administers the landmark, remains concerned that a terrorist with a small bomb strapped under a coat or hidden in a backpack could blow up the monument from the inside. To

CHANGES AT THE WASHINGTON MONUMENT
Restoring the National Mall's openness, with one obstrusive exception.

retain the visual purity of the obelisk, Olin proposed using an old building
at the bottom of the hill for security screening and taking visitors through
an underground passageway to the monument. But opponents argued that
the plan would disfigure the National Mall.

In a compromise that should satisfy no one, a security pavilion was
attached to the base of the monument. Despite its attempt to blend in
with the monument's huge blocks of Maryland marble, it sticks out like a
fat toe, a small but telling reminder of how far America has to go before
it can resolve the competing agendas that shape its public buildings and
public spaces.

POSTSCRIPT

*The security pavilion at the base of the Washington Monument remained in
place in early 2010, though a National Park Service spokesman said the agency
planned to move the facility to an area at the bottom of the monument's hill. No
timetable was set, however. Seeking a more balanced approach to the design of
federal office buildings, courthouses, border stations, and other structures, the Gen-*

eral Services Administration in 2007 issued the Site Security Design Guide, *a primer for architects and others working with the agency. The guide observes that "protection often has come at the expense of the workplace and the surrounding environment, with no significant risk reduction." It calls instead for careful analysis of perceived risks and the use of multi-purpose security measures, such as grass berms that would block bomb-laden vehicles, provide attractive open space, and reduce storm-water runoff.*

The transparency of such designs as the 2007 San Francisco federal building, by the firm Morphosis, proved the effectiveness of this approach. Yet the anxieties spawned by the September 11 attacks were never far from the surface, as became clear in 2009, when the Customs and Border Protection agency of the Department of Homeland Security stripped large yellow letters spelling "UNITED STATES" off the facade of a newly opened upstate New York border station. A spokeswoman for the customs agency told New York Times *architecture critic Nicolai Ouroussoff: "The sign could be a huge target. . . . Anything that would place our officers at risk we need to avoid."*

Hubs of Frustration

AIRPORTS—A SYMBOL OF OUR FREEDOM OF MOVEMENT—HAVE
BECOME DEHUMANIZING

SEPTEMBER 10, 2006

When the two hijackers slipped undetected through a security checkpoint at the Portland, Maine, airport at 5:45 a.m. on September 11, 2001, Americans had no clue of the horrors that were about to unfold that day. Nor could they grasp that the nation was about to enter a new era of security-conscious design that would plunge American airports into chaos.

What has happened to air travelers since has become the stuff of twisted legend, from the 50-minute waits to get through the security checkpoint at Denver International Airport to the 600-foot lines of frustrated passengers waiting to be screened at Chicago's Midway Airport. For travelers, the terrorist attacks further dehumanized an experience that was already a cattle call. For airports, the predicament spawned by 9/11 (and before it, the bombing of the Oklahoma City federal building in 1995) has been never-ending in its nightmarishly changing scope.

There had been hijackings before, of course, but this was the first time hijackers had turned planes into missiles aimed at skyscrapers. Then came the shoe bomber and, most recently, the foiled plot to simultaneously blow up several transatlantic airliners with liquid explosives. These days airport managers and architects even have to worry that airports themselves might become terrorists' targets.

All this has put enormous pressure on a type of building that, more than any other, represents Americans' cherished freedom of movement. And that pressure inevitably filters down to architects, who are scrambling to reconcile the traditional goal of speeding passengers along as quickly as possible with the new imperative to slow things down in order to screen passengers and bags for weapons, explosives, and other items, even toothpaste and shaving cream.

Reconciling speed and security, however, is not the only issue. Airports are places, not just conduits of movement. They are mini-cities where we eat, shop, and do business. Now more than ever, the issue is how to humanize them—how to take these sprawling machines for moving people and transform them into something at least a little more livable.

"You can make travel more pleasurable if you design a building where you orient people well, where there are light and views," said Chicago architect Helmut Jahn, who has designed airport buildings around the world, including the United Airlines Terminal at O'Hare International Airport.

That is Jahn the architect talking. Now listen to Jahn the frequent flier: "Travel has become an absolute pain. It's no fun getting on and off a plane."

A look at recently retrofitted facilities in three airports—Newark Liberty International, from which United Airlines Flight 93 took off on September 11 before crashing into a field near Shanksville, Pennsylvania; Midway, the nation's fastest-growing airport; and O'Hare, the nation's busiest—shows how architects have been at pains to improve the lot of frustrated travelers. But this survey also reveals the limits of what designers can accomplish in aging terminals; the shortsightedness that helped cause long backups at security checkpoints; and the ongoing turbulence of a transportation network that was overburdened before September 11 and continues to stack the odds against the passenger.

NEW REALITIES AT AIRPORTS

Many travelers think of airports simply as enormous, interchangeable structures, not as architecture. Yet airports *are* designed, and the way they are shaped—or misshaped—can have a profound impact on the traveler's experience.

In a typical airport security checkpoint, Transportation Security Administration (TSA) screeners herd travelers through tightly bunched corrals of

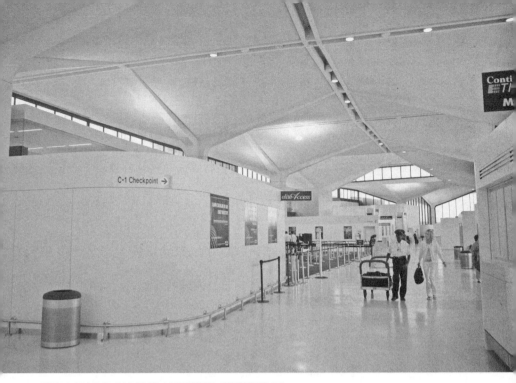

WALLS AROUND BAGGAGE-SCREENING MACHINES AT
NEWARK LIBERTY INTERNATIONAL AIRPORT
Struggling to make the new security apparatus unobtrusive.

metal detectors and X-ray machines. The screeners bellow at passengers to take laptops out of their bags and to take off their shoes. The passengers can be excused for feeling like the cows at the old Chicago stockyards.

It is all a far cry from 1988, when Jahn completed the airy, greenhouse-like United Airlines Terminal at O'Hare. In this striking work of architecture, passengers were supposed to glide effortlessly from a spacious, skylit ticketing pavilion to "flow-through" ticket counters on their way to soaring, barrel-vaulted concourses. The design was based on the widely accepted premise of the era: Ease of motion was paramount; security was an afterthought. "The whole thing was predicated on that movement," said Chicago architect Martin Wolf, who worked with Jahn on the project.

In the years that followed, as airlines routed vast numbers of passengers through O'Hare and other hubs, air travel became an exercise in frustration. September 11 made things much worse, turning a relatively seamless process into a cumbersome, time-consuming, physically demanding hassle.

The trouble starts from the beginning of the journey. The passenger, having already endured a long wait just to get to the ticket counter, is forced to haul his luggage to a baggage-screening machine, present his ID and boarding pass to a screening agent, then head for the security checkpoint, where he must face yet another stress-inducing line. Electronic ticketing has streamlined this process somewhat, but the space-hogging baggage-screening machines installed after the terrorist attacks remain a problem, as a recently completed retrofit of Newark Airport's Terminal C suggests.

Like the rest of the 1970s-era airport, Terminal C has ticketing areas framed in cross-shaped concrete columns that rise to lofty, folded concrete ceilings and broad, light-emitting bands of glass. But after 9/11, baggage-screening machines the size of small SUVs intruded on the terminal's concourses, blocking passengers' pathways and forcing them to lug their bags from ticket counters to the machines.

As designed by Graf & Lewent Architects, an Elmhurst, New York, airport specialist, the $3.2 million rehab puts the machines behind ticket counters, where they are hooked up to hidden conveyor belts. With the machines relocated and the lines leading to them gone, the concourse has been restored to its former width, allowing passengers to move freely through the terminal and to deposit their bags directly at the ticket counter. But this openness is by no means widespread.

The aging terminal is crammed with shops and other amenities for which it wasn't originally designed. As a result, Graf & Lewent principal Steve Lewent was forced to put some of the baggage-screening machines on the flanks of the ticket counters—or even, at one end of the terminal, in the middle of the concourse. The machines and the boxy white walls built around them create ungainly roadblocks, taking up nearly half of the concourse's width and making the terminal look as though it had been invaded by a herd of white elephants.

For the passenger, the overall experience is improved but hardly ideal.

FIXING "THE MIDWAY STRANGLER"

The outcome is better at Midway, where city officials recently opened a $10.7 million security pavilion meant to correct a major flaw in the airport's five-year-old expansion: a single checkpoint area that caused long backups of passengers and was dubbed "the Midway Strangler."

The expansion consists of a light-filled, modernist ticketing pavilion east of Cicero Avenue that is linked by an enclosed pedestrian bridge to concourses and departure gates west of Cicero. Designed by Kansas City, Missouri–based HNTB Architecture, with A. Epstein and Sons International of Chicago, the project opened in March 2001. Yet only nine months later, it was well on its way to becoming seriously outmoded. "Nobody dreamt that there would be the security criteria there are today," said Allen Pomerance, Epstein's project manager for the expansion and the security pavilion.

The original design grew from the faulty assumption that the six security checkpoints on the west side of the bridge would process 600 passengers per lane per hour, a breakneck rate of 10 people a minute. After 9/11 the rate dropped to 400 passengers per hour, according to Erin O'Donnell, the Chicago Department of Aviation's managing deputy commissioner at Midway. Then, as more people returned to flying, it slowed to just 200 passengers per hour, three times as slow as the initial forecast.

With the checkpoint turning into a choke point in 2003, Mayor Richard M. Daley called the long lines a national disgrace and lambasted the TSA over the delays. But his administration was partly to blame. Asked why the original design did not include two bridges, Pomerance replied that Midway was intended "to be a low-cost airport for low-cost airlines." City aviation officials, he said, were explicit that there would be only one bridge.

The security pavilion, a 10,000-square-foot rectangular structure attached to the north side of Midway's concourse building, takes some modest steps toward undoing the damage done by the original design. It offers travelers 9 new security checkpoints, bringing the total to 15. When the project is completed later this month, Midway will have 20 security checkpoints, more than three times as many as it had on 9/11.

The outcome is hardly an architectural triumph, but it is at least serviceable. While space in the new security pavilion is tight, natural light streams through its glass facade, a welcome departure from the dungeon-like atmosphere of most security corrals. The lines for screening haven't disappeared, but they are no longer as long as two football fields. Passengers aren't panicking.

At Midway, form has finally caught up with function.

BALANCING SECURITY AND MOBILITY

At O'Hare, Jahn is engaged in a far more extensive undertaking: a major overhaul of the three passenger terminals for domestic travel, a project originally pegged at a cost of $315 million and now behind schedule and over budget. Aimed at easing congestion in crowded ticketing pavilions and baggage areas, the job is remaking Terminals 2 and 3, simple boxes of steel, glass, and concrete completed in 1961 by C.F. Murphy Associates, the predecessor of today's Murphy/Jahn. The finished portions of Terminal 3 show how Jahn has deftly balanced security and openness.

TERMINAL 3 AT O'HARE INTERNATIONAL AIRPORT
Reasonably and creatively addressing the issue of risk.

Like an umbrella protecting travelers from rain and snow, a new steel canopy extends more than 40 feet over column-free sidewalks and lanes of the upper-level roadway where passengers arrive. The canopy reaches another 20 feet inside the terminal, leaping over a moat-like opening that used to separate Terminals 2 and 3 from the roadway and is now filled by escalators, elevators, and glassed-in vestibules.

It all seems very normal, which is precisely the point: post–September 11 security concerns have threatened this type of casual drive-up arrival sequence as never before. In 2002, for example, a master plan for Los Angeles International Airport by the firm Landrum & Brown floated the radical idea of a remote check-in complex where passengers would park, check their bags, and then take a people-mover to terminals. The since-discarded plan, which sought to protect terminal buildings from vehicle-delivered bombs, was a conspicuous overreaction to 9/11, an admission that terrorism would now be the driving force behind all major decisions in how Americans went about their lives.

Jahn's design, which was prepared before September 11 and responded to issues raised by the Oklahoma City bombing, wisely forgoes this fortress mentality. Its strikingly transparent wall of frameless glass, supported by vertical cables, is insulated with an inner layer of laminated glass to prevent a bomb blast from turning the glass into deadly shards. Pedestrian traffic through the terminal flows more easily because the architect shifted baggage-screening machines behind ticket counters.

Unfortunately, Jahn's redesign doesn't include a revamp of the security checkpoints, which are controlled not by the city of Chicago but by the TSA. "We've tried over the years to have some influence on the design [of the screening checkpoints]," Jahn said. "They just have their standard stuff. It's horrible."

Nonetheless, the project is a model for airport retrofits. We cannot design a world that makes us 100 percent safe. Invulnerability is an illusion. Recognizing this, Jahn and his clients have accepted a certain level of risk and carefully layered their response into a remarkably open design, in which defensive measures are skillfully integrated into the architecture rather than grotesquely applied.

For the beleaguered passenger, the design represents a welcome step forward in the quest to make the post–September 11 airport experience less of a dehumanizing cattle call.

THE PROMISE AND
PERILS OF REBUILDING

WHILE CITIES AROUND THE NATION ADJUSTED TO THE "NEW NORMALCY" OF tightened security in the wake of September 11, New York City also had to confront the reality of ground zero and the prospect of filling that hole in its midst. After the six plans made public in the summer 2002 were disparaged by both critics and the public, the state agency in charge of the redevelopment sponsored what it called an "innovative design study," inviting some of the world's most distinguished architects to participate. In effect a master plan competition, the study would raise great expectations that proved impossible to fulfill.

A Brilliant Tightrope Walk at Ground Zero

ONE PLAN FOR THE WORLD TRADE CENTER SITE RISES
ABOVE THE REST

DECEMBER 22, 2002

Architecture now has a Harry Houdini and his name is Daniel Libeskind. Alone among the modernists who brought forth bold new visions for ground zero, the Berlin-based Libeskind escaped the seemingly inescapable trap of crushing commercial space and monstrous mega-structures. He avoided,

THE LIBESKIND PLAN FOR GROUND ZERO
A design that promised to balance between commemorating the dead and building a living city.

too, the pitfall of the postmodernists—a nostalgic throwback to the days when no one worried about hijacked jets smashing into buildings.

Libeskind's plan for the former World Trade Center site offers at once a deeply moving memorial to those who died in the terrorist attacks of September 11, 2001, and a joyous but dignified celebration of New York's street life and skyline.

It is a brilliant work of urban design that performs exactly the right tightrope walk for ground zero—balancing the acts of commemorating the dead and building a living city. Yes, it can be improved, but among the field, which includes at least three other world's tallest building schemes, it is without peer, proving that bigger is only better when it addresses the ground as well as the sky.

The design is all the more stunning when you realize that the Polish-born Libeskind, who became a U.S. citizen in 1965, has never completed a large-scale office building. His best-known previous project is the Jewish Museum Berlin, which is shaped like a fractured Star of David and packs such an emotional punch that it drew thousands of visitors even before it was filled with objects. That structure established Libeskind as a poet of tragedy; this latest design cements that reputation.

FIGHTING THE DEVELOPERS

None of the other six architectural teams invited to submit designs for the site came close—not Lord Norman Foster of Britain and his "kissing" (but out-of-place) twin towers; not New York superstars Richard Meier and Peter Eisenman, who produced a brute tic-tac-toe grid of a high-rise; certainly not Skidmore, Owings & Merrill of New York, which would have crammed ground zero with a glum forest of nine skyscrapers.

Now one has to hope that New York planning officials will have the wisdom and the courage to choose Libeskind's design early next year, when they are scheduled to adopt a ground zero master plan. More important, they and the public probably will have to fight the city's infamously avaricious real estate developers from tearing the Libeskind plan to shreds.

Already the developers are hissing that all the architects' proposals are mere fantasies and the market will—and should—be the prime shaper of the 16-acre site. Which is, in a sense, true: the new designs are simply suggestions of what might go at ground zero. But if only the market matters, and not the public realm, then we have just been treated to one of the greatest charades of all time and can fully expect an urban planning disaster to be heaped upon the human tragedy already executed by the terrorists.

INTERESTING, BUT . . .

New York officials invited the seven teams to brainstorm new ideas after the initial round of six ground zero plans were derided by critics and the public alike for their stultifying sameness and for overstuffing ground zero with office space.

The officials wanted real diversity—and they got it, though a close examination of the new designs recalls the ongoing relevance of a remark by the late, great Chicago architect Ludwig Mies van der Rohe: "I don't want to be interesting; I want to be good." Most of the new plans are more interesting than good. They are rich in ideas, but they would not create a richly textured cityscape.

There are several mega-structures, which consist of interconnected sets of high-rises rather than conventional freestanding buildings. Their architects offer a wide variety of reasons to justify such structures, including more escape routes if terrorists strike again. It sounds great until you confront the scaleless gigantism of what actually would get built.

The five interconnected towers by the team called United Architects, which would form a curving "veil" around a memorial, are easily the most spectacular of this bunch—a glass mountain that perfectly captures the intense energy of Lower Manhattan. But look more closely and you see that more care has gone into creating free-form, so-called blob architecture in the air than making spaces attuned to human beings on the ground.

Foster's twin towers are a disappointment for such a distinguished architect—faceted like a double diamond, to be sure, but bulky and unsettling, more fit for Shanghai than New York. The architect talks a good game about lively street markets, but his plan ultimately consists of two towers isolated in a park.

Meier, Eisenman, and associates propose a hulking L-shaped group of five towers with interconnected, cantilevered walkways. Their ideal is a grand civic space like Rockefeller Center. The reality is a supersize picket fence, graceless and uninspiring. Worse, they would spread the memorial into the surrounding neighborhood, defusing the emotional intensity of a single concentrated site.

And so the mega-structural monstrosities go, from the THINK team's pair of giant, largely unoccupied lattices (unthinkable because they would cost so much and contain so little) to Skidmore's bizarre cluster of nine high-rises, which manages to be even more densely packed and commercially oriented than the original six plans by New York architects Beyer Blinder Belle and collaborating firms.

A PIECE OF TRADITIONALISM

After seeing these nightmarish *Blade Runner* landscapes, it is a relief to encounter the traditional urbanism of the plan by Peterson Littenberg Architecture & Urban Design. These designers call for setback towers, grand boulevards, and memorials like an amphitheater, whose seating capacity would duplicate the number of September 11 victims. But the Peterson Littenberg scheme is the architectural equivalent of comfort food. It goes down easy—too easy. It never truly comes to terms with the emotional enormity, the psychic shock, of what transpired when the terrorists struck.

Addressing that tragedy is the great strength of Libeskind's design, which is why victims' families reportedly wept when the architect introduced his plans.

At the core of Libeskind's vision, both physically and emotionally, is the memorial—a sunken space, 70 feet below street level, that would extend down to the foundations that once supported the twin towers. The memorial would leave exposed a portion of the foundation, or slurry, wall that held back the Hudson River when the twin towers collapsed, symbolizing the resilience of democracy.

At ground level, cultural buildings would wrap around the fringes of the memorial. One of them, a large cube, would cantilever precariously, but poetically, over the sunken space. Libeskind also includes an exuberant, elevated walkway that encircles the site. "Now everyone can see not only ground zero," he said, "but the resurgence of life."

All this has far more emotional power than the trite suggestion several teams made for covering the footprints of the twin towers with ground-level reflecting pools, or Foster's soulless idea of a walled memorial precinct.

In contrast to the mega-structures, which offer streets and parks in the upper reaches of the skyscrapers, Libeskind wisely restricts his public spaces to ground level, realizing that pulsing sidewalks are every bit as much the essence of New York as tall buildings.

Yet his towers are reasonably good—at once familiar and edgy, recalling the romantic spires of Lower Manhattan but displaying crystalline tops and shafts that evoke the explosions that transformed the site. They're a family of midsize freestanding buildings, like those at nearby Battery Park City, and one of them would be surmounted by an iconic spire that the architect calls a "vertical park."

RESTORING THE SPIRITUAL PEAK

Forget the cloying, patriotic symbolism of the tower's height—1,776 feet. What matters is the way its gardens spiral gracefully toward the heavens, recapturing the spiritual essence of the "Tribute in Light," the ghostly towers of light that captivated the nation earlier this year on the anniversary of the attacks. A skyscraper, Libeskind said, restores "the spiritual peak to the city, creating an icon that speaks of our vitality in the face of danger and our optimism in the aftermath of tragedy."

There are pragmatic, as well as aesthetic, reasons to support his plan. In contrast to the mega-structures, its skyscrapers could be built one by one, as the now-dormant market for new office space in Lower Manhattan gradually revives. Moreover, its vertical park appears to be uninhabited, so a developer wouldn't need to rent office space to tenants skittish about being in a supertall tower.

But the ultimate appeal of Libeskind's design is that it superbly marries the poetic with the pragmatic, remembering and renewing. It has roughly as much office space as the original six designs and its competitors in the latest round. Yet miraculously, it wriggles out of these chains and gives us something magic.

POSTSCRIPT

This critique foretold two outcomes: Libeskind's triumph in the master plan competition—and the gutting of his plan thereafter. In early 2003, the Lower Manhattan Development Corporation (LMDC) chose two finalists for the master plan competition: Libeskind's and the design by THINK, whose two latticework structures, each 1,665 feet tall, would have straddled the footprints of the destroyed twin towers. A vicious political battle ensued, with advocates of the THINK team deriding Libeskind's design as a morbid pit while Libeskind labeled THINK's design "skeletons in the sky," a comment for which he later apologized. On February 26, 2003, a committee of representatives of the LMDC, the Port Authority of New York & New Jersey, New York governor George Pataki, and New York mayor Michael Bloomberg selected Libeskind's plan.

To naive optimists unschooled in the cut and thrust of Manhattan real estate, it must have seemed as if brighter days lay ahead for ground zero. But the leaseholder of the 16-acre site, developer Larry Silverstein, treated Libeskind's plan as a mere concept. He turned instead to the New York office of Skidmore, Owings & Merrill (SOM), with whom he already was drafting plans for a massive office building at ground zero. By this time, Pataki had coined a patriotic new name for the iconic skyscraper—"Freedom Tower."

Under Silverstein's leadership, SOM's David Childs would design the tower, with Libeskind relegated to the role of commentator rather than true collaborator. The result of their awkward collaboration, made public in late 2003, preserved only superficial elements of Libeskind's design, including an off-center spire and the symbolic height of 1,776 feet. The design, said New Yorker architecture critic Paul Goldberger, recalled "the old cliché about a camel being a horse designed by a committee." In 2005, when Pataki and Bloomberg unveiled yet another Freedom Tower design, Libeskind would be almost completely out of the picture.

Tower of Banal

LATEST FREEDOM TOWER DESIGN ERASES ORIGINAL VISION OF
REMEMBRANCE AND RENEWAL

JULY 3, 2005

The unveiling of a new and fortress-like Freedom Tower for ground zero—
"Fort Zero," screamed the front page of the *New York Post*—is the latest
and most visible sign that the redevelopment of the former World Trade
Center site is slouching toward mediocrity.

The problems, evident in almost every aspect of the rebuilding, threaten
to undermine the carefully conceived balance between remembrance and
renewal that was the hallmark of Daniel Libeskind's brilliant, competition-
winning master plan.

What they add up to is death by a thousand cuts rather a single mortal
blow—and the danger that unless public officials stop their blather about
everything going smoothly, the rebuilt ground zero will turn out to be a
whittled-down version, rather than a sparkling realization, of Libeskind's
bold outline for the scarred Lower Manhattan site.

The evidence of erosion extends beyond the banality of the redesigned
tower, which would be topped by a less-than-inspiring spire and set atop a
nearly windowless, 200-foot-tall pedestal—a city-dulling response to police
fears that a vehicle-delivered bomb could kill scores of people with deadly
flying glass.

Among the other problems:

- Essential features of Libeskind's 2002 master plan—from a spiky,
  off-center tower with life-affirming vertical gardens to a subterranean memorial framed by the scarred foundation wall that held the
  Hudson River at bay after the twin towers collapsed—have been
  eliminated or seriously compromised.
- A newly chosen ground-level memorial that is meant to be the site's
  spiritual centerpiece—consisting of a tree-lined park marked by
  square, sunken reflecting pools that evoke the destroyed twin towers—is itself threatened by a variety of factors, such as a grotesquely
  overscaled cultural center that would loom over it.
- A performing arts center, to be designed by Frank Gehry and one of
  the major cultural elements meant to leaven the site's focus on commemorating the dead, has been relegated to a second round of fund-
  raising for the redevelopment of ground zero, seriously diminishing
  its chances of ever being built.

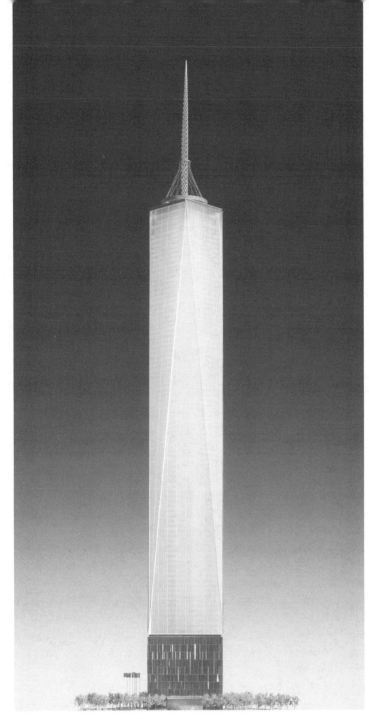

A MODEL OF FREEDOM TOWER
The skyscraper as fortress, a city-dulling response to terrorist fears.

The postponement and the gradual erosion of Libeskind's vision reflect the perhaps impossible challenge of shoehorning onto a 16-acre site, roughly two-thirds the size of Chicago's Millennium Park, not only the memorial, the performing arts and cultural facilities, but also millions of square feet of office space as well as a major transit terminal.

Adding to the sense of tumult as New York governor George E. Pataki and New York City mayor Michael Bloomberg made public the revised Freedom Tower proposal, a group of families who lost relatives on September 11 was in Washington, DC, asking the White House and Congress to halt plans for one of the museums that is to occupy the cultural center alongside the memorial.

The opponents charge that the museum, called the International Freedom Center, is being shaped by left-wing advisers who blame the United States for the world's problems. Whether one agrees with them or not, they may be right about one thing: the once-sharp focus of ground zero redevelopment plans on commemorating the tragedy of September 11 and building a great new urban center in Lower Manhattan now risks being diluted by extraneous clutter.

Officials of the Lower Manhattan Development Corporation, the state-chartered agency in charge of redeveloping ground zero, insist everything is on track, citing a planned late summer groundbreaking for Santiago Calatrava's much-praised transit center and a groundbreaking for the memorial next year. "We're hitting all our major milestones," says Joanna Rose, an LMDC spokeswoman, even though Freedom Tower's completion date has now been pushed back a year to 2010.

Trying to meet a schedule is one thing. Delivering aesthetic quality is another. The new plan for Freedom Tower—which was hastily redesigned after the New York City Police Department raised concerns in recent weeks that an earlier version of the skyscraper would be vulnerable to a car or truck bomb—shows the danger of rushing to meet a deadline.

Designed by David Childs of the New York office of Skidmore, Owings & Merrill—the handpicked architect of developer Larry Silverstein, who holds the lease to the World Trade Center site—the 82-story, 1,776-foot tower is conceived as a monument to standing tall in the face of terrorism. Just one problem: its 200-foot-tall base, which would consist of blast-resistant concrete walls sheathed in metal, reveals just how much we've got our guard up.

In a bizarre twist, the office tower is set atop the base as if it had been lifted above the ground and placed on a pedestal. The base will be filled with an 80-foot-tall lobby and, above it, mechanical equipment.

New York is a city of vibrant street life and serendipitous sidewalk meet-ings, yet it's hard to imagine anything that casual happening alongside this brute base. Because the character of public spaces invariably is shaped by the buildings alongside them, the tower's looming presence will inevitably weigh on the memorial immediately beside it.

The tower's skyline silhouette—a glass-sheathed square that would slope back at its corners to form what from some angles will appear to be a monumental obelisk—is better, but hardly winning. Though it has an appealingly simple shape, it still doesn't hold up its end of the skyline conversation with the Empire State and Chrysler Buildings. Their art deco spires conspicuously outclass its cable-stayed antenna, which represents a lackluster stab at Buck Rogers dazzle.

Worse, the tower fails to culminate the upward spiral of the shorter, slice-topped office buildings that someday may rise at ground zero, a flour-ish of Libeskind's master plan that has now disappeared. His proposed tower, with its asymmetrical, garden-filled spire, represented not just the progressive environmental agenda of energy-saving architecture; it was the summit of a great urban complex, a new kind of Rockefeller Center. Childs's skyscraper, by comparison, is far more self-referential, as if it were a showy tower rising in downtown Houston.

It was therefore disappointing to hear Libeskind effusively praising a design that undercuts the very things he sketched with such skill in 2002 and then fought to preserve when he and Childs wrangled over the first redesign of the Freedom Tower a year later. More and more, Libeskind seems like a human fig leaf—a master planner who provides political cover for officials who, in reality, have given him no real authority.

MEMORIAL ALTERED

The competition-winning memorial—designed by the young New York architect Michael Arad and the veteran Berkeley, California, landscape architect Peter Walker—also undermines Libeskind's master plan in sig-nificant ways. It eliminates, for example, the wide-open pit that would have revealed to sidewalk passersby the foundation wall that was the most stirring artifact of the September 11 attacks.

Ironically, the memorial itself is in danger of being compromised, and the story behind that story is a telling example of the complex web of juris-dictions, infrastructure, and political pressures at ground zero. The height of the cultural center alongside the memorial was bulked up to roughly 100 feet to accommodate mechanical systems for the subterranean concourses of Calatrava's transit station, whose elegant, birdlike aboveground reception hall is to be built to the center's east. Now, according to LMDC spokeswoman Rose, an effort is being made to reduce the building's height.

One could go on—and on. There have been fights over the ramps that will lead downward to the memorial's reflecting pools. (They are now conventional switchbacks, providing a far less subtle transition between ground level and the pools than the L-shaped ramps Arad originally devised.) There have even been battles over the arrangement of the names of the victims. Should they be randomly located or should they reflect such things as clusters of coworkers or what World Trade Center tower, north or south, the victims worked in?

There still are potential bright spots at ground zero, such as Calatrava's transit hub, though they are becoming ever more difficult to find. At least Libeskind's restoration of the street grid, a welcome contrast to the superblock of the old World Trade Center, remains intact. The history of the once-controversial, now-revered Vietnam Veterans Memorial in Washington, DC, reminds us that great public works have the ability to transcend the political firestorms attending their creation. Even so, it is increasingly more difficult, especially in light of the grotesquely fortified Freedom Tower, to expect that the grand promise of ground zero will ever be fulfilled.

POSTSCRIPT

As of early 2010, construction was under way at ground zero, with the memorial due to open on September 11, 2011, and the Freedom Tower (now called 1 World Trade Center) scheduled for completion in 2013. But little has gone right. In 2006 Childs redesigned the tower's base, sheathing it in blast-resistant glass instead of metal, yet the skyscraper still seemed likely to be a forbidding presence. Also in 2006, when Silverstein unveiled plans for ground zero office towers by a trio of distinguished architects (Norman Foster and Richard Rogers of London, as well as Fumihiko Maki of Tokyo), the critical consensus was that the site remained overpacked with office space. By early 2010, only Maki's skyscraper, known as Tower 4, was under construction.

Problems even engulfed Calatrava's promising transportation hub. Its costs escalated to $3.2 billion from $2 billion, partly because the 2004 Madrid train bombing and the 2005 attack on London's public transit system forced the architect to incorporate costly new security measures. To save money, the rooftop wings of the center's aboveground pavilion were made fixed rather than moving, as at Calatrava's exuberant 2001 addition to the Milwaukee Art Museum (see p. 131). Officials pushed back the transportation hub's opening to 2014, five years later than originally planned.

RECLAIMING THE PUBLIC REALM

DESPITE THE TRAVAILS AT GROUND ZERO, THE URBAN STAGE STILL OFFERED MOMENTS of undiluted joy and beauty. They were evident, most notably, at Chicago's Millennium Park, which set new aesthetic standards for urban parks and became a model, in contrast to the grinding inertia at ground zero, for how big cities get big things done. To be sure, the park had its own contentious history and cost overruns. It opened in 2004, four years late, and the tab was roughly half a billion dollars, more than three times the original price tag. Once the dazzling public space made its debut, however, those problems somehow faded from view. To walk into the park was to step into the urban future—and to escape, if only briefly, from the traumas of the present.

A People's Park for the Future

WHY MILLENNIUM PARK HAS INSTANTLY—AND INTERACTIVELY— ESTABLISHED ITSELF AS CHICAGO'S NEW TOWN SQUARE

AUGUST 29, 2004

Of all the scenes that have played out since Millennium Park opened six weeks ago, this is the one that says the most: children race around the black granite reflecting pool of the Crown Fountain, waiting for the giant human faces projected onto twin glass-block towers to spit their jets of water.

THE CROWN FOUNTAIN
Where joy—and the new interactivity—reign.

The kids come dressed for the occasion—not in regular clothes, but in bathing suits. They line up where they know the shower will fall, and they scream with delight when they get it, bunching beneath the white foam that seems to shoot out of the mouths of these human gargoyles but actually comes from computer-controlled pumps.

That this inventive multimedia spectacle takes place a few blocks from stately old Buckingham Fountain offers a telling contrast. At Buckingham Fountain, which the Chicago Park District keeps trapped behind a fence, all you can do is stand by and watch water shooting out of sea creatures' mouths. The scene is almost prim, something for men in straw boaters. But at the Crown Fountain, the atmosphere is raucous, festive, and, above all, interactive. It's the difference between architecture as object and architecture as event—and it is among the reasons that Millennium Park has instantly established itself as a triumphant, if still imperfect, public space.

Remember the so-called experts who predicted back in the 1990s that the widespread use of computers would suck people into the virtual realm of "chat rooms," dooming the public realm? Millennium Park offers a striking refutation of that thesis, though, ironically, the computer has played an essential role in shaping both its objects and the expectations of the people who encounter them.

City officials estimate that more than a million visitors have poured through the park since its July 16 opening. Even if those numbers are exaggerated, as such crowd calculations are wont to be, the park's drawing power is beyond dispute. Its spectacular works of art and architecture—the Crown Fountain, by Barcelona artist Jaume Plensa; the *Cloud Gate* sculpture, by London artist Anish Kapoor; and the Jay Pritzker Pavilion, by Los Angeles architect Frank Gehry—resemble planets that exert a collective gravitational pull, attracting masses of onlookers by day and night.

A LOOK AT THE FUTURE

What the visitors really are seeing is the future—a new kind of urban park. And that is altogether appropriate because Chicago is the city where Americans have long come to glimpse the face of tomorrow.

The first skyscrapers busted the clouds over the Loop in the 1880s. The World's Columbian Exposition of 1893 flaunted the first Ferris wheel and revealed that urban planning could make crowded, chaotic cities orderly and beautiful. In the postwar era, the "glass houses" of Ludwig Mies van der Rohe changed the contours of skylines around the world.

Millennium Park already belongs to that litany of innovation. It has proved to be as different from the serene greenswards of the great nineteenth-century landscape architect Frederick Law Olmsted or the formal, French-influenced parks of Daniel Burnham as a sleek, fold-up cell phone is different from a hand-cranked telephone.

True, Millennium Park isn't as rigorously contemporary as Bernard Tschumi's Parc de la Villette in Paris, with its bright red, neo-constructivist follies punctuated in a vast grid. In contrast, owing to its location in historic Grant Park, Chicago's new park is a hybrid of the Beaux-Arts and the modern, with the major pieces plugged into its room-like outdoor spaces.

Still, Millennium Park is clearly not a conventional sculpture garden, with a few timid pieces of public art dropped into a field of trees and grass. Here, the jumbo-size objects, not nature, are the focus of attention. They stand closely bunched, almost jostling one another, as much an extension of the crowded Loop as a respite from it. Noting the dense crowds and the disparate collection of objects, some observers have likened the experience to a theme park.

I want to come back to this theme park business, especially because I think it's wrong. But first, I'd like to tease out what we know about this 24.5-acre, $475 million park that we didn't know when it opened. Parks look very different with people in them. Happily, Millennium Park looks better, at least in six ways I've observed:

First, the principal objects in the park have proved themselves to be remarkably interactive as well as remarkably inventive.

Cloud Gate was dazzling enough when it sat by itself, an enormous jelly bean–shaped sculpture that tantalizingly met the ground at just two points. It is even more enticing with people around and inside it. Its highly polished, mirrored surface seems to reach out and grab the sky, pulling the clouds so close that visitors press their fingers against the sculpture's smooth, silvery surface—a chance to touch the untouchable.

Within the cone-like, 28-foot-high space beneath the sculpture, park-goers inevitably look up, broad smiles on their faces, to see their miniaturized reflections in its domed ceiling. The sculpture is distinctly architectural, not just an object in space, but an object that shapes space. The exquisitely refined glass-block towers of the Crown Fountain accomplish the same feat, carving out a joyous precinct.

Behind all the fun is a big shift: the people visiting Millennium Park no longer want to passively observe painterly scenes of nature, as parkgoers did in Olmsted's day. That was an industrial-age ideal, when the charge was to provide a relief from the crowded, polluted city. This is a post-industrial park, in which people come to actively engage with what they see, just as they engage with their computers.

Second, it's good that one architect or master planner didn't design all of Millennium Park.

Give one person near-complete control of a huge cultural precinct and you risk getting too much of a good thing, as at Richard Meier's Getty Center in Los Angeles. Meier is a great architect, but "All Richard Meier All the Time"—all so annoyingly perfect—shouldn't be anybody's idea of an ideal city. The slightly chaotic variety of Millennium Park—which was designed by a variety of architects, sculptors, and landscape architects—easily beats the imposed order of the Getty. Many hands, in short, are better than one.

Third, Millennium Park has found new ways to perform the age-old role of the park as a social mixing chamber, a place where people of different races and classes can drop their guard and mingle.

CLOUD GATE
A state-of-the-art sculpture that collects the skyline, the sky, and admirers from around the world.

Gehry's magnificent steel trellis over the Great Lawn of the Pritzker Pavilion—about as long as two football fields and as wide as one—does this best. It's a great unifying dome, so different from Ravinia, where the concertgoers in the pavilion and those on the lawn inhabit two different worlds.

The same impulse extends to the architect's snaking, wonderfully loopy BP Bridge over Columbus Drive: it's a bridge, in a sense, to nowhere because there's not much to do on the Daley Bicentennial Plaza side of it. People cross it, then they come back to where they started. But something unexpected transpires in between.

The bridge's river-like shape forms eddies, where, on occasion, parkgoers pause and talk to one another. It is, in other words, both place and passageway, and it is one of the many spots in Millennium Park that create triangulation—a third thing that encourages two perfect strangers to drop their guard and strike up a conversation. In a metropolitan area like Chicago that is polarized along the lines of race and class, we need such places desperately.

Fourth, Millennium Park sets new standards for providing access to the disabled without compromising aesthetic quality.

Here are images I'll always remember from the park: a boy in a wheelchair who was able to direct himself, with a little help from his father, into the Crown Fountain's shallow reflecting pool; a lady in a motorized wheelchair who was driving her way over the hardwood ramp on Gehry's bridge; a blind man with a white cane walking around *Cloud Gate*, his hands feeling the outline of the sculpture as he tried valiantly to sense what all the excitement was about.

Scenes like these teach new lessons of inclusivity and universal access.

Fifth, Millennium Park is as lively by night as it is by day. Evening concerts are one reason why. The other is lighting, and Millennium Park does lighting as artfully as it does objects.

At night, for example, the glass-block towers of the Crown Fountain, which are lit from within, become beacons of red, yellow, and purple. The silhouettes of people against the towers are equally arresting, as is the theatrical lighting of the still-maturing Lurie Garden and the metal shells of the Pritzker Pavilion.

All this suggests that urban parks can have a vibrant nocturnal life instead of being creepy places where you worry about muggers.

Sixth, Millennium Park has turned out to be a whole that's more than the sum of its parts. It has been a delight to watch the unintended outcomes, such as the BP Bridge turning into a balcony for the Pritzker Pavilion or the SBC (now AT&T) Plaza becoming a lookout point for jazz concerts at the McCormick Tribune Plaza beneath it.

Beyond these surprises, the park's mix of the classical and the contemporary has come off surprisingly well. The juxtaposition of old and new not only makes the new pieces seem newer. It embeds the park with a sense of time, as if it weren't all built up at once but had grown organically over decades.

Does this assortment of pluses mean Millennium Park is perfect? Hardly. Aesthetically, the park needs more subtlety, the carefully arranged progression of temptation, vista, and discovery that the landscape promises to provide when it is fully grown.

Socially, the park needs to become more nurturing, a place with more benches and other nooks where people can sit and gather and partake of each other. For all its innovations, it remains what urban parks have always been—a place where office workers go to have lunch, couples go to kiss, and people go to watch other people.

It cannot sustain itself—it will burn itself out—if it is solely about spectacle.

Which brings us to that knotty question about whether this is a new Disneyland. In Millennium Park, it's true, we move from one alluring object to another, as we would in a theme park. The objects, for the most part, are discrete events, formally unrelated to one another, as if they were the national or company pavilions at a world's fair. But the theme park comparison ultimately falls apart.

A theme park like Disneyland is about artifice—the creation of sanitized, sentimental environments, like Main Street USA, that restrict perception through the narrow lens of nostalgia. Art does not narrow perceptions. Art expands them, which is precisely the sort of creative jolt that *Cloud Gate* and the other objects in the park deliver.

Theme parks cordon themselves off from the world; Millennium Park sits right at the doorstep of one of the world's great cities, and there is no charge to enter it. It's a real public space, not a gated fantasyland—an art park, not a theme park.

So, yes, Millennium Park is a new kind of urban park: a park that is more about objects than the ground beneath them; a park that is more about participation than passivity; a park where the boundaries between sculpture, architecture, and landscape design blur—all to great aesthetic effect.

Yet Millennium Park still has a road to travel before it truly fulfills its social promise. It needs to be about both object and ground, architecture as spectacular event and architecture as simple everyday reality.

Six weeks in and counting, the park represents an extraordinary achievement as well as a tantalizing glimpse into the future—the city as a work of art.

The Millennium Park Effect

IT HAS EMERGED AS A SPARKLING EXAMPLE OF HOW BIG CITIES CAN GET BIG THINGS DONE

JUNE 26, 2005

A new catchphrase was in the air after Frank Gehry's shimmering Guggenheim Museum made its spectacular 1997 debut in the tattered shipbuilding city of Bilbao, Spain: "the Bilbao effect." The term, which sounded like weather forecasting jargon, spoke to the way a dazzling avant-garde work of architecture could instantly warm a city's artistic and business climates, attracting tourists by the planeload and turning a forgotten industrial outpost into a world cultural mecca.

Now, as Millennium Park approaches its first birthday, Chicago has a fresh variation on that theme: "the Millennium Park effect."

The joyful post-industrial playground, which has brazenly discarded the old industrial-age model of the serene urban park, is blowing equally strong winds of change across the cityscape around it. It has altered a museum's plans, boosted real estate prospects, and (perhaps) opened doors for more innovative architecture in a city whose design scene had grown stale as recently as a decade ago. Despite opening four years behind schedule and at more than triple its original $150 million budget, it has emerged as a sparkling example of how big cities can get big things done.

In the national conversation, Millennium Park is being hailed in some quarters as a template for cooperation among business and political leaders—in sharp contrast to the feuding among powerful interests that has turned the rebuilding of ground zero into a textbook case of civic inertia. "One of the great new models for a new kind of urban park," the *New Yorker*'s architecture critic, Paul Goldberger, recently told television host Charlie Rose.

For the Chicagoans who live with Millennium Park, it should be just as important that the 24.5-acre park has evolved into a widely used public space, one that is as receptive to the brown-bagging Loop office worker as to the tourist intent upon ogling *Cloud Gate*, which everybody calls "The Bean."

It is impossible to construct a park this ambitious and expensive—the project's total cost, seemingly ever rising, is now said to approach $500 million—without stirring controversy. Indeed, other members of the architectural commentariat have labeled the project a sculpture garden on steroids and a "yes, but" saga, as in "yes, it's great, but the process that led to it was a mess."

Yet those arguments are easily refuted by the transformation the park has wrought: what used to be an eyesore at the northwest corner of Grant Park—an urban scar of surface parking lots and working commuter railroad tracks at the foot of Chicago's skyline—is now a showcase public space. It has simultaneously healed the scar and brought new life to the urban tissue around it. Consider:

- In 2001, three years before the park's opening, the Art Institute of Chicago boldly reversed course and shifted the location of its new

THE JAY PRITZKER PAVILION
A festive focal point for Chicago's cultural life, gathering crowds beneath its heroic trellis.

wing from a site south of the museum to another plot on its north—right across Monroe Street from the future location of Millennium Park. Last month the museum announced that it intends to build a superlong footbridge, designed by Italian architect Renzo Piano, that will link the park to the new wing.

- A recent study prepared for the city of Chicago predicted that the park would provide a $1.4 billion boost to residential development in the surrounding East Loop area during the next 10 years, as measured by the increased value per square foot of properties and the number of units to be built.

- The park's influence was evident in 2004 when the innovative plan for a new Spertus Institute of Jewish Studies, which calls for a facade of folded glass to be slipped into the historic Michigan Avenue street wall, sailed through the city approvals process. That would not have happened 10 years ago, when the city was locked in the iron grip of aesthetic traditionalism. And the park's pull is still on display in the thick crowds on the sidewalks south of the Michigan Avenue Bridge—once-scruffy territory where, not long ago, shoppers from the fancy North Michigan Avenue retail district wouldn't have dared tread.

To be sure, Millennium Park remains an imperfect work in progress—the black-glass Exelon pavilions (including a new visitor center) look drearily Darth Vaderish, there are too many officious security guards decked out in bright yellow shirts, and the painstaking process of sanding away the welding seams on *Cloud Gate* won't be finished until at least the end of the summer.

But the park seems, if anything, to be gaining in popularity, rather than falling victim to the "been there, done that" syndrome of tourists with short attention spans.

In a sense, the front-page news treatment given to stories about the costly, delay-plagued completion of *Cloud Gate* shows how deeply the park's chief icon has embedded itself within Chicago's civic psyche. More important, the park's new emphasis on humanizing the spaces in between its icons means that it offers something more than spectacle—and that it is well on its way to achieving its potential as a great democratic space, a mixing chamber for people of different races and classes, who normally live entirely segregated from one another.

That shift is most evident at the Crown Fountain by Spanish sculptor Jaume Plensa, where extra-long cedar benches were installed last fall to give parkgoers a place to sit as they watch the human gargoyles spit water from the twin glass-block towers. Unfortunately, the benches already have cracks in them and may get worse after enduring more of Chicago's notorious freeze-and-thaw cycles. But for now, they are lined with people, and the fountain, more than ever, is an urban stage where the players are the children running through the fountain and the audience consists of tourists, office workers, and anybody else who wants to be where the action is.

Maybe it's the universal appeal of watching kids cool themselves in the water on a hot summer day—the oasis phenomenon—but, for whatever reason, people drop their guard and converse. "Is the water cool?" a female office worker sitting on one of the benches asked a little girl, who was drying herself off after running through the fountain. "I don't think I can come back to work wet."

Parks work best when they give people lots of choices about what kind of spaces to inhabit—action-filled or contemplative, grand or intimate. And Millennium Park is getting better at that, notably in the new Boeing Galleries just east of the Crown Fountain and Wrigley Square. Designed by the Chicago office of Harley Ellis Devereaux, this pair of understated, granite-paved outdoor spaces serves as a display area for exhibitions and, in the bargain, it offers plenty of ledges and shaded areas where people can sit.

Of equal interest has been the way the park's existing spaces, like the Great Lawn that spreads southward from Gehry's Pritzker Pavilion, have assumed new identities as people work them into their daily routine. The lawn now serves as an old-fashioned meadow, a passive park space where people picnic, read a book, throw a Frisbee or a baseball, or just stare up at the sky (or the skyline) through the dome-like steel trellis that sweeps over the lawn.

Who would have thought it—Gehry's dynamic, neo-baroque architecture, which always seems to be careering toward chaos, offering a serene respite? It's been equally surprising that Gehry's pavilion, which was expected to be the park's centerpiece, has been upstaged by *Cloud Gate*, which now ranks with the Picasso sculpture in Daley Plaza as a symbol of Chicago.

Ultimately, such design quality goes a long way toward rebutting the criticism of Millennium Park. So does the way its creation echoes the troubled run-up to the World's Columbian Exposition of 1893 in Chicago's Jackson Park. There was wrangling over where to hold the fair in Chicago; rancor over Daniel Burnham's selection of leading eastern architects from Chicago architects who felt snubbed; and the belated opening of the fair's centerpiece, the first Ferris wheel.

Against that backdrop, Millennium Park's expensive, delay-inducing shift from its original timid Beaux-Arts plan can be seen in proper perspective: the park, like the 1893 fair, is an instant city. And such cities do not unfold neatly, as in an urban planning textbook.

Perhaps because of the rapid recovery that followed the Great Fire of 1871, it is in Chicago's blood to build instant cities, to brawl over them as they are under way, and to dazzle the world with them once they are done. That is the story at Millennium Park, although the jury is still out on whether it will be the leading edge of an architectural renaissance or a fleeting exception to the mediocrity of the current building boom. Whatever the outcome, just one year into the park's life, "the Millennium Park effect" has energized Chicago with the power of a lightning bolt.

POSTSCRIPT

In the years that followed, Millennium Park became more than a crowd-pleasing combination of art and architecture. It evolved into a crossroads of Chicago's polyglot culture. As Chicago Tribune *arts critic Howard Reich observed in 2006,* the park offered a multicultural range of entertainers (African American gospel choirs, Mexican mariachi bands, and Brazilian crooners), while myriad languages (German, French, Spanish, Russian) could be heard before performances by the Grant Park Orchestra and Chorus. The park, Reich wrote, had become "our town square, our meeting place, our focal point for the arts—at least when the winter winds aren't howling."

Nationally, Millennium Park inaugurated a wave of new art parks in American downtowns, including Seattle's Olympic Sculpture Park (2007), the Citygarden Park in St. Louis and the John and Mary Pappajohn Sculpture Park in Des Moines (both 2009), along with the Virginia B. Fairbanks Art & Nature Park in Indianapolis (planned to open in 2010). Though the particulars of the designs differed, the overall object was the same: to breathe new life into cities, as Millennium Park had done, with bracing combinations of sculpture and landscape architecture.

2 | THE
BUILDING
BOOM

BEFORE THE RECESSION HALTED THE START OF MAJOR CONSTRUCTION PROJECTS, Chicago was Shanghai-on-the-Prairie—a symbol of the real estate boom that was changing the face of downtowns throughout America. Cement mixers whirred, construction cranes were everywhere, and a skyscraper seemed to be popping up on just about every corner. Not every city enjoyed such growth, of course. Yet with the boom came concerns that the surge of construction would turn out to a mixed blessing for the cityscape.

In Chicago, at least, this was not a boom of office towers, like the one that had transformed the Loop in the 1980s. It was primarily a surge of residential buildings, specifically apartment and condominium high-rises. Their presence reflected how new cultural attractions like Millennium Park and the beautification programs of Mayor Richard M. Daley had changed perceptions of the once-gritty Loop and its environs. Instead of fleeing downtown for the suburbs, as they had done in the 1960s, people flocked to it, creating a new market for urban living.

Only time would reveal that this construction binge was the most visible part of a nationwide housing bubble that would burst in 2007. But the boom's depressing environmental consequences were readily apparent. Far too many of the Chicago towers were eyesore slabs plopped on parking-garage podiums. They offered density without good design, urbanization without urbanity. The overbuilding of the age was even apparent in such mundane structures as branch banks and a bulked-up showcase McDonald's, fit for the age of swelling McMansions and oversize SUVs.

WRETCHED EXCESS

Monuments to Mediocrity

THE DEMANDS OF BUSINESS TRUMP THE ART OF ARCHITECTURE
IN A SURGE OF HIGH-RISE RESIDENTIAL CONSTRUCTION

AUGUST 10, 2003

Chicago likes to think of itself as America's architectural capital, but it's turning into Blah-ville.

If you doubt that, take a stroll to the new Grand Plaza apartment building, where two hulking towers are plopped on a massive parking garage and shopping complex at 540 North State Street. While a rooftop deck boasts three putting greens and each apartment has its own marble threshold, Grand Plaza's exterior consists of monotonous concrete walls and cartoonish triple-tiered setbacks. The style—one hesitates to use the word here—is the Robert Taylor Homes public housing project meets *Batman*'s Gotham City.

Cass Gilbert once defined a skyscraper as "a machine that makes the land pay," but at least his Woolworth Building in New York City was a thing of soaring neo-Gothic beauty. Grand Plaza, whose towers are 57 and 37 stories tall, does not soar. It's the product of a spreadsheet syndrome that values private amenities over architecture's public face.

Such monoliths are becoming far too commonplace. Chicago has long enjoyed a reputation as a city that superbly balances the demands of busi-

GRAND PLAZA
A symbol of the spreadsheet syndrome that values private amenities over architecture's public face.

ness and the art of architecture, but the present building boom—the nation's largest surge of high-rise residential construction—is throwing that balance grotesquely out of whack.

Wherever you glance these days—on either side of North Michigan Avenue, just west of South Lake Shore Drive or along the Chicago River— you are apt to see a towering construction crane, hear the whir of a cement mixer, and exclaim, "What went wrong?"

Some of these buildings, such as the 57-story Park Millennium apartment tower at 222 North Columbus Drive, look as though they might enjoy a second career as missile silos. Others turn the remaining historic structures, such as the old Medinah Temple (now a Bloomingdale's home furnishing store), into orphaned set pieces, islands of quality in a sea of architectural junk.

For years, urban planners dreamed of a "24-hour downtown" where you could live, work, and play. Now that the dream is being realized, however, it is turning out to be an aesthetic nightmare.

There are exceptions to the trend, such as the bold Skybridge condominium high-rise in Greektown, in which the empty space between two towers is surmounted by a trellis-like bridge of steel. Yet even Mayor Richard M. Daley spoke out in February against the bland concrete hulks that are blighting the cityscape, though he conveniently forgot to mention that his bureaucrats had approved these very buildings.

More important, the mayor made the wrong prescription for Chicago's design ills, calling for a new wave of exciting, "cutting-edge" designs, when simple boxes, beautifully refined, would do just as well. For years, that was the Chicago way, exemplified by the artistry of Louis Sullivan and Ludwig Mies van der Rohe. Asking today's hacks to do unique, world-class buildings, à la Frank Gehry, is like handing firecrackers to a four-year-old.

To be sure, these are the kind of problems cities want. The new residential towers have created thousands of construction jobs, expanded the tax base, and provided a built-in clientele for fancy stores and fine-dining restaurants. Chicago's astonishing vitality is the envy of smaller midwestern cities such as St. Louis and Milwaukee. Yet a vital city is not the same thing as a healthy city.

A healthy city is more than a collection of megabuck high-rises. It's a place where traffic moves instead of crawls; where shops and entertainment make lively, mixed-use districts instead of sterile in-town, dormitory suburbs; where parks and other open spaces create civilized clearings instead of wall-to-wall steel and concrete. There is a difference, in short, between carefully managed growth and unchecked Dodge City growth.

As Chicago rewrites its antiquated 1957 zoning ordinance, it is approaching these essential quality-of-life issues with the usual timidity, tweaking on the margins instead of addressing the problem's core: a failure on the part of public officials, developers, and architects to respond creatively to dramatic shifts in urban life, including the city's reinvigoration and its simultaneous suburbanization.

NATION'S LEADER

Chicago is anything but the Second City when it comes to new residential construction. Experts say it easily outpaces New York City, where there is far less "dirt"—developer-speak for prime open land—in and around Manhattan.

Since the current surge began in 1998, developers have completed—or started construction on—nearly 70 condominium and apartment high-rises in the greater downtown area, according to Tracy Cross, president of a Schaumburg-based real estate market analysis firm. Add a few more, and in the span of less than decade, Chicago will have built nearly as many high-rises as there are in all of Milwaukee.

The boom picked up steam in the early 1990s when developers converted old warehouses into inexpensive loft condominiums, then singles and young couples snapped them up. Downtown housing prices rose quickly, high enough by the late 1990s that loft developers were ready to make the leap from mid-rise warehouses to high-rise condos.

Loft owners traded up to the high-rises. At the same time, suburban home prices soared because baby boomers were flocking from the city to choice suburbs. That trend enabled empty nesters to cash in on their homes and to move downtown. Cross calls the phenomenon "the gerbil effect," comparing the flow of people between city and suburbs to the circular motion of a gerbil on a wheel.

All of a sudden, where there once had been surface parking lots, three-flats, and abandoned rail yards, high-rise residential buildings popped up. Prices escalated dramatically. Speculators entered the market, buying units they could "flip" to make a quick killing. The height of the towers rose in tandem with the stock market, leaping from a modest 20 stories to the 70-story Park Tower, a hotel-condo combo that, at 844 feet, is Chicago's 10th tallest building.

Then the stock market bust of 2000 and the September 11, 2001, terrorist attacks led to a dramatic decrease in sales. Today some high-rises have entirely unsold "see-through floors," and owners are offering free rent and other breaks to lure tenants and buyers. Even so, hoping to ride the next economic wave, developers are gearing up for more towers. Earthmovers have broken ground, for example, on the first high-rise at Lakeshore East, a $1.5 billion, 26-acre project that will rise on a former nine-hole golf course and driving range just south of East Wacker Drive and west of Lake Shore Drive. It could be home to as many 10,000 people.

As the boom moves to such high-profile locations, there is added urgency in the question "What kind of city is it giving us?"

The answer is not a happy one if you look at the monuments to mediocrity being churned out by two of the most prominent figures in the construction surge—Joel Carlins, founder of Magellan Development Group, and Jim Loewenberg, president of Near North Properties and head of his own architectural firm.

The two often work together, sometimes teaming with other developers, and Loewenberg typically does their designs. Their buildings are so widely reviled by architecture buffs that they have spawned a new lexicon. Former planners for the city speak of the "Loewenberg-ization" of the Near North Side, which increasingly is marred by the pair's high-rises. In such projects as One Superior Place, a 52-story concrete slab of an apartment building at 1 West Superior Street, the team has produced designs of sterile symmetry and unarticulated surfaces that recall the old housing blocs of East Berlin.

VARIATION ON A DISMAL THEME

The aforementioned Grand Plaza, whose design architect was Anthony Belluschi (with Loewenberg serving as project architect), is a twin-towered variation on this dismal theme—slightly zippier, with its chamfered tops, but ultimately overgrown and under-detailed.

Some of the pair's other projects are comically bad. At 222 North Columbus Avenue, the blank-walled, concrete top of their Park Millennium apartment tower looks menacingly monolithic, as if the building were harboring nuclear warheads. "The top got away from everybody," Loewenberg admitted.

In general, though, he is unapologetic. His designs grow from the philosophy that people rarely look above the bottom of a high-rise and that what they really want is decoration at the base of the building and high-quality apartments. Aesthetic refinements? They're frills. "We design to a budget," Loewenberg said.

That attitude is as cynical as it is lamentable, an abrogation of the architect's responsibility to design for the broader public as well as the client. Ludwig Mies van der Rohe designed to a budget and his 860–880 North Lake Shore Drive apartment towers, at once efficient and elegant, became the glass houses that remade skylines around the world.

Loewenberg's stance is so glaringly off base that one is tempted to write off the uglification of Chicago as the product of a single architect. But, in reality, there are lots of bad buildings out there, and they arise at least partly from "the gerbil effect," with the influx of suburban buyers exerting a subtle, but profound, influence on the urban fabric.

The difference between a condo tower in New York and one in Chicago is that the Chicago tower will have a base, roughly four to nine stories tall, that houses a parking garage where condo and apartment dwellers store their cars and SUVs. The apartment floors begin only after the parking garage ends.

It's a small difference with large consequences. It means that in New York, you look up from the sidewalk to the second floor and you see somebody's curtains. In Chicago, you look up and see, in most cases, a blank wall of concrete or opaque glass, because the city requires builders to cover parking garages rather than leaving them exposed.

From farther away, the Chicago buildings often have a split aesthetic identity—the base is clad in one material, usually brick, the condo tower in another, typically poured-in-place concrete. Usually, there is little visual integration between the two parts, as there is in the graceful corncob-shaped towers of Bertrand Goldberg's Marina City.

Such crude combinations are the defining characteristic of "plop architecture," also known as "tower on a podium" design. In the last five years, it has become pervasive, from Grand Plaza to the twin-towered River East Center at Illinois Street and Columbus Drive, by DeStefano + Partners. There, a 58-story condo tower and a 17-story hotel sit like chess pieces atop a 100-foot-tall base that houses movie theaters, a health club, and shops.

Though the lower floors of the podiums are often lined with stores or restaurants, these hulks could not be more different from the delicate scale of the Greenwich Village town houses that Jane Jacobs once championed as an antidote to chilly steel-and-glass high-rises standing on barren plazas. In an attempt to solve the old problem of a sterile pedestrian environment, planners are also allowing the huge podiums to come right out to the lot line. That has created a new problem—faceless, overwhelming bulk.

OVERPOWERING THE GOOD

Stack several examples of "plop architecture" alongside one another, as developers are doing on State and Dearborn Streets west of Michigan Avenue, and you get a case study in sky-blocking canyonization. The skyscrapers are shoehorned in so tightly that rare examples of architectural quality, such as Solomon Cordwell Buenz's finely scaled, 59-story Millennium Centre, almost cease to matter.

Instead of the old narrow band of high-rises along Michigan Avenue, there is a new thicket-like extension of the Loop, spreading across River North, Michigan Avenue, and Streeterville, whose infrastructure is increasingly overtaxed. On Streeterville's narrow roads, such as North St. Clair Street, it can take 15 minutes to go three blocks, a troubling sign of creeping Manhattanization.

There is precious little public open space in the areas east and west of the Boul Mich, a striking shortcoming for a mayor who has made the greening of Chicago a hallmark of his tenure. What good are Daley's plants and flowers when they are competing with an overgrown patch of architectural weeds?

Elsewhere downtown, the problem is not too many towers in too little space, but a suburbanization of the skyline, as one sees at Central Station,

MUSEUM PARK TOWERS
Banal neoclassicism that flops as architecture and urban design.

the dormitory-like, suburb-in-the-city now taking shape on a former abandoned rail yard that stretches southward from Roosevelt Road.

Central Station's first high-rises—the 20-story Museum Park Tower 1 and the 21-story Museum Park Tower 2, both by Pappageorge/Haymes architects—make a better stab at composition than the disjointed Loewenberg buildings. The trouble is they ape the classical design of the nearby Museum Campus. Worse, they're set in a staggered arrangement that opens up views from within condominium units but fails to form the kind of cliff-like wall one sees along North Lake Shore Drive.

The outcome, as is plain to anyone traveling along South Lake Shore Drive, is a group of buildings that resemble a suburban high-rise complex or, perhaps, an insurance company headquarters in Hartford, Connecticut. That impression is not dispelled by another Central Station structure, the Prairie House, a tiered mid-rise condo building by DeStefano + Partners. It would look equally at home in the suburbs and is just as derivative as the two Museum Park Towers, though it is imitating Frank Lloyd Wright.

There's a disappointing lack of vision here. City planners are supposed to keep developers and architects honest by setting certain minimum design standards. But at Central Station, River North, and River East, the planners allowed the construction of high-profile gateways to downtown that undercut Chicago's claim on being America's foremost architectural city. There's no way that should be allowed to happen at Lakeshore East, where Carlins and Loewenberg are the lead developers.

REFORM AND REGULATION

Daley's recent "no more ugly buildings" declaration recalls the movie *Amadeus*, in which the king tells a perplexed Mozart that his latest composition has "too many notes." The mayor's blast was a shot from the hip rather than a carefully articulated policy. It doesn't require developers to downscale or reshape their projects—merely to prettify them.

Not surprisingly, Chicago's planning commissioner, Alicia Berg, defends Daley, saying it was appropriate for the mayor to speak out. "His message was, 'C'mon, you guys can do better,'" she said. "It was sort of a general call."

As part of zoning reform, her department is advocating a lower threshold for proposed designs to undergo the intensive "planned development" review process. (Currently, such a review kicks in when a project is 600 feet tall or two acres in size.) Planners also are trying to limit the number of so-called non-accessory parking spaces in downtown highrises—spaces used by shoppers and other visitors—to reduce the parking podiums' bloat. And Berg wants to create a formal advisory committee of architects, landscape architects, and engineers that makes recommendations to her department as part of the review process.

The commissioner seems to be heading in the right direction, but one wonders if stronger measures and more fundamental solutions are needed.

Chicago is known as a freewheeling city, yet it also has a tradition of regulated growth. In 1893, for example, the city capped heights at 130 feet, and its 1923 zoning ordinance created setback formulas that helped shape such beloved towers as the Wrigley Building. These measures correctly recognized that while it is improper to mandate a style, there is a seamless continuum between architecture and urban design.

The right rules matter. City officials are ill-advised if they think they can get rid of the architectural blahs by demonizing one firm (Loewenberg already has lost one job in the wake of Daley's pronouncement). It would be far better to rejigger the rules of the development game so all firms would be more likely to do better designs.

In that spirit, how about downzoning the North Michigan Avenue district and upzoning areas around CTA elevated stops elsewhere in the city? How about some mandatory dos and don'ts, such as "Buildings along Lake Shore Drive and Wacker Drive should be of the highest architectural quality"?

Why not mandate—or at least encourage—that the bases of tower-on-a-podium buildings be wrapped in town houses, a step that already has tamed some of the monsters? Or, better yet, why not do away with "plop architecture," convening a range of experts (developers, architects, and planners) to come up with better models?

Forget star buildings by star architects. Ultimately, a city is only as good as the basic building blocks—the background buildings—that it comprises. Architects such as Graham, Anderson, Probst & White and David Hovey have completed high-rise projects in River North and downtown Evanston that show how architects can design background buildings on a budget and still give something back to the city. The challenge is not to squelch Chicago's astonishing residential building boom, but to guide it to serve the public good.

POSTSCRIPT

With the 2004 passage of a new zoning ordinance, the first comprehensive rewrite of its zoning code since 1957, Chicago enacted several measures that sought to address issues raised in this critique and one by the architecture critic Lynn Becker in the Chicago Reader. *The threshold for proposed designs to undergo the intensive "planned development" review process was lowered, ensuring that more high-rises would be subject to planners' scrutiny. In addition, the city limited the amount of non-accessory parking in high-rise buildings and created design standards for downtown buildings, including guidelines meant to preserve the character of pedestrian-oriented streets. "This is the first time that zoning in Chicago will address more than just height, bulk, and location, which is all the current code does," commented Peter Skosey, vice president of the nonprofit Metropolitan Planning Council.*

Separately, the city established an advisory panel that functioned as an advocate for general improvements in the development process, though not as a design review board for specific projects. Such measures helped stop the spread of the bland high-rises that were so prevalent in 2003. But experience would reveal that it is impossible for even the most well-meaning city government to legislate good design.

Once Grand, Now Bland

THE BOOM IN BRANCH BANKS IS SHORTCHANGING THE
CHARACTER OF NEIGHBORHOODS

FEBRUARY 23, 2005

Banks used to be about ritual and permanence. They resembled Greek
or Roman temples, with the banker playing the secular priest, dispensing
loans instead of benedictions. Banks inspired awe, though their built-for-
the-ages classicism was really a form of salesmanship, designed to convince
depositors that their money would be safer in the bank's vault than stuffed
in a mattress.

No more. Now banks want to look like Starbucks, not the Parthenon.
Around Chicago and the nation, branch banks are popping up like mush-
rooms—or, to put it another way, multiplying like cockroaches. Defying
predictions made in the 1990s, when online banking boomed and banks
trimmed spending on bricks and mortar, face-to-face banking is back. But
its architecture, on the whole, is disappointingly faceless.

In storefronts, strip malls, and even parking garages, many of the
branches are as visually generic as cell phone outlets, convenience stores,
or fast-food restaurants. Indeed, the new mini-banks—let's call them
McBanks—are the early 21st century's answer to the fast-food restaurants
of the late 20th century: loved for their convenience, loathed for their
cookie-cutter McArchitecture.

Instead of raising aesthetic standards, the new banks are raising blood
pressure. That's not simply because they look so bland, but because they
have pushed out corner drugstores and other retailers that make neighborhoods livable. They also are drawing fire because they don't generate sales
tax revenue, as stores do.

Not surprisingly, bankers and their design consultants take a different
view. They are giving customers what they want, they say—a convenient
combination of online, ATM, telephone, and in-person banking. Invariably, they use the word "intimidating" to describe the old banks, saying
that they were as cold and impersonal as Department of Motor Vehicles
branches.

In contrast, the new banks fall all over themselves to glad-hand you.
Teller lines and roped-off areas are out. Now tellers and managers dress in
the unpriestly garb of "business casual." Banks from Sarasota, Florida, to
San Jose, California, share branches with Starbucks. "A scone with your
loan?" the trade journal *American Banker* quipped in a recent story.

While these amenities undoubtedly appeal to customers, they don't address the one thing that the branch bank boom hasn't altered: banks, like all buildings, still have the capacity to add to or detract from the cityscape. And that raises a vexing question: Is it possible for a bank to be approachable and functional without being dumbed down architecturally?

THE NEW FACE-TO-FACE BANKING

As computer use boomed in the 1990s, it appeared that banks were ready to sever their historic ties with human interaction. They invested heavily in online operations and sliced spending on new buildings. Actual banks appeared ready to disappear into the ether of the Internet.

But a funny thing happened on the way to a placeless banking universe: plenty of customers still wanted to look into the eyes of a banker. And banks discovered that branches provided them with the perfect platform to sell customers not just checking accounts, but insurance and other financial services that used to be off-limits because of federal regulations dating back to the Great Depression.

As a result, the number of branch banks around the country has steadily increased to more than 80,000, according to the American Bankers Association, a Washington, DC–based trade group. While 36 million U.S. households banked online in 2004, a nearly fivefold increase from 1998, more than 9 of every 10 households still visits a branch bank once a month.

Chicago is the epicenter of the branch-banking boom, largely because old Illinois laws that restricted the spread of branch banking recently have been relaxed. Bank One, for example, added 60 branches last year, giving it 310 branches in the six-county Chicago area and northwest Indiana. Upstart Washington Mutual, based in Seattle, claims 150 in the region.

Yet the new face-to-face banking is dispiritingly banal compared to the old bank temples. The only thing remotely Greek or Roman about a Washington Mutual branch is the bank's code name for the design—"Occasio," which is Latin for "favorable opportunity."

"Our customers, as we interviewed them, didn't talk to us about building something that resembled a mausoleum," explained Karen Curtin, Washington Mutual's senior vice president for innovation and customer insight. "Banks can be intimidating. They wanted a place where they would come in and feel comfortable."

A downtown branch at 431 North Orleans Street, which follows the Occasio prototype created for Washington Mutual by Dayton-based Design Forum, reveals the strengths and weaknesses of this approach.

A WASHINGTON MUTUAL BRANCH BANK
Convenient banking, impoverished architecture.

The branch is shoehorned into a street-level storefront of an exposed-concrete parking garage. The exterior—it's a stretch to call it a facade—has windows that let passersby see inside instead of the massive columns that offered the old banks real and symbolic protection. The lone feature that distinguishes the little bank's exterior is a bright blue awning. If you squint, it could be the awning for a White Hen convenience store.

Inside, the space is decidedly untraditional. Kiosk-like "teller towers" let customers stand alongside tellers instead of facing them across the barrier of granite counters and teller cages. A children's play space encourages busy families to bring their kids to the bank. Warm colors—purples, greens, and yellows—have more in common with a Starbucks than the cool white marble banks of yore.

Give the Occasio branches their due: they organize banking in a way that responds to the relaxed American lifestyle, and they do so in a way that is visually fresh—crisp and clean-lined rather than tarted up with paste-on stone columns. They are performing well economically, Curtin said, though she declines to provide specifics.

Still, there's a disturbing sameness to them. The branches don't so much defile city and suburban downtowns with tastelessness as drag them down with cookie-cutter banality. Multiply that banality over and over, as McBanks cluster in city neighborhoods or suburbs, and you wind up with a bigger problem: too many banks in too little space.

At the Armitage Avenue–Halsted Street intersection in Lincoln Park, a Citibank, a North Community Bank, and a mansion-like Bridgeview Bank hold down three of the four corners. To the west along Armitage, squeezed into storefronts, are a Fifth Third Bank, a Bank One, and a National City Bank.

Merchants are right to view the influx warily, and not just because most of these banks look like yokels at a party of chic urbanites. The influx threatens to sap Armitage of its retail identity, displacing one-of-a-kind boutiques with could-be-anywhere branches. In addition, as the merchants argue, the banks put a damper on retailing because they close before the other stores and (excluding ATM service) aren't open at night or on Sundays.

"Merchants there say they would rather have their worst competitors open up a shop across the street than have another bank come in," said Charles Eastwood, chief of staff for Alderman Vi Daley (43rd), in whose ward the district is located.

CURBING MCBANKS

In response, Daley introduced an amendment to the city's new zoning code that the Chicago City Council passed earlier this year. In its final form, the measure requires a bank to get a special-use permit if it wants to build a new branch within 600 feet of an existing bank in an area designated a "pedestrian retail street." The law covers several North Side retail strips, such as Armitage.

Yet the Chicago law is a blunt instrument compared with the more sophisticated set of tools being used in the North Shore suburb of Lake Forest. Its regulations were put in place after Cincinnati-based Fifth Third Bank announced in 2003 that it would construct a new branch in the suburb's western business district, upsetting residents because the district already had three banks and the new one would displace a dry cleaner, an interior design shop, and other retailers.

Concerned that Lake Forest would be left with a glut of buildings suitable for nothing but banks, the suburb imposed a 90-day moratorium on new bank construction and passed a law requiring a special-use permit for banks. But unlike Chicago's new measure, the law gives the suburb leverage to control such things as whether a new bank's materials and design are compatible with its neighbors. It also allows Lake Forest to pressure banks so their buildings can be converted to other uses, particularly stores.

The first bank built under these requirements, a new Bank of America at 780 North Western Avenue, sits a couple of blocks north of Howard Van Doren Shaw's brilliant Arts and Crafts–style Market Square shopping center. Designed by Timothy Morgan Associates of Lincolnshire, it looks nothing like a grand old banking temple or a new strip-mall bank. Instead, the two-story structure offers an attractive mix of permanence and flexibility.

A simplified version of an old-fashioned Main Street commercial building, the branch sports handsome brick arches and other traditional touches. But its street-level window bays are the most revealing detail. If the bank was to go out of business, a store could easily put those show windows to good use. "You could see this being a Gap or an Abercrombie & Fitch," said Tom Broadfoot, an assistant manager at the bank. Even the vault could be reused, he joked, if the bank became a jewelry store.

The new Bank of America is a decent, civilized building, modestly matching the scale and character of the storefronts along its street while ceding pride of place to the picturesque towers of Market Square. This is good contextual architecture, free of postmodern pastiche or mock traditionalism. It suggests a different and more enlightened direction for bank design, one that recognizes that the old days of grand bank temples are gone, but that a bank's responsibility to shape the public realm remains as significant as ever.

POSTSCRIPT

Local regulations didn't curb the spread of branch banks, but the recession did, albeit marginally. As the economy went into free-fall in 2008, Washington Mutual failed, the biggest bank collapse in American history. New York–based JPMorgan Chase (which had previously acquired Bank One) purchased the bank and announced in 2009 that it would shutter 209 Washington Mutual locations nationwide, including 57 in Chicago and its suburbs. But such consolidation proved the exception rather than rule. As the New York Times *reported in 2009, bankers were loath to shut down local branches, even though they were costly to maintain. The chief reason: closing the branches risked making customers think about moving their deposits elsewhere.*

A Mickey D's on Steroids

WHEN SUPERSIZE ISN'T NECESSARILY BETTER

APRIL 17, 2005

Just as the McDonald's restaurants of the 1950s expressed a buoyant, space-age modernism, so the beefy new downtown McDonald's that just made its splashy debut delivers a telling statement about its time: the age of swelling McMansions, gargantuan gas-guzzling SUVs, and baseball players who bulked up by injecting themselves with steroids.

In this high-profile flagship restaurant at 600 North Clark Street, which holds down the western gateway to downtown, the supersize meets the retro and the result is the ultimate Big Mac Attack—a massive version of the old McDonald's outlets and a missed opportunity to lift the River North area of Chicago out of its theme-park muck.

To be fair, the new McDonald's has its moments, and they range from a highly transparent glass facade that creates a dazzling nighttime beacon along Ontario Street to the reproductions of classic modern furniture that adorn its surprisingly upscale interior. But on the whole, this showcase project is as disappointing as a stale batch of French fries.

A MCDONALD'S FOR THE 21ST CENTURY

Last year, when Oak Brook–based McDonald's asked three top Chicago architects—Helmut Jahn, Martin Wolf, and Daniel P. Coffey—to cook up plans for replacing the landmark Rock 'n' Roll McDonald's that occupied the site for 20 years, it had a chance to write a new essay in innovation, one that would be as fitting for the start of the 21st century as the midcentury McDonald's restaurants were for their time.

Jahn, for example, suggested a combination of the superscale road signs celebrated by Philadelphia postmodernist Robert Venturi and his own high-tech aesthetic: a curving steel-and-glass pavilion, tucked behind a nearly 100-foot-tall, perforated metal set of the Golden Arches. Cars would have slipped under one side of this giant "M," pedestrians the other. A tree-lined esplanade promised to lead those on foot to the two-story pavilion, where the latest in electric lights would have projected whimsical images, such as a Big Mac that disappeared with each successive bite. The design was wonderfully fresh, a transparent, multimedia spectacle that integrated the latest technology into a powerful aesthetic whole.

Instead, McDonald's discarded the three architects' plans and clung to the familiar look of its 1950s restaurants and their trademark space-age features—parabolic arches, a tilted, wedge-shaped roof, and glass windows canted upward and outward, like those in an airport control tower. That look was largely crafted by Richard and Maurice McDonald, then adapted by Ray Kroc, the brothers' franchising agent, for the McDonald's he opened in northwest suburban Des Plaines in 1955. Kroc later bought out the McDonald brothers and became the driving force behind McDonald's growth.

It's easy to understand why the company decided to celebrate the 50th anniversary of the Des Plaines McDonald's and the genius who molded its worldwide empire. Got a brand identity that millions of baby boomers love? Don't mess with it. But why not do something bold, especially in the first city of American architecture?

A LACK OF SIMPLICITY

Designed by Daniel Wohlfeil, McDonald's director of worldwide development, the new franchise outlet is burdened by the need to marry the company's old image with its new demands for space.

The statistics are telling: the Des Plaines McDonald's was a one-story, 900-square-foot structure with no indoor dining and no drive-through lanes. In that spartan setting, you went to the walk-up windows and ordered. In contrast, the new Chicago model has two stories of indoor dining

A SHOWCASE MCDONALD'S
A supersize version of the original McDonald's, cooked up for the age of excess.

for up to 300 patrons, two drive-through lanes, and 24,000 square feet of space, including a cappuccino, espresso, and gelato bar (McDonald's answer to Starbucks). Simple and modestly scaled, it's not.

Wohlfeil has arranged the restaurant in three parts that logically descend in a tier from Ontario Street on the north to Ohio Street on the south: First, the blown-up version of the old McDonald's, which sports 60-foot-tall arches (more than double the height of the originals); then a shorter midsection topped by a curving indoor seating area that looks out on a "green roof" of mulch, rocks, and greenery; and, finally, a tail end that duplicates the diminutive scale of the Des Plaines McDonald's—only the original now becomes a mere canopy for the drive-through lanes.

As urban design, the showcase McDonald's is not so terrible. The big pavilion holds down the Ontario-Clark corner, shaping a comfortable sidewalk space for pedestrians. That's better than plopping down the restaurant like a spaceship in the middle of the block.

The building's state-of-the-art, self-supporting glass walls do more than allow it to shine at night. They open the interior to the outside, taking advantage of skyline views and bringing the vitality of Chicago inside—a welcome departure from nearby, inward-turning theme attractions like the hideous Rainforest Cafe.

GROTESQUE, NOT CUTE

Yet as architecture, the new McDonald's is hardly Grade A. The key problem is its shift in scale, which is comparable to taking a cute little '50s ranch house and blowing it up to twice its normal size. If you could actually do that, the ranch house would look grotesque rather than cute. And so it is with the new McDonald's.

As Philip Langdon wrote in his 1986 book *Orange Roofs, Golden Arches*, the old McDonald's outlets had "a feeling of skyward momentum, symbolic of an aerospace age in which man could hurtle himself into the heavens." Here, however, what used to seem nimble and light comes off as blockbusting and weighty. Even the innovative details, such as the spider-shaped metal fixtures that hold the floor-to-ceiling glass walls in place, appear strangely oversize and clunky.

The inside is more successful, particularly the second floor, where the absence of internal columns (made possible because the arches help hold up the roof rather than being merely decorative, as in the original McDonald's) creates an airy, free-flowing space. On the floor's north side, horizontal wood slats create intimate rooms within a room, and these spaces are filled by Ludwig Mies van der Rohe's Barcelona chairs and other classics of modern furniture. Mies in a McDonald's? Well, why not? Though the furnishings create an incongruous mix of high culture and low, museum and commercial emporium, they nonetheless signal McDonald's intent to bring a new sophistication to its restaurant interiors.

A curving seating area along the floor's south side is done with similar flair, featuring a decade-by-decade wall display of McDonald's history and furniture to match (including some very 1960s Egg chairs).

All this is fun, but in the end, it's more nostalgic than of the moment—a way for McDonald's to shrewdly associate itself with classic design and thus underscore its advertising theme of "forever young." To truly stay forever young, though, you have to be willing to take a risk and reinvent yourself. This project, sadly, turned out to be more about oversize recycling than bracing reinterpretation.

POSTSCRIPT

While the showcase McDonald's in Chicago was a disappointment, the aesthetic ambition of its interior signaled a praiseworthy trend: the upgrading of design standards at thousands of the chain's U.S. outlets. In prototypes rolled out in 2006, McDonald's ditched its outdated exteriors, with their screeching ketchup-red and mustard-yellow mansard roofs, for a tastefully muted modernism with a sprinkle of dynamic asymmetry. McDonald's also transformed its harsh plastic-heavy interiors into soft earth-toned places where customers might linger with a laptop in an upholstered chair beneath a stylish pendant light. The quality of the interiors created by individual franchise operators varied widely, but the shift reflected how much design expectations in America had risen, in large part because of the influence of Starbucks. Its outlets offered a multi-sensory mix of hip furniture, piped-in jazz, and aroma-heavy coffee. The combination was much-admired—until Starbucks over-expanded and announced in 2008 that it would shut down scores of stores.

A Gallery of Rogues

FOR EVERY GEM PRODUCED BY THE LONG-RUNNING BUILDING BOOM, THERE ARE EVEN MORE CLUNKERS

JANUARY 27, 2008

There is the ideal Chicago, the showcase city glimpsed on the Chicago River boat tour that glides past the Wrigley Building and other glorious skyscrapers. And then there is the real Chicago, a Dickensian construction zone where it is simultaneously the best and the worst of times.

Come see it, if you dare.

On North Michigan Avenue, shoehorned behind the mountain-like mass of the InterContinental Chicago hotel, there's Avenue East, an orange-and-white hulk designed in the colors of a Creamsicle. Just north of McCormick Place stands Museum Park Place, a stubby slab that addresses South Lake Shore Drive with a superscale tic-tac-toe grid in screeching red.

Farther north on the Drive, in the big Lakeshore East project, there's the Lancaster, a tinselly glass tower that looks like it dropped in from China. And then, on East Chicago Avenue, you stumble upon the Bernardin, a postmodern cartoon with a parking-garage base wrapped in a comically bad, neo-Italianate stage set, right down to the keystones above faux windows.

This rogues' gallery of condominium and apartment towers, all either new or completed in the last few years, reveals a trend that Chicago's boosters will find hard to swallow: for every authentic gem produced by the long-running building boom, such as Helmut Jahn's quietly elegant condo tower at 600 North Fairbanks Court, there are more gewgaws— structures that offend not only because they're poorly designed but also because they erode the city's extraordinary sense of place.

It has been nearly five years since Mayor Richard M. Daley attacked an earlier wave of exposed-concrete apartment and condominium towers that resemble monotonous, Soviet-style housing and issued his headline-generating "no more ugly buildings" edict. But while city planners have improved their review procedures since then, no bureaucrat can legislate good design.

And so we are confronted with irreversible visual carnage, as on South Lake Shore Drive, where drivers gazing out the windshield confront a crazy quilt of structures—mock-classical, mock–Prairie style, and Dallas Freeway Modern. Yes, they're selling like hot cakes, but real estate success has never looked so cheap.

The bigger story here reaches beyond Chicago to boomtowns across America and the world: this is a time of urbanization without urbanity; of star architects who are their own brands, not the standard-bearers of larger movements; of idiosyncratic, do-your-own-thing "icon buildings" rather than broadly accepted norms that generate satisfying cityscapes.

"Individualism is emphasized to a greater extent now," said Neil Harris, professor emeritus of art history at the University of Chicago and author of *Chicago Apartments: A Century of Lakefront Luxury*, an authoritative study

of Lake Shore Drive's historic apartment high-rises. "Why should buildings be any different?"

Though fear of recession, the sagging stock market, and an oversupply of units could slow the building boom or eventually bring it to a halt, many developers at least publicly maintain that they will forge ahead with new projects, including the Santiago Calatrava–designed, 2,000-foot Chicago Spire. That may or may not be good news, depending on your threshold for architectural mediocrity.

Since 1998, developers have completed or started construction on more than 160 buildings in Chicago's greater downtown area that are at least 12 stories tall (the widely accepted definition of a high-rise), according to Gail Lissner, a vice president at Appraisal Research Counselors. That's more high-rises than there are in all of Detroit (126), St. Louis (105), or Milwaukee (83), according to the Emporis building database. In just 10 years, then, Chicago has built the equivalent of an entire downtown. But quantity is hardly commensurate with quality, as seen by a snapshot contrast of elegant North Lake Shore Drive with its ugly-duckling counterpart to the south.

COMMONALITY WORKS

Why is it better up north? As Harris points out, the apartment towers that went up along the Drive in the 1920s were built in proximity, so they had the effect of imitating a cliff. Their styles ran the gamut from neo-Gothic to neo–Renaissance revival, but they shared a common scale and common materials (brick, limestone, and other masonry). As a result, they constituted something of a family where the whole was more than the sum of the individual parts.

"Those buildings helped one another," Harris said. "They fit. It was almost as if they had been designed by the same architect."

But it's a different story down south at Central Station, the dormitory-like, vertical suburb that's taking shape on 80 acres of formerly abandoned rail yards that stretch southward from Roosevelt Road. The workhorse Chicago firm of Pappageorge/Haymes is one of Central Station's chief architects, and its initial efforts have been desultory.

As if to compensate for the stodgy classicism of its 20-story Museum Park Tower 1 and 21-story Museum Park Tower 2, Pappageorge/Haymes's just-completed 23-story Museum Park Place flaunts an aggressive red

AVENUE EAST
The "Creamsicle" building, shoehorning square footage behind the Magnificent Mile.

supergrid, which expresses the building's structure. The result is a "look at me" one-liner, the kind of thing you'd expect to see along a freeway in Houston or Dallas. While there are some good strokes here, such as the human-scaled town houses at the tower's base, even Daley's design guru bemoans the results.

"It's a huge missed opportunity in many ways along Lake Shore Drive," said Sam Assefa, the mayor's deputy chief of staff for economic and physical development.

STRIVING TO DO BETTER

The other big residential project now materializing along the Drive, Lakeshore East, has its own aesthetic problems, as Jim Loewenberg, the chief architect and co-developer of the widely panned concrete hulks in River North, strives to do better—and rises to the level of mediocrity.

While this sunken 28-acre parcel near the Aon Center offers a handsome contemporary park at its core and is drawing thousands of residents to once-fallow downtown land, its architecture couldn't be spottier.

Along Columbus Drive, you see architect Jeanne Gang's 82-story, under-construction Aqua tower, with its strikingly undulating balconies. But ringing the park are several subpar Loewenberg-designed high-rises, such as the Lancaster, a 30-story condo tower whose bowing expanses of glass have a nervous, jittery look, like the mirror-glass towers in the opening credits of the 1970s TV show *Dallas*.

Lakeshore East speaks to the quality gap between the profession's stars and its anonymous rank and file. It's like a baseball team that has a couple of power-hitting .300 hitters while everybody else bats .100. You may get a home-run building here or there, but the overall quality of the architecture is anything but all-star.

SHOEHORNING HURTS

That same lack of skill is evident in smaller projects, such as Avenue East, the 28-story condo tower tacked onto the back of the InterContinental. The design, by the little-known firm of Built Form Architecture, employs its Creamsicle palette of orange-toned concrete and white metal panels—a failed stab at creating a light, contemporary response to the weightiness of the eclectic old hotel. But the new building jarringly crowds the InterContinental instead of setting it off, as a beautifully detailed glass tower would have done. This is shoehorning, plain and simple, and the big question is why city planners allowed it without demanding better architecture.

THE BERNARDIN

A painful reminder that architects should be taught to practice traditional design instead of learning to despise it.

Assefa responds that the city has established a stricter design review process since many of the offending towers were approved and that the outcome will be better architecture and urban design in such high-profile locations as the south edge of Grant Park. He's right—sort of.

The city's added scrutiny pushed Pappageorge/Haymes to improve its initial design for the under-construction One Museum Park. The curvy, glassy 62-story tower at Roosevelt and the Drive already commands that corner and promises to frame Grant Park, even if it looks like something out of a *Buck Rogers* comic book.

But smaller buildings such as the 26-story Bernardin, designed by Antunovich Associates and named for the late Joseph Cardinal Bernardin, still don't meet the size threshold for extensive design review. So we face the prospect of more towers like this one, with tarted-up parking-garage podiums and poorly proportioned mansard roofs. Chicago has the character to absorb such pounding. Yet why not insist on something more sophisticated than a 3-D cartoon?

LESSONS LEARNED?

Surely the answer does not lie solely in regulating the end product of architects' work, but in teaching them how to produce better buildings from the start. As Ned Cramer, the editor in chief of *Architecture* magazine, observed recently, architecture schools need to start teaching traditional design rather than teaching their students to despise it.

The great 19th-century English critic John Ruskin once wrote: "When we build, let us think that we build forever. . . . [L]et us think, as we lay stone on stone, that a time is to come when those stones will be held sacred because our hands have touched them, and that men will say, as they look upon the labor and the wrought substance of them, 'See! This our fathers did for us.'"

That is certainly preferable to leaving a legacy of architectural mug shots.

GEMS AMID THE ROUGH

NOT ALL THE BUILDINGS PRODUCED DURING THE BOOM YEARS WERE DUDS. IF you knew where to look, you could find sparkling exceptions. A trio of examples by some of Chicago's most talented practitioners—Ralph Johnson, Andrew Metter, and Jeanne Gang—showed how the brute material of concrete, so prevalent in the rash of mediocre high-rises, could be transformed into visual poetry. Along with fine residential work by other Chicago architects, these projects revealed a rejuvenation of modernism and the city's continued capacity, when the circumstances were right, to produce design of the highest quality.

A Sparkling New High-Rise

THE CONTEMPORAINE, BY RALPH JOHNSON,
HERALDS THE REVIVAL OF MODERNISM

MARCH 21, 2004

There's something fresh and wonderful at 516 North Wells Street in Chicago: an exposed concrete high-rise that's butterfly light rather than tombstone heavy.

The new 15-story condominium building, known as the Contemporaine and designed by Ralph Johnson of Perkins+Will, represents a welcome departure from the hulking residential towers that have deadened the Chicago cityscape of late. Yet it has a broader significance. It is one of several high-rises in Chicago that are frankly—and winningly—modern.

These buildings show that the Chicago tradition of taking the utilitarian and transforming it into art is far from dead. Their high level of design quality also begs this question: Why should we (and City Hall) be willing to accept such awful stuff elsewhere?

Besides the Contemporaine, the bright spots include Johnson's 39-story Skybridge at 1 North Halsted Street, where a trellis-like bridge surmounts the empty space between two towers; Lucien Lagrange's 27-story Erie on the Park at 510 West Erie Street, which flaunts V-shaped structural braces; and Brininstool + Lynch's 20-story Vue20 tower at 1845 South Michigan Avenue, a boxy but attractive high-rise that asserts itself on the skyline with a projecting aluminum sunshade.

These just-completed buildings have a lot in common. They reinterpret the architectural language of 20th-century modernism, but they do things that classic modernist designs don't. They have lively, articulated tops. They relate to the street rather than standing aloof from it. They are, in short, good neighbors, which incorporate the lessons of postmodernism to make a better modernism.

DEBT TO LE CORBUSIER

As Johnson freely acknowledges, the Contemporaine, like Skybridge, draws inspiration from the Swiss-born architect Le Corbusier. The later designs of this 20th-century master resembled enormous pieces of abstract sculpture, with rough-hewn concrete walls that retained the imprint of their wooden molds. Earlier, as in his legendary Villa Savoye, Le Corbusier put his buildings on stilt-like columns to emphasize their lightness.

Anyone looking at the exposed and unpainted concrete walls of the Contemporaine or its tall and very slender concrete columns will instantly recognize Johnson's debt to Le Corbusier. The building is not brutally tough, but surprisingly refined, remaining small enough to ensure that the concrete never becomes overwhelming. Johnson is thus able to provide a model for better residential high-rises, his composition of clearly articulated parts creating a singular whole.

The most surprising of those parts is the four-story parking garage at the Contemporaine's base. It's not the typical decorated podium, its garage

THE CONTEMPORAINE
An elegant essay in glass and concrete.

hidden behind walls of tarted-up concrete. Rather, it's faced in floor-to-ceiling glass, just like the condos above it. Through its modest scale, it relates perfectly to the Contemporaine's motley surroundings, which range from old Victorians to Binny's Beverage Depot, complete with a neon sign shaped like a bottle.

This is the first Chicago garage in recent memory to exhibit such alluring transparency. It ought to help convince the planners at City Hall that a garage can be attractive without pretending it is not a garage. Johnson further enlivens the garage by expressing the diagonal ramp that leads up to it from the street.

The dynamism evident in that gesture pervades this entire building, with Johnson relying on both erosion and projection to endow his design with sculptural excitement. He carves out the tower's corner to emphasize its ground-level entrance and plays the same game in the sky, drawing your eye to a soaring void at the building's top. A 45-foot-tall, curving concrete column further marks the entrance, with balconies perched thrillingly atop it, like the plates a magician twirls on a stick.

PINWHEELING ENERGY

The balconies are equally inventive. While some run across the face of the building, others pop out like mini–diving boards. All have elegant glass walls, not typical picket fences that resemble prison bars. Instead of being draped symmetrically across the exterior, they thrust in different directions, giving the Contemporaine a pinwheeling energy.

Other refinements, such as a horizontal slot between the garage and the 11-story residential tower, underscore the impression that the building consists of floating parts. At the summit, a concrete wall folds over the big void like a piece of origami. Along with a thin, curving column that echoes the one at the entrance, the folded wall endows the Contemporaine with a skyline presence that other new high-rises conspicuously lack.

Sometimes beautifully sculpted buildings can be utterly uninhabitable. But not this one.

Johnson has thoughtfully laid out the 28 condominium units, which are targeted to what real estate agents like to call the "upper bracket" (the units range in price from $364,000 for a 2-bedroom, 1-bath to $1.45 million for a penthouse). Floor-to-ceiling glass helps bring the outside inside, making the units seem more spacious. Exposed concrete ceilings are not for everybody, but the units, with their hardwood floors and Euro kitchen furnishings, are elegant in an edgy sort of way. The lone functional problem comes in the parking garage, where the ramp carrying traffic both up and down is narrow and very steep.

Vue20—which, like the Contemporaine, was backed by the CMK Development Corporation—shows how the principles underlying Johnson design can be applied to a less expensive building. In this case, Brininstool + Lynch handsomely reinterpret the architect Louis Sullivan's idea of the skyscraper as a three-part composition, comparable to the base, shaft, and capital of a classical column. True to its name, the high-rise offers striking city and lakefront views through its floor-to-ceiling glass.

More upscale than Vue20, Erie on the Park has its own modernist precedent, its V-braces recalling the structurally expressive X-braces of the 100-story John Hancock Center. Lagrange has designed its apartments not simply as cubes of space, bloodless and rational, but as dramatic interiors where movement is boldly choreographed to achieve maximum visual impact with minimal square footage.

Buildings like these offer a much-needed reminder: Architecture is the art we live with—and live in. We're in the age of spectacle buildings, fantastic sculptural creations such as Frank Gehry's Walt Disney Concert Hall in Los Angeles and Santiago Calatrava's Milwaukee Art Museum addition. These cultural landmarks are terrific (and they draw tourists), but the risk is that their bling will blind us to larger issues, from the new imperative to conserve scarce resources through ecologically sensitive "green" design to the ever-pressing need to provide spirit-lifting shelter. Contemporaine and its counterparts answer the call for better housing that creatively shapes the contours of our lives, both inside and out.

Pleasant Dreams

LIGHTER-THAN-AIR SERTA HEADQUARTERS ELEVATES
THE ORDINARY

MARCH 8, 2009

The new headquarters for the mattress people at Serta is no architectural snooze. It is, rather, a quiet beauty that floats lightly, almost dreamily, above the land, evoking Ludwig Mies van der Rohe's Farnsworth House, the supremely elegant modernist masterpiece that rises on steel stilts along the Fox River.

THE SERTA INTERNATIONAL CENTER
A model suburban office headquarters that touches the earth lightly.

That is a high compliment, but this building deserves it because, unlike the 58-year-old Farnsworth House, which Mies designed as a weekend retreat, Serta is a workaday structure filled with offices and cubicles and machines that beat up mattresses. The Serta headquarters makes visual poetry, in other words, out of the prosaic stuff of everyday life.

Just north of the Northwest Tollway in Hoffman Estates—in the 780-acre Prairie Stone business park that contains a visual hodgepodge of office buildings, hotels, and stores—the headquarters was designed by Andrew Metter of the multifaceted Chicago design firm once called A. Epstein and Sons International and now known simply as Epstein.

Metter, 57, is one of Chicago's most underrated architects, a non-star who bears similarities to the better-known and more original Glenn Murcutt, the Pritzker Prize–winning Australian architect who likes to quote the Aboriginal proverb: "Touch the earth lightly."

Although Metter is a commercial architect while Murcutt specializes in houses, both men prefer a portfolio that is local, not global. Like Murcutt, Metter is almost obsessively deliberative, taking his time with buildings instead of cranking out junk. Almost naively, in this age of cynical, globe-hopping "starchitects" for whom architecture is a confidence game of "can you top this?" imagery, Metter still believes in the power of good design to make the world better, if only in small ways.

All these things come together at the Serta global headquarters, which houses 110 employees of the nation's number 3 mattress maker (following rivals Sealy and Simmons) and is a showcase for the company to display its products to retailers and other buyers.

Metter got the job when Barbara Bradford, Serta's senior vice president of marketing, felt dissatisfied after interviewing other architects. She went for a ride to find buildings she liked and came upon an ocean liner–like, Metter-designed office and warehouse building in Prairie Stone. Intrigued, she walked in the lobby and asked the receptionist who designed it. "Andy Metter," replied the architecturally attuned receptionist.

Occupying a small portion of a 20-acre site filled with prairie plants and a picturesque retention pond, and formally known as the Serta International Center, Metter's new building is an artful two-parter. Part 1 is a two-story, steel-framed rectangular block that houses common areas such as a research and development center, an auditorium, and a lunchroom. Part 2—framed in concrete and filled with offices, conference rooms, and small showroom areas—consists of a single story that bends like the letter S and extends outward from the rectangular block.

The ensemble, shaped by Metter with Epstein project architect Daesun Park and Terry Ryan of Jacobs/Ryan Associates Landscape Architects of Chicago, is much more than the sum of its details.

Whether you view Serta from the tollway or from the walking paths in Prairie Stone, it presents a captivating tension, at once echoing the dominant horizontality of the prairie landscape and seemingly levitating above it. This effect stems principally from the fact that the building's floor level is raised four feet above the ground, a feature that Metter dramatizes with protruding window bays and concrete brows that wrap around the exterior like a Möbius strip. He also lets the ground slope beneath the structure's southwest edge, making it appear to float.

The design thus symbolizes environmental responsibility and delivers on that message with a range of deftly integrated green features. The raised southwest corner, for example, lets rainwater flow beneath it into the retention pond.

Unfortunately, there is too much pavement as one approaches the Serta headquarters, a consequence of the need to create a turnaround for trucks and other vehicles. But the design entices you inward with such alluring details as a pair of gently sloping, exquisitely detailed ramps that lead to the raised office floors. Metter conceived of them, like sleep, as a threshold to another world.

Metter's interior plan is fundamentally sound, putting corridors for visitors along the hard-edged entrance side while placing offices for employees toward the softer, more expansive prairie views. Following the European model of the thin, light-grabbing building, the floors are just 63 feet wide, giving everybody access to views and natural light. Metter controls natural light with a variety of features, including frosted glass, hand-operated sunshades, and the aforementioned upper concrete brows.

A post-tensioned concrete roof creates long spans and prevents intrusive columns from disrupting the work spaces. Employees can open hopper windows to let fresh air stream in—a welcome change from the hermetically sealed suburban office buildings that allow people to see nature without sensing it. Metter has shaped almost every aspect of the interior, right down to the chic jet-black coffee bars. While Serta does not have a fancy food court, the two-story block in the center of the building offers employees another amenity: a second-floor lunchroom that overlooks the prairie and has an outdoor wooden deck.

Equally well handled is the high-ceilinged R&D center, a factory-like space where the company makes prototype mattresses and subjects potential products to equipment such as the Cornell Mattress Testing Machine. (This brute rams a 230-pound weight into a mattress 100,000 times to test whether it can retain its shape and firmness.) Long slats of channel glass let diffused daylight seep into the big R&D center, dramatically reducing the need for artificial light.

True, the showplace headquarters cost anywhere from 10 to 30 percent more than a typical suburban office building, depending on how you define "typical." But for Serta, which wanted a "statement building" and was willing to pay for it, the benefits are clear: a workplace that should help to attract and retain good employees; better internal communication because of the interior's openness; and an image that projects the identity of a forward-thinking industry leader.

This is the Chicago area's finest suburban office building since architect Ralph Johnson's 2002 Crate & Barrel headquarters in Northbrook, but it has a wider significance than that superlative suggests. Here, the desire for a "statement building" did not produce a self-aggrandizing one-liner.

Instead, Metter and his clients created real architecture: a building that serves its users, enhances its site, and raises the task of making mattresses to the level of art.

Waves of Creativity

THE AQUA TOWER, BY RISING STAR JEANNE GANG, IS ONE OF CHICAGO'S BOLDEST AND BEST NEW SKYSCRAPERS

NOVEMBER 8, 2009

Aqua, the spectacular new Chicago skyscraper with the sensuous, undulating balconies, is the pearl of the long-running, now-ending Chicago building boom, a design that is as fresh conceptually as it is visually.

A skyscraper typically consists of repetitive right-angled parts, a money-saving device that frequently produces aesthetic monotony. But in this defiantly non-Euclidean high-rise, almost nothing seems to repeat. Its white, wafer-thin balconies bulge outward, each slightly different from the next. They race around corners and shoot upward in fantastic, voluptuous stacks. This is a new vision of verticality, and it makes Aqua one of Chicago's boldest—and best—skyscrapers in years.

Located just north of Millennium Park at 225 North Columbus Drive, the 82-story tower is still in the finishing stages, so it is impossible to fully assess whether its function is as successful as its form. Nonetheless, it can be said that Aqua is remarkable on several counts.

It is one of the world's tallest buildings designed by a woman and the first skyscraper from Chicago's Jeanne Gang of Studio Gang Architects, who is only 45 years old. Aqua also is a real estate miracle: its financing documents were signed in late August 2007—just before the credit crunch hit. Had the tower been delayed by 60 to 90 days, said the building's architect-of-record and co-developer, Jim Loewenberg, it might never have been built.

None of this would matter without Gang's singular design, whose three chief components are hotel space (for now, without an occupant) on floors 4 through 18, apartments on floors 19 through 52, and condominiums from floors 53 to 81. There are also shops, parking, and town houses.

Essentially, then, Aqua is a residential skyscraper, a place to live (or sleep) rather than a place to work. And it takes full advantage of the aesthetic freedom afforded by that identity, which means it doesn't have to be tidy and buttoned-down, like a corporate headquarters.

The story of how this tower came to be is already the stuff of legend: In 2004 Loewenberg, a veteran Chicago architect and developer who had blighted River North with banal high-rises, was seated next to Gang, a rising star whose then-tallest independently completed work was a Rockford community theater with a 90-foot-tall fly tower. The occasion was a Harvard Club dinner where Frank Gehry was the speaker. Loewenberg was looking for a young architect who would produce an out-of-the-box design for a tall tower at his big Lakeshore East residential complex, which rises west of Lake Shore Drive and south of the Chicago River. In Gang, he found one.

Responding to the site for the proposed tower, which was surrounded by a forest of nearby high-rises, she and her colleagues produced a novel concept: a skyscraper whose balconies would be stretched outward, by anywhere from 2 to 12 feet, to capture views that would not be available otherwise. If you lived on the east side of the tower, for example, you wouldn't just see Lake Michigan. You would be able to peer through the thicket of adjoining high-rises and glimpse Millennium Park.

In turn, Gang sculpted the balconies into a larger visual order inspired by the layered topography of limestone outcroppings along the Great Lakes. Reflecting her talent for giving poetic form to mundane materials, the design seized on the plasticity of concrete. When the plan was unveiled in 2006, it prompted raves from critics—and no small amount of private sneering from some of Gang's male competitors, who clucked that the balconies would be mere decorative appendages. Yet the nearly finished outcome richly fulfills the promise of Gang's concept. The balconies elevate an otherwise-ordinary concrete-framed structure to the level of art.

From afar, to be sure, the balconies don't have much of a skyline impact and the high-rise even can resemble a flat slab. But as you move closer and see Aqua from oblique angles, the balconies become a stunning presence, flowing like ocean waves across the facade and forming organic, irregularly shaped towers within the tower. Crucially, the thin metal pickets on the balconies fade from view, allowing the skyscraper's sculptural forms to predominate.

In the 1920s, the great flourishes of tall buildings came in richly decorated bases and highly articulated tops. The middle was almost an afterthought, simply a way to connect these two parts. At Aqua, the old base-middle-top formula is out. The top is conspicuously flat. It is the middle, with its playful bulges, that is the star.

AQUA FROM BELOW
Undulating concrete balconies that flow across the facade like waves.

The balconies, it turns out, were not a wild extravagance. The premium for them, Loewenberg said, was about 1½ percent of the building's $325 million construction cost, which works out to about $4.87 million—not a bad deal considering all the buzz they generated.

Contractors built the balconies by loading Gang's specifications for the curving edges directly into a surveying tripod with a built-in computer. That allowed them to bend steel formwork to precisely the contours Gang and her colleagues had designed.

In a further display of the virtues of customization, Gang tweaked the balconies for sun-shading, making them deeper on Aqua's south than on the north. She and Loewenberg also put as many balconies as possible next to living rooms, thus forming visual extensions of the living spaces. Finally, the oval "pools" of glass between the balconies use a tinted, reflective glass (as opposed to the clear glass employed elsewhere) to prevent apartments from overheating.

These features allow Aqua to rise above a criticism frequently leveled at such "wow" buildings—that they are simplistic one-liners where form overrides function. At Aqua, there is a reason for everything. If the tower indulges in expressionism, it is at least a rationalized expressionism, grounded in midwestern practicality.

The only problem has to do with the forest of skyscrapers that formed the balconies' reason for being: this showstopping, but hemmed in, tower lacks an effective stage on which to preen. You wish you could set it alongside the Chicago River, where it could show off like its curvaceous 1960s antecedent, Marina City.

Aqua's other great virtue is that it is skillfully woven into the fabric of the city, setting it apart from Marina City, whose corncob-shaped highrises meet the ground awkwardly. The tower sits on a beautifully sculpted two-story base, which is rectilinear enough to shape the street, but not so squared-off that it's a visual bore. Atop the base is an outdoor activity level, one of Chicago's largest green roofs, that forms a "fifth facade." When residents of Aqua and occupants of nearby buildings look down on it, they see irregularly shaped pathways and swaths of green, not an ugly asphalt roof.

Gang further joined her tower to the city with two boldly sculpted concrete staircases that let pedestrians walk from Columbus Drive (which occupies the highest level of a multilevel street system) to Lakeshore East's ground-level park at two different points. One is a switchback with corrugated concrete walls; the other, a spectacular helix. These aren't just staircases. They're architectural events.

The most dramatic space of the tower's interior is a clear-span, first-floor hotel ballroom, which is not sealed off from the outside world, as ballrooms tend to be, but offers pleasant views of the nearby park. Only when you venture upstairs do the functional advantages of the balconies—and some possible disadvantages—become clear.

Aqua's apartments, which range from convertibles to two-bedrooms and have 8-foot ceilings, are not exactly spacious. Without the balconies, they might have felt claustrophobic. With the balconies, they are at least livable. Some offer striking views, not only of the cityscape but also of the curving, sheltering underside of the balconies above. That impact is even more pronounced in the mostly unoccupied condos, which range from studios to penthouses and typically have ceilings close to 9 feet high (roughly 13 feet in the penthouses).

Gang speaks of the balconies as an "inhabited facade," conjuring visions of urban cliff dwellers enjoying a communal outdoor space on the side of a skyscraper. Given that Aqua's uppermost balconies reach 200 feet higher than those at Marina City, it's going to be fascinating to see whether people actually use them or shy away because of fear of heights.

While the minimal presence of the thin metal pickets is just right when Aqua is seen from street level, some condo dwellers may feel the need for a greater sense of enclosure.

That caveat aside, Aqua can be deemed a smashing success, a building that takes us in dazzling new aesthetic directions yet still manages to respond to both its urban environs and to the environment as a whole.

The tower has enough energy-saving features to strive for a LEED (Leadership in Energy and Environmental Design) silver rating from the U.S. Green Building Council. It has already won an award from the People for the Ethical Treatment of Animals because birds will be able to see its curving balconies and therefore will be less likely to fly into the tower.

So credit Gang for an extraordinary debut on the big stage, one that adds to Chicago's allure as laboratory for skyscraper innovation. And credit Loewenberg for a risk-taking act of enlightened patronage. The risk has paid off. At Aqua, to paraphrase F. Scott Fitzgerald in *The Great Gatsby*, the building boom finally has produced something commensurate with our capacity for wonder.

DOES SUPERTALL

MEAN SUPERB?

THE CHICAGO BUILDING BOOM WOULD REACH ITS APOGEE OF AMBITION WITH THE unveiling of plans for, and the start of construction on, three skyscrapers designed to be more than 1,000 feet tall: the Trump International Hotel & Tower, the Fordham (later Chicago) Spire, and the Waterview Tower. The first two of these so-called supertalls grabbed all the headlines—the Trump Tower, because of its association with the flamboyant New York developer and reality TV star; the Spire, because of a startling, twisting design by the Spanish architect Santiago Calatrava and its colossal proposed size of 2,000 feet. Both buildings provided long-running sagas that riveted the public as they went through shifts in design, function, and (in the Trump Tower's case) height. Only Trump's was built, opening in 2009 after the boom went bust. Half a world away, in the Persian Gulf city-state of Dubai, the ultimate supertall arrived at the beginning of 2010, revealing how Chicago architects were exporting their skyscraper expertise overseas. Originally called the Burj Dubai, and then abruptly renamed in honor of the Abu Dhabi sheikh who bailed Dubai out of its 2009 debt crisis, the Burj Khalifa—at once excessive and elegant—climbed an astonishing half mile into the sky.

The Donald's Dud

TRUMP'S SKYSCRAPER, SHORTENED BY THE POST-9/II FEAR OF
HEIGHTS, REACHES ONLY FOR MEDIOCRITY

DECEMBER 19, 2001

It won't be the world's tallest building. And it's no architectural world-beater, either.

Actually, I find it hard to say which is more disappointing about Donald Trump's plan for a bloated blob of a skyscraper on the prime riverfront site now occupied by the Chicago Sun-Times Building—the mediocrity of the design or the facile, thumbs-up reviews it's getting from Mayor Richard M. Daley's top planners.

When Trump and his joint venture partners at the Sun-Times' parent company, Hollinger International Inc., announced the massive, mixed-use project in the summer of 2001—hinting that it might bring the world's tallest title back to Chicago—the flamboyant New York developer pledged that he would deliver quality architecture, not his typical brand of glitz. Then he signaled that he would make good on that promise by picking a talented Chicago architect, Adrian Smith of Skidmore Owings & Merrill, whose credits include one of Chicago's top postmodern skyscrapers, the much-admired NBC Tower.

But Smith's scheme, shown to city officials last week, fails to live up to the skyline standard set by its neighbors, including the Wrigley Building and the rest of the great ensemble of 1920s skyscrapers that flank the Michigan Avenue Bridge.

This shortcoming is all the more galling because Smith had designed a far superior plan for the Trump skyscraper, a beautifully sculpted, gracefully tapering tower that almost incidentally would have been the world's tallest. Yet due to concerns that such an iconic presence might become a terrorist target, that design was shelved after September 11 and replaced with the present plan, considerably shorter and squatter.

The discarded plan underscores a stark set of choices facing Trump, who still must sign up office tenants and obtain financing, as well as city officials, who still must grant approval to the developer: Will the highly visible project, known as the Trump Tower Chicago, only be about real estate and private needs, or will it also be about architecture and the quality of the public realm? Will Daley and his aides stand up for good design, or will they give away the store?

The plan now on the table calls for a 78-story, 1,073-foot office and condominium tower that would replace the 7-story Sun-Times Building at

401 North Wabash Avenue. The high-rise reflects potential office tenants' desire for large floor sizes (up to 45,000 square feet, nearly as big as Sears Tower). It also responds, though not satisfyingly, to the unique geometry of its site, which sits along a bend in the Chicago River.

The glass-sheathed building would not be a square or a rectangle, hemmed in by the Chicago street grid, but a parallelogram whose north and south fronts slice diagonally, following the river's bend. In addition, the flat-topped tower would step back as it rises, its notches acknowledging the profile of the frilly white Wrigley Building to the east and Ludwig Mies van der Rohe's IBM Building, an austere black slab, to the west.

There would be five levels of below-street parking as well as ground-floor shops. The high-rise's major public amenity would be a three-tiered river walk on the building's south side, with one level outdoors and the other two covered to permit shoreline strolling in bad weather.

NOT DOING IT WITH MIRRORS

Perhaps because they won small but significant victories on urban design issues like the river walk, city officials had nary a discouraging word for the Trump plan. Indeed the *Sun-Times* reported City Hall's reaction to be "a near endorsement."

"It's going to be exciting architecture," gushed Alicia Berg, the city's planning and development commissioner.

Another City Hall official, who declined to be identified, seemed positively relieved that Trump didn't want to clad the building in his trademark mirror-glass. "It isn't the sort of Krystle Carrington, mindlessly glitzy thing," this official said.

Yet now that the plan has been made public, it's clear that the key issue is not glitz, but girth. This is an awfully chunky building, and Smith's decision to make it a parallelogram only adds to its feeling of enormous bulk. The reason: the unconventional shape accentuates the skyscraper's size because two sides of the tower will come into view from key locations.

Seen from Lake Michigan or the Michigan Avenue Bridge, the building's eastern and southern fronts (the latter as long as a football field) would appear to be a single, massive wall. The high-rise seems less a skyscraper than a sky-blocker.

Admittedly, the tower will appear far trimmer from the north and south when the viewer sees its knife-like corners. But that is simply to acknowledge that this plan works from just about every vantage point except the most important one—the view from the lake and the bridge, which takes in the Wrigley Building, the Tribune Tower, and the two 1920s skyscrap-

ers (333 and 360 North Michigan) south of the bridge. Nearby are such midcentury classics as the IBM Building and the corncob-shaped towers of Marina City.

This is one of Chicago's greatest urban spaces, and the quality that nearly all of its skyscrapers share is that they are not only tall, but about being tall, with design features that accentuate their verticality and draw the eye upward to focal points like the Wrigley Building's clock tower or the Tribune Tower's neo-Gothic crown.

Trump's tower, by contrast, is a skyline dud, resembling a bunch of boxes piled on top of one another. It is equally unsatisfying when compared with the building that still sets the standard for marking a bend in the river and is Chicago's finest postmodern high-rise, 333 West Wacker Drive. That 36-story tower, by New York's Kohn Pedersen Fox, succeeds not only because its curving, green glass wall follows the river's curve, but also because that arc plays beautifully against a wafer-like, flat-walled backdrop that gives the building a subtle, elegant top. In other words, 333 West Wacker has what Trump's proposal now conspicuously lacks—exquisite overall geometry and an equally skilled articulation that makes the parts as satisfying as the whole.

The Michigan Avenue Bridge district will be permanently marred if Trump's behemoth is built as currently designed. So it is baffling to hear city officials saying "hosanna" when they still have the leverage to press the developer and his architect to come up with a better design.

BETTER DESIGN IS OUT THERE

Actually, that shouldn't be too hard; a terrific design for this site already exists, as I learned when I saw an architectural model of the pre–September 11 design during an interview in Smith's office.

That proposal is for a 2,000-foot-tower, including communications antennas, that is shaped like a diamond rather than a parallelogram. It has notches, setbacks, and vertical features that would make it a soaring skyline object worthy of its setting. Even scaled down to the size of the present plan, its trim vertical look would make it a knockout.

It is easy to understand why, with the shock of September 11 still fresh, Trump doesn't want to build such a tall tower. Clearly the floor plans of this skyscraper, smaller and more irregular than those in the present scheme, would complicate efforts to lease space to commercial tenants. Yet

PLAN FOR TRUMP TOWER
A bloated blob of a skyscraper, unworthy of its showcase site.

the point isn't so much the alternative plan as what it stands for: the notion that the skyscraper can, and should, be a thing of breathtaking beauty.

In any tall building, there is a tension between designing from the inside out to snare tenants and designing from the outside in to make the building sympathetic to its surroundings. Yet the best skyscrapers resolve the demands of both art and economics, form and function. That still could happen here, at least if there is the right sort of encouragement from city officials and the right kind of accommodation from a developer who seems eager to shed his image as a prince of glitz.

POSTSCRIPT

In 2002, responding to concerns raised by this critique, Smith made public a dramatically revised version of the Trump skyscraper, which achieved a far better balance between form and function. By slicing off the previously pointed ends of the parallelogram-shaped tower, the architect cut the building's river frontage to 380 feet from 500 feet. In turn, the proposed skyscraper grew to 86 stories, 8 stories taller than in the original plan, and it gained an asymmetrical spire that initially promised to be a strong visual focal point. The Chicago City Council quickly approved the proposal.

In 2004—aided by the wave of publicity from his popular reality TV show, The Apprentice, *and its signature line, "You're fired!"—Trump attracted scores of condominium buyers, so many that the office portion of the project was eliminated and its residential component expanded. Later that year, Trump obtained financing, bought out Hollinger International's stake in the joint venture, and held a ceremonial demolition of the Sun-Times Building. The* Sun-Times, *for its part, would relocate to a drab riverfront high-rise at 350 North Orleans Street.*

As 2004 came to a close, Trump—who had flown to Chicago to promote his latest venture (Donald Trump, the Fragrance) at the former Marshall Field's store on State Street—attended a secret meeting with Daley in the mayor's City Hall office. In the weeks leading up to the meeting, the developer had decided to discard the tower's spire because he could not sell antenna space. But Daley, who wanted the skyscraper to have an eye-catching top, told Trump to put the spire back. When the Chicago Tribune *revealed the meeting, the headline read: "Daley to Trump: 'You're Spired!'" The completed skyscraper would open in 2009 (see p. 116).*

Scaling Aesthetic Heights

THE FORDHAM SPIRE ADAPTS TO OUR WORLD IN
A STUNNING NEW WAY

JULY 31, 2005

Let's set aside, for a second, the hardheaded question of whether Spanish architect and engineer Santiago Calatrava's twisting 2,000-foot Chicago tower will ever get built. In a way, it doesn't matter. The unveiling of a design for the dazzling but still-evolving 115-story hotel and condo tower marks a major milestone in an ongoing revolution: the skyscraper and the tall office building no longer are synonymous.

For more than a century, they were. When the great Chicago architect Louis Sullivan articulated the famous principle "form ever follows function" in 1896, he was writing an influential essay, "The Tall Office Building Artistically Considered." It aimed to impart grace upon a then-new and offensively cantankerous building type—the skyscraper—which was blocking views, darkening streets, and making buckets of money for ruthless capitalists.

"This sterile pile, this crude, harsh, brutal agglomeration," Sullivan called it.

More recently, all the holders of the world's tallest building title have been office buildings, from the Empire State Building to Sears Tower to the pagoda-inspired Taipei 101 in Taiwan. To think about building tall, in other words, has been to think about tall office buildings. And it was to assume that downtowns would be places of work—noisy, dirty, perhaps industrial—and that people would live outside them in quieter city neighborhoods or leafy suburbs.

But as Calatrava's design reveals, life and cities have changed, and the skyscraper is free to adapt to those changes in stunning new ways. Though far from faultless, it is one of the freshest and most captivating skyscraper plans Chicago has seen in decades, fully taking advantage of the possibilities offered by its status as a place to live rather than work.

Tall residential buildings are apt to be thinner than tall office buildings, placing residents closer to the views for which they paid so dearly. Such towers do not have to project the business-like image of a corporation, whether it be Sears Roebuck & Co. or the Seagram's liquor empire. They also reflect the fact that cities, at least Chicago, no longer are the brutal industrial beasts of Sullivan's day, having been softened and suburbanized by the likes of Mayor Richard M. Daley. This is the age of the post-industrial city, which is as much a place to play as a place to

work. Calatrava's tower reflects that shift, flaunting a Baroque dynamism that could not be more different from the gridded, hard-boiled Chicago architecture of old.

There have been tall residential towers before, of course, as well as tall mixed-use buildings that included apartments. Architects in Chicago have designed such buildings in a variety of ways: the mansion in the sky (Park Tower); the skeletal, structurally expressive high-rise (the John Hancock Center); the slab plopped on an enormous base (Water Tower Place); and the organic high-rise, whose sensuous curves takes its visual cues from nature (Marina City and Lake Point Tower). Calatrava's tower, which the architect compares to the twisting trunk of a tree, clearly belongs to the latter tradition.

TOO MUCH PRODUCT?

What's different today is the scale—and profusion—of tall residential buildings either planned or under construction in Chicago. And three of them are not just any tall buildings, but supertall buildings, which aim to crack the barrier of 1,000 feet: Calatrava's tower, which would be called the Fordham Spire and would rise on a riverfront site just west of Lake Shore Drive; the under-construction Trump International Hotel & Tower, which, at 1,361 feet, will be just 90 feet shorter than Sears Tower; and the planned Waterview Tower at 111 West Wacker Drive, a thin setback tower that would rise to 1,047 feet. The plans alone are a stunning rebuke to the post–September 11 prophets who predicted the death of the skyscraper.

The luxury condo boom has some real estate experts predicting that the Fordham Spire, where typical units are expected to carry the lofty price tag of $1 million to $2 million, will never materialize because there is simply too much product out there. But it would be foolhardy to dismiss the $500 million project, even if the odds for it being built appear to be as long as the tower itself.

If Trump, the star developer, had the "X" factor of his reality TV show, *The Apprentice*, working in his favor, the developer of the Fordham Spire, Chicago's Christopher Carley, chairman of the Fordham Co., has his own "X" factor: a star architect, Calatrava, who rivals Frank Gehry in his ability to create attention-getting icons.

As anyone who has been to Calatrava's lyrical, bird-like Milwaukee Art Museum addition knows, his startling, almost surreal buildings have the capacity to alter the rules of everyday life, or at least make people behave in

PLAN FOR THE FORDHAM SPIRE
The tall residential building, artistically reconsidered.

seemingly non-rational ways. The Milwaukee Art Museum's budget grew astronomically as the $125 million addition progressed, and the museum is working to retire $25 million in debt associated with the project.

Calatrava's planned tower, which would house 300 apartments and a 5-star hotel, would sit atop a tiered 4-story parking podium. The podium would double as a pedestal for a sculptural, glass-faced skyscraper in which each successive floor would rotate slightly from the one below it, making it appear as if the tower were twisting into the sky. The building's roof would stretch to the height of 1,458 feet, 7 feet taller than Sears Tower. Its steel spire would soar to roughly 2,000 feet, surpassing Sears and the planned 1,776-foot Freedom Tower in New York as the nation's tallest building.

Superlatives like this do not come cheap. Despite the tower's straight-forward internal structure, Carley acknowledged that the skyscraper will cost at least 35 percent more per square foot than a typical residential high-rise. "The Calatrava factor," he calls it, with a smile.

While other architects have proposed twisting towers, few have been done with such panache. Already being compared to a drill bit, the tower would whir without interruption into the sky, meeting Sullivan's standard that a skyscraper should be "every inch a proud and soaring thing, rising in sheer exultation . . . without a single dissenting line." In a sense, it shows that skyscrapers can return to the slender, romantic forms of the 1920s, before air-conditioning and the desire for huge office floors made office buildings bulge with ungainly girth.

IN HARMONY

Yet Calatrava's song of the sky would not be a show-off solo; his twisting forms would engage in a memorable skyline dialogue with Lake Point Tower's undulating curves. Nor would this skyscraper be a flashy eye-grabber whose beauty is only skin-deep. The design integrates sculpture, structure, and space in a way that recalls the tree-inspired high-rise plans of Frank Lloyd Wright. Its floors would cantilever beyond its trunk-like concrete core and circle of columns, opening unobstructed views. Still, Calatrava must figure out how to incorporate the balconies Carley wants for some condo units without compromising the purity of the tower's sculptural form.

There are other issues to confront, including the way the skyscraper clumsily emerges from its podium, a move that recalls a stripper popping out of a cake. In an interview after the unveiling, Calatrava said he wants to eliminate the podium and have the tower come directly to the ground, where it would be surrounded by crescent-shaped gardens. The base of the tower would still contain restaurants and shops. Yet ditching the podium raises the question of how the tower can transform itself to a pedestrian-friendly scale at ground level, an issue that takes on added weight because it will rise near the adjoining river walk.

Traffic congestion is another concern since this enormous building would be reached by a narrow, out-of-the-way road called East North Water Street. Calatrava said he is exploring an exit off Lake Shore Drive, presumably off the lower level, that would provide direct access to the skyscraper. Whether his solution works or not, it shows that Daley should be taking neighbors' concerns about congestion seriously rather than dismissing them as "not in my backyard" complaints.

EVOLVING POINTS OF REFERENCE

There is, finally, the question of whether a tower this tall belongs along the lakefront and whether it would be wise to change the way the skyline now tiers down gracefully toward the shoreline. Calatrava makes the persuasive case that the tower's site, close to the meeting of the lakefront and the Chicago River, deserves to be marked like "a symphony finale." In addition, he accurately points out, our skyline reference points are forever changing. The Hancock Center seemed shocking when it was built in the late 1960s. Now people revere it. Perhaps the same would happen with the Fordham Spire. But the public deserves to see more drawings of what this tower would look like from various locations around the city and from the pedestrian's point of view.

Despite those concerns, the design has an extraordinary sense of possibility. So much of what has been built in the current residential building boom has been visual junk—hulking concrete condos and faux pieces of history. Carley deserves credit for breaking out of that box and asking Calatrava to vault to a higher standard. This could be a great tower, one that meaningfully extends Chicago's innovative design tradition into the 21st century and explores new possibilities of the residential skyscraper artistically considered.

Now comes the hard part: getting it built.

POSTSCRIPT

The city of Chicago granted zoning approval for the Fordham Spire in 2006, but Carley was unable to obtain sufficient financing for the project and his option to purchase the 2.2-acre site expired. Later in 2006 an Irish developer, Garrett Kelleher, executive chairman of the Shelbourne Development Group, announced *that he had acquired the property and would fund the development of the sky-scraper, which he renamed the Chicago Spire. The tower's cost was now placed at $1.2 billion, more than double the original estimate, while its height was pegged at 124 stories. Initially, Kelleher's plans called for the building to house 300 con-dominium apartments and a 20-story hotel. But all that would change, along with Calatrava's original design, when the third version of the skyscraper was unveiled.*

Let's Twist Again

THIRD TIME'S THE CHARM FOR THE CHICAGO SPIRE—OR IS IT?

DECEMBER 11, 2006

I just had a revelation about Santiago Calatrava's latest proposal for the twisting, 2,000-foot Chicago Spire as I was driving south on Lake Shore Drive and staring at the John Hancock Center. The mighty X-braced Han-cock is 1,127 feet tall. Stack another tower nearly as high atop it and you have some idea of how enormous Calatrava's new skyscraper would be. We're talking condos piled 2,000 feet into the sky, nearly twice the Han-cock's height. That's a huge leap in scale, not an itty-bitty tweak.

The distinction is critical because we're likely to hear from Dublin-based developer Garrett Kelleher and city officials that this design is a mere revision of the original plan—and that it only needs a quick once-over from city planners before it gets the inevitable Chicago City Council rubber stamp. Nothing could be further from the truth. With the needle-thin broadcast antenna gone and its airspace replaced by sellable condo space, this is practically a whole new building.

And it is not, all things considered, a better one.

The tower's newly truncated top, which Calatrava advertises as simpa-tico with the simple profiles of Sears Tower and the Hancock, is a sky-high letdown. Why soar 2,000 feet into the air for what is essentially a buzz cut? With its pinprick spire, the tower was an exultant urban presence, the pin-nacle brilliantly culminating its upward drive. Now, for good reason, I'm getting e-mails from unhappy readers offering the following suggestion: Paint the Chicago Spire red and call it the "Twizzler Tower." Tellingly, the nickname is not being conferred with the same affection as the tower's previous sobriquet, "The Drill Bit."

I am not saying this skyscraper, which would rise just west of Lake Shore Drive and near the north bank of the Chicago River, should not be

PLAN FOR THE CHICAGO SPIRE
A sky-high letdown, resembling a stick of licorice.

built. I am saying it demands the highest level of scrutiny so it can fulfill the highest standards of design.

Provided Kelleher can disprove skeptics and get it built, the Spire will become the postcard image of Chicago for the next 50 years, maybe the next 100. Calatrava, who is capable of superb work when he doesn't lapse into showstopping excess, can do better. And with time and money, he almost surely will. The point is that he needs to be pushed by his client—and by the city. The last thing we need is what transpired when the Chicago Plan Commission approved an earlier version of the project in March: aldermen fawned over Calatrava, turning his appearance into a performance rather than a public hearing.

At root, the question about the revised plan (which now stands at 160 stories and eliminates a hotel once envisioned for the skyscraper) is this: Has Calatrava turned new functional and financial requirements to his advantage—or has he sold out the integrity of the original design?

That tension is most evident on the skyline, where Kelleher's desire to nearly triple the number of residential units for sale to 1,300 from 450, has put the architect in a bind. Before, his tower didn't just twist. It gracefully tapered, getting noticeably thinner as it climbed into the sky. Now, it looks straighter, flatter, less voluptuous, and more Twizzler-ish. And it meets the sky weakly, its enormous curving ribs culminating in tiny metal fins that are preposterously small, like so many extended pinkies.

All this is not a veiled suggestion that Mayor Richard M. Daley should do what he did with Donald Trump and order a spire atop this skyscraper. But this much is clear: Calatrava and Kelleher should rethink the tower's top and refine its middle.

The big gesture of the twist is not enough. God has to be in the details throughout. Based upon renderings I saw last week, the project has miles to go before it achieves the level of refinement evident in another twisting tower, Skidmore, Owings & Merrill's planned Infinity Tower in Dubai, or even Calatrava's own "Turning Torso" tower in Sweden. (For those new to architecture, twisting towers are all the rage these days.)

There is more reason for concern at ground level, and it's related to what's happening in the sky. With the number of proposed units almost tripled, Kelleher's potential for profit grows exponentially, as does the threat of aggravating Streeterville's already clogged streets. The tower, which would be the nation's tallest building, would rise on a tiny side street called East North Water Street. When the skyscraper had just 450 units, that incongruity might be glossed over. No longer.

There are some positive features in the redesign, but even they invite further scrutiny. By shifting the tower slightly to the north and putting all parking underground, Calatrava and Kelleher create the possibility for ample public open space between the tower and the Chicago River. In the same holistic vein, they are proposing two Calatrava-designed pedestrian bridges along the lakefront in an attempt to make the tower less of an isolated object.

But who would pay for the bridges: the city or the developer? And I wonder whether the public space along the riverfront promenade would be usable or ceremonial. Would passersby be encouraged to use it, or would they be made to feel as if they were encroaching upon somebody else's high-priced turf? The answers will determine whether the proposed improvements turn out to be genuine amenities or mere attempts by the developer to justify his enormous increase in sellable space.

Once so promising, the twisting tower has now reached a crucial stage. It still has the capacity to enliven and enrich Chicago's skyline and its streets. Literally and aesthetically, it remains head and shoulders above the city's mediocre residential high-rise norm. The issue is whether city officials, especially Daley, will drive the architect to deliver the greatest possible benefits to the public realm. Calatrava is certainly capable of achieving them.

In the following months, Calatrava backed away from the banal, nearly flat-topped version of the Spire and played with numerous alternatives. He finally settled on a much-improved design in which the skyscraper would appear to make a 360-degree twist as it moved from the ground to a sharply articulated, cone-shaped summit.

With an eye toward winning the support of community groups and park advocates, the architect revised and expanded plans for the tower's surroundings, not only for the project's 2-acre site, but also for the adjoining 3.2-acre site of the planned DuSable Park (located to the east across Lake Shore Drive), whose construction Kelleher pledged to help finance.

Among the improvements in Calatrava's plan: a grand, circular plaza set between the tower and the north bank of the Chicago River; pedestrian passageways leading beneath Lake Shore Drive's superstructure to the new park; and the boldly configured landscape of the park itself. The design thus promised to succeed as a work of skyline sculpture and as a building that engaged the city around it. The Chicago Plan Commission approved the new Spire proposal on April 19, 2007. Foundation work began that summer, creating (for a time) an entirely novel situation in Chicago: three supertall towers under construction simultaneously.

How to Build Today's Supertalls

ELEGANCE, NOT MACHISMO, IS BEHIND CHICAGO'S
UNPRECEDENTED REACH FOR THE SKY

AUGUST 19, 2007

A white hard hat on his head, the earnest look of a professor on his face, Bill Baker has a ready metaphor to reveal the hidden structural logic behind Chicago's unprecedented reach for the sky. Mimicking the cores of concrete that shoot up the center of today's supertall skyscrapers, Baker stands like a soldier at attention, his feet touching. But the silo-like cores are too thin to single-handedly brace the towers against howling winds. So Baker extends his left arm and puts it on the shoulder of a colleague standing with him in front of Donald Trump's ever-growing skyscraper on the Chicago River's north bank.

"That steadies me," said Baker, a partner and structural engineer at the Chicago architecture, engineering, and planning firm of Skidmore, Owings & Merrill. "It's like ski poles."

He has just illustrated the essence of a relatively new but little-noticed way of erecting skyscrapers: massive arms of steel or concrete extend outward from a building's core and grab high-strength structural columns along the perimeter, bracing the building against gravity and the overturning force of the wind. This is the method, called core and outrigger, that is propelling a skyscraper boom unlike any other in Chicago. Today, for the first time in its history, the city has three supertall skyscrapers—those 1,000 feet or higher—under construction simultaneously. And owing to shifts in both physics and aesthetics, they aim to become icons of a new post-industrial, post–lunch bucket city—less about old-fashioned machismo than new-age elegance.

"It's the difference between somebody who is a gymnast and a dancer," said Zurich-based architect and engineer Santiago Calatrava, designer of the now-under-construction Chicago Spire, in a telephone interview from his native Spain. "We try to be elegant—we are not being athletic. We are not showing muscles."

At this stage, the most visible of the new giants is the Trump International Hotel & Tower, which now reaches more than 500 feet into the air on its way to a total height of 1,361 feet, 90 feet shorter than Sears Tower. Then there is the Waterview Tower, where the superstructure has just popped out of the ground at the southwest corner of Wacker Drive and Clark Street. This hotel and condominium skyscraper eventually will stretch to 1,047 feet, a foot taller than New York's celebrated Chrysler Building. Finally, there is the Spire, the twisting 2,000-footer at 400 North Lake Shore Drive, which will be the nation's tallest building and the world's tallest all-residential structure. For now, it consists of a few holes in the ground, into which contractors will drive steel and concrete caissons reaching 120 feet down to bedrock.

While other places have far more supertall towers under way—the Middle East playground of Dubai has a staggering 15, according to the Emporis international building database—Chicago offers something that no other city can: a chance to view the present generation directly alongside the previous generation, consisting of Sears Tower, the Aon Center, and the John Hancock Center. That trio of giants, which was based on the structural concept of a "framed tube," redefined the skyline's silhouette between 1969 and 1974.

EVOLUTION OF THE ART

"What's going on here is fairly phenomenal," said Antony Wood, executive director of the Chicago-based Council on Tall Buildings and

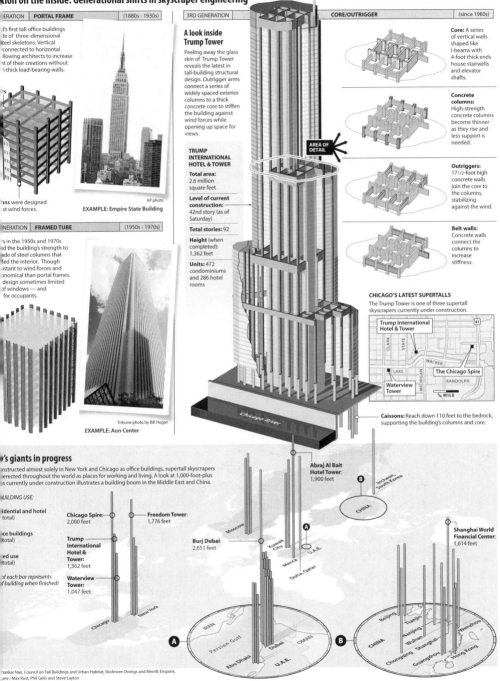

tion on the inside: Generational shifts in skyscraper engineering

| ERATION | PORTAL FRAME | (1880s - 1930s) | | 3RD GENERATION | | CORE/OUTRIGGER | (since 1980s) |

PORTAL FRAME (1880s - 1930s)

d's first tall office buildings
de of three-dimensional
eel skeletons. Vertical
connected to horizontal
llowing architects to increase
nt of their creations without
n thick load-bearing walls.

ns were designed
st wind forces.

EXAMPLE: Empire State Building
AP photo

FRAMED TUBE (1950s - 1970s)

s in the 1950s and 1970s
ed the building's strength to
ade of steel columns that
led the interior. Though
istant to wind forces and
onomical than portal frames,
design sometimes limited
f windows — and
for occupants.

EXAMPLE: Aon Center
Tribune photo by Bill Hogan

A look inside Trump Tower

Peeling away the glass skin of Trump Tower reveals the latest in tall-building structural design. Outrigger arms connect a series of widely spaced exterior columns to a thick concrete core to stiffen the building against wind forces while opening up space for views.

TRUMP INTERNATIONAL HOTEL & TOWER

Total area: 2.6 million square feet

Level of current construction: 42nd story (as of Saturday)

Total stories: 92

Height (when completed): 1,362 feet

Units: 472 condominiums and 286 hotel rooms

AREA OF DETAIL

Core: A series of vertical walls shaped like I-beams with 4-foot thick ends house stairwells and elevator shafts.

Concrete columns: High-strength concrete columns become thinner as they rise and less support is needed.

Outriggers: 17 1/2-foot high concrete walls join the core to the columns, stabilizing against the wind.

Belt walls: Concrete walls connect the columns to increase stiffness.

CHICAGO'S LATEST SUPERTALLS
The Trump Tower is one of three supertall skyscrapers currently under construction.

Trump International Hotel & Tower

The Chicago Spire

Waterview Tower

CLARK · STATE · LAKE · WACKER · RANDOLPH · MICHIGAN · 41 · 1/4 MILE

Caissons: Reach down 110 feet to the bedrock, supporting the building's columns and core.

's giants in progress

nstructed almost solely in New York and Chicago as office buildings, supertall skyscrapers erected throughout the world as places for working and living. A look at 1,000-foot-plus s currently under construction illustrates a building boom in the Middle East and China.

UILDING USE:

idential and hotel
total)

ce buildings
total)

ed use
total)

f each bar represents
building when finished)

Chicago Spire: 2,000 feet

Trump International Hotel & Tower: 1,362 feet

Waterview Tower: 1,047 feet

Freedom Tower: 1,776 feet

Burj Dubai: 2,651 feet

Abraj Al Bait Hotel Tower: 1,900 feet

Shanghai World Financial Center: 1,614 feet

Chicago · New York · Moscow · Kuwait City · Mecca · Doha, Qatar · U.A.E. · IRAN · Persian Gulf · Abu Dhabi · Dubai · U.A.E. · OMAN · CHINA · Beijing · Tianjin · Nanjing · Wuhan · Shanghai · Wenzhou · Chongqing · Guangzhou · Hong Kong

A · B

Jackson, South Korea · CHINA

hankar Nair, Council on Tall Buildings and Urban Habitat; Skidmore Owings and Merrill; Emporis,
ine / Max Rust, Phil Geib and Steve Layton

HOW TO BUILD A SUPERTALL

The engineering heavy-lifting behind Chicago's unprecedented reach for the sky.

Urban Habitat, an international organization of architects, engineers, planners, and builders. "It's a unique place to watch the evolution of the skyscraper art."

That evolution is inseparable from the work of structural engineers such as Baker, who tend to work in the shadows of more celebrated architects. But maybe that is changing. The current cover of the trade journal *Architectural Record* carries the headline "Engineering the New Architecture." The lead story is titled "The Engineer's Moment." The point, as author Nina Rappaport asserts, is that engineers are assuming an expanded role in design rather than simply laboring as "consultants after the fact."

"They're very important," agreed Chicago architect Adrian Smith, who collaborated with Baker on both the Trump Tower and the Burj Dubai, the under-construction, mixed-use tower in Dubai that is expected to hit a record-shattering height of around 2,650 feet, more than half a mile into the sky. "The architects can conceive things to be built," added Smith, who left Skidmore last year to start his own firm. "But very rarely do they have the expertise for how to keep it up and build it in the most efficient ways. You need a team of structural engineers to do that."

Indeed, structural engineers have played an integral role in the development of tall buildings for nearly 125 years. Their contribution begins with architect-engineer William Le Baron Jenney, who was the first to use an internal frame of metal to support the floors and outer walls of a skyscraper in his 9-story Home Insurance Building, completed in Chicago in 1885 and demolished in 1931. With its rigidly connected girders and columns, this method of skeletal construction, also known as the "portal frame," liberated the skyscraper from the constraints of thick, load-bearing masonry walls and reached its apogee in the 1,250-foot Empire State Building of 1931.

Three decades later, the portal frame gave way to the framed tube, in which the building's outer shell bore the forces of the wind and much of its own gravity loads. The Hancock Center, a collaboration of Skidmore, Owings & Merrill architect Bruce Graham and engineer Fazlur Khan, led this charge in 1969 with its industrial-strength X-braces and persuasive efficiency. The steel-framed, 100-story "Big John" was built for the same cost as a 45-story office building with a conventional structural cage. The Aon Center (originally the Standard Oil Building), Sears Tower, and New York's World Trade Center all followed its pathbreaking example.

Still another revolution would sweep aside the framed tube in the 1980s and 1990s. It was spawned by architects' desire to break free from the aesthetic bonds of structural expressionism and by the irony that the closely spaced perimeter columns in some of the framed-tubed skyscrapers were cutting off the very panoramic views that their great height made possible.

Instead, following the example of Chicago's never-built Miglin-Beitler Skyneedle—a super-skinny 125-story office building proposed in 1988 and designed by New Haven, Connecticut, architect Cesar Pelli with New York structural engineers Thornton Tomasetti—architects shifted from steel to new, high-strength concrete and dispensed with the framed tube for the combination of a concrete core attached to perimeter super columns.

Here, science met art in a shift that allowed supertall towers to be both tall and thin. And the trend goes on.

The Spire, for example, will have a height-to-width ratio of 10–1, compared with Sears' much-chunkier 6½–1. It will, its backers claim, be the most slender supertall skyscraper in the world. The roof at the Trump Tower, for its part, will reach slightly higher than its counterpart at the Hancock Center (1,133 feet versus 1,127 feet). But the building will be 25 feet narrower at the base, a skinniness already apparent in the building's flatiron-like appearance when seen from the north, south, and west.

While such narrowness leads to fewer units per floor, it also means that "no part of the interior is very far from a window," said R. Shankar Nair, the former chairman of the Council on Tall Buildings and Urban Habitat and the structural engineer for the Waterview Tower. The lost square footage is made up by simply stacking more units in the sky.

The core-and-outrigger system "is the standard for supertall skyscrapers today," Nair explained.

But unless you are standing on Wacker Drive and peering into a cleft in the Trump Tower's glass wall that is left open for the hoists that whiz up and down the tower's south side, all the structural heavy lifting is largely concealed from view. Baker, a genial man with gold-colored, wire-rimmed glasses, is happy to show it off, however.

His tour of the tower, the tallest American skyscraper to be built since Sears Tower in 1974, begins near the entrance to the hoists, where a sign on the wall encourages frequent use of non-greasy suntan lotion and simple, soap-like dispensers stand ready to pour out the goo.

Above a construction elevator entrance, another sign—this one displaying a picture of the tower's namesake pointing at the viewer like Uncle Sam in the old "I Want You for U.S. Army" recruiting poster—urges: "'Safety First' or You're Fired!"

CORE LOOKS DIFFERENT

Nearby is the tower's core, which rests on caissons reaching down 110 feet to bedrock. The core looks very different from the core of a framed tube skyscraper. In such a building, Baker explained, the center of each floor is porous, with elevators and exit stairs inserted into shafts formed by irregularly spaced columns and surrounded by drywall partitions. "It's not a structural core that helps resist wind loads," he said.

At the Trump Tower, however, there is no mistaking the core's heft. At the tower's base, it measures 150 feet long by 45 feet wide and is made of high-strength, steel-reinforced concrete. The core consists of five parallel walls, each shaped like an I beam, with ends 4 feet thick. Escape stairs and elevators are placed inside. Such walls presumably would have been far more difficult to pierce than the porous cores of the World Trade Center's twin towers, which collapsed after fuel-laden, hijacked jetliners knifed through them on September 11, 2001.

Baker declines to discuss the threat of terrorism, but Calatrava, who has designed a similarly robust core for the Spire, speaks directly to the issue. "Being so massive, it creates a kind of enormous protective barrier for the escape stairs and elevators," he said of the Spire's core.

Soon, like a no-frills version of a glass-walled atrium hotel elevator, one of the hoists clambers to the Trump Tower's 29th floor, a vantage point from which you seem to be hovering in a helicopter over the Chicago River. It is no accident that the three supertalls are clustered within less than a mile of one another and form a new "gold coast," this one not along the lakefront but along the river. Peering outward from the freshly installed windows on the 29th floor, where the distance between columns is a generous 25 feet, you see rumbling elevated trains that resemble centipedes crawling through the Loop. The clock tower of the neighboring Wrigley Building looks like an oversize toy. Because the Trump skyscraper rises from a bend in the river, it offers straight-shot views down the waterway and out to Lake Michigan.

600 WORKERS

In the future, the super-rich will enjoy such glamorous vistas. But today the skyscraper resembles a vertical factory, a hive of 600 construction workers—ironworkers, drywallers, plumbers, surveyors, and others—laboring away inside.

The windows come shrink-wrapped in crates that travel up the hoists, which is far more efficient than having the project's two tower cranes carry them into place. The structural columns narrow as the tower rises because they don't have to bear as much weight. Less bulk means more room for condo and hotel dwellers—and less money spent on concrete and rebar. On the upper floors, there are portable toilets on wheels for workers. At the Burj Dubai, Baker said, there even are upper-level dining areas for the construction workers, which saves them the trouble of traveling down 140 or so stories to eat lunch. (When completed in 2009, the tower is expected to have 160 stories.)

Now Baker descends concrete fire stairs to the 28th floor, where the outriggers can be found. They turn out to be 17½-foot-high, 5½-foot-wide walls of concrete that reach out like arms from the core to the super columns on the tower's perimeter. Set perpendicular to the outriggers, and just as high, are so-called belt walls of concrete that, like a belt holding up a pair of pants, tie together the super columns.

"You want all the columns to work together, not like individual pickup sticks," Baker says.

Air-handling equipment, electrical transformers, water pumps, and other mechanical equipment will be threaded through openings in the outriggers. The ceilings above the outriggers are 30 feet high. With exposed concrete everywhere, the spaces have the feel of a nuclear reactor—or, maybe, a spot for an edgy get-together. "Great for a party," Baker quipped.

In the 1980s, conventional wisdom held that it no longer made sense to build supertall office buildings. More height would necessitate more material, it was said, and would leave more building surface to be blown around by the wind. In addition, more elevators would chew up more valuable floor space, rendering such towers uneconomical.

BENEFITS OBVIOUS

Yet while it does take more time (and, thus, more money) to build the complex outrigger floors, the benefits of this method are now clear. They represent, in some respects, a return to the principles of the first skyscrapers that arose in Chicago, albeit at supersize scale.

In the core-and-outrigger system, a tower can be more open to the outside than in a framed tube, taking advantage of surrounding views and bringing in more natural light. In addition, most new core-and-outrigger skyscrapers are residential and mixed-use buildings, which means they need far fewer elevators than office buildings.

There are other practical advantages. The enormous weight of the concrete core and super columns helps reduce the wind-caused oscillation that can lead to whitecaps in toilets and swinging chandeliers. What this new way of building tall will mean for the public realm remains unclear. A visit to the three-level riverfront walkway at the base of the Trump reveals a strikingly open, handsomely proportioned public space, with views every bit as compelling as those upstairs. Yet new structural techniques by no means guarantee aesthetic success. Architecture remains a mix of technology and art, and the outcome of that story will become apparent only when the new giants finally assume their place on the skyline. For now, quiet engineering heroics are at center stage, making possible Chicago's next round of architectural fireworks.

POSTSCRIPT

The fireworks would have to wait. In early 2008, in an ominous sign that the collapsing housing market would have a major impact on Chicago's high-rises, construction on the Waterview Tower stopped at the 26th floor, leaving the skyscraper's concrete superstructure looming over Wacker Drive. Chicago-based Teng, the tower's developer and designer, announced that the Beijing Construction Engineering Group Co., Ltd., would arrange for more than $300 million in construction financing to finish the job. But as of early 2010, building had not resumed.

As the recession deepened and credit markets seized up, construction on the Chicago Spire also ground to a halt. Later in 2008, Calatrava filed a lien seeking more than $11.3 million from developer Garrett Kelleher's Shelbourne Development Group. Kelleher's spokeswoman insisted that construction eventually would go forward, a view seconded by the architect during a public appearance in Chicago in 2009. But the project was still stalled in early 2010. All that remained of the Spire's colossal ambition was a giant hole in the ground, 76 feet deep and 110 feet across.

A Skyscraper of Many Faces

IN TRUMP'S CONTEXT-DRIVEN CHICAGO SKYSCRAPER, BEAUTY IS
IN THE EYE—AND THE VANTAGE POINT—OF THE BEHOLDER

SEPTEMBER 27, 2009

Chicago's architecture aficionados felt a sense of dread eight years ago: Donald Trump was coming.

THE TRUMP INTERNATIONAL HOTEL & TOWER FROM THE CHICAGO RIVER
Better than expected from "The Donald," despite its riverfront bulk and a subpar spire.

The flamboyant New York real estate developer, whose buildings gave new meaning to the word "flashy," was planning a massive skyscraper, perhaps as tall as 150 stories, on the riverfront site of the 7-story Chicago Sun-Times Building at 401 North Wabash Avenue. It was as if Godzilla were about to wade ashore from Lake Michigan and breathe fire on the skyline.

Yet now, after the fear spawned by the September 11 terrorist attacks shortened it, *The Apprentice* hyped it, and the housing market's collapse left nearly a third of its interior unsold, the 92-story Trump International Hotel & Tower is finally here—not vulgar, sometimes enthralling, far exceeding original expectations, but still short of Chicago's soaring architectural standards.

This shiny, glass-sheathed tower—the seventh tallest building in the world, the tallest in America since the 1974 completion of Sears Tower, and the tallest structure its height-obsessed developer has ever built—is a good building, not a great one.

It meets the ground superbly and touches the sky weakly. It is exhilaratingly thin from some angles and unpardonably squat from others. Its reflective silver-blue curtain wall provides a poetic, ever-changing palette for the sky and passing clouds. Yet it lacks a memorable, consistently effective skyline silhouette, like the mighty X-braced John Hancock Center, or a fresh take on the residential skyscraper, like the soon-to-be-finished Aqua tower and its spectacularly undulating balconies.

Chicago architect Adrian Smith and his former colleagues at the Chicago office of Skidmore, Owings & Merrill designed the $850 million hotel and condo skyscraper. (Smith left SOM in 2006 to start his own firm.) It stacks more than 2 million square feet of shops, parking, a health club, a hotel, and condos on a narrow riverfront site, which is not unlike cramming an oversize McMansion onto a typical suburban lot. How to prevent such girth from crushing everything around it?

Smith's response grows from his philosophy of contextualism, which seeks to acknowledge and enhance a building's surroundings rather than parachute in an alien object. Wisely, he did not boldly express the tower's bones in the manner of the muscular Hancock Center, a strategy that would have overwhelmed the Trump skyscraper's surroundings. Instead, he looked outward for inspiration, treating the skyscraper's environs as an unfinished canvas that his building would complete.

Three vigorous setbacks (at the 16th, 29th, and 51st floors) roughly match the roof heights of the Wrigley Building's base, the River Plaza residential high-rise at 405 North Wabash, and 330 North Wabash by Ludwig Mies van der Rohe. From the 51st floor, the tower shoots skyward to its roof at 1,133 feet. A glass-sheathed drum that screens mechanical equipment reaches to 1,174 feet and then the skyscraper's gray, fiberglass-covered spire climbs to its summit at 1,361 feet 6 inches—just 6 inches shorter than one of the World Trade Center towers destroyed in the September 11 terrorist attacks.

The approach yields a handsome telescoping tower, reminiscent of the classic skyscrapers of the 1920s, that is infinitely superior to the exposed-concrete condo towers, plunked atop parking podiums, that have disfigured downtown in recent years. Yet that is to assess the Trump Tower by the lowest possible standard. Like the former Sears (now Willis) Tower, the Trump Tower changes constantly in profile as you move around it. But unlike either that building or the Hancock, its skyline quality is disappointingly irregular.

The skyscraper is at its most persuasive when it is viewed in fragments rather than as a whole, or from angles that conceal its considerable bulk.

From Wabash Avenue, its long ends seemingly sheared off by the buildings on either side of the street, the tower bursts into view—taut, thin, and elegant. Like the Chicago Board of Trade Building, it takes full advantage of its unusual site, which makes it appear to rise from the middle of the street. Stand at State Street and Wacker Drive, and the Trump Tower resembles a supersize version of D. H. Burnham & Co.'s Flatiron Building in New York, its prow-like end suggesting a ship slicing through space.

From a variety of distant points, the tower looks remarkably thin, even compared with the white stalk of the Aon Center. For that, credit Bill Baker, SOM's chief structural engineer, who masterminded a high-strength structural system, whose massive concrete core and arm-like outriggers allow the big building to be so skinny (and so open, when residents look from the inside out).

Among the best details is the skyscraper's richly textured curtain wall, its vertical proportions, stainless-steel fins, and bands of louvers echoing Mies's spare modernist language at 330 North Wabash. The wall is a dazzling light catcher, coloring the skyscraper in pale hues of blue, silver, gray, and white. As a result, the Trump Tower simultaneously blends in and stands out, as notable for its subtle, ever-shifting luminosity as for its strong (though not quite iconic) stepped-back silhouette.

VIEWPOINT MATTERS

But neither the exemplary structural engineering nor the top-drawer curtain wall can resolve the conundrum posed by the tower's parallelogram-shaped footprint and the density piled onto it. When the Trump skyscraper is seen from the Michigan Avenue Bridge and other high-profile vantage points, its illusion of thinness vanishes. With nothing to hide them, the long and short sides of the tower come into full view, and they make the skyscraper seem more like a beached whale than a giraffe gracefully sticking its long neck above the treetops.

What also holds back this tower from greatness is the way it meets the sky. Its toothpick-thin spire halfheartedly complies with Mayor Richard M. Daley's edict to put a spire on top; it's no more than a flagpole without a flag. The cartoonish drum beneath the spire fails to achieve a graceful transition between the body of the tower and its summit. There is nothing quite so frustrating as a skyscraper, like this one, that invites you to make the journey into the sky—and then falls flat once you get there.

Yet if the Trump Tower is pleasing, but imperfect, on the skyline, it is consistently good at ground level, reversing the outcome of 1970s supertall towers like Sears, which excelled in the air but flopped on the ground with their anti-urban, windswept plazas.

In the most important stroke, Smith placed the Trump Tower to the site's western edge, appropriately tethering it to the large-scale 330 North Wabash and Marina City, and thus ensuring that it would not pygmyize the delicate Wrigley Building. The westward shift also carved out space for a big, lushly planted public plaza, designed by SOM and Chicago landscape architect Peter Schaudt. With dynamic curves that echo the skyscraper's rounded corners, the still-to-be-completed plaza can be counted upon to offer baroque flights of stairs and striking riverfront views that will lure pedestrians by the score.

PLAYFULNESS AND GRACE

Smith further opened the site by lifting the skyscraper's mass on stilt-like columns that rise 40 feet above street level. This made way for the tower's three-tiered river walk, which provides a convenient covered shortcut between Michigan and Wabash Avenues—a major upgrade from the stark walkway outside the old Sun-Times Building.

Other pluses at the base include a rebuilt, rerouted section of Wabash Avenue; cantilevered steel-and-glass canopies that elegantly mark the tower's entrances; a playfully spiraling ramp that leads to and from the tower's parking garage; and undulating, highly transparent glass walls that open views of the tower's hotel and condo lobbies. Trump and his architects deserve credit for not succumbing to the post–September 11 syndrome of fear and making the tower a fortress.

And what of the Trump Tower's interior? It actually offers much to the public, including an understated mezzanine-level bar and a sleekly contemporary 16th-floor bar and restaurant. Both have striking water and skyline views, though their prices tend to be sky-high. The core-and-outrigger structural system creates a pleasing openness in the skyscraper's 486 condos, which have 10-foot ceilings and floor-to-ceiling glass. The 339 hotel rooms, which can be purchased by individual buyers and rented to hotel guests, are equally expansive and stylishly appointed. Unfortunately for Trump, only about 70 percent of the units are sold. The vacancies include the 14,260-square-foot, 89th-floor penthouse, which resembles a private observatory with 16-foot ceilings and stunning views in every direction. Its advertised $30 million price tag, Trump acknowledged in an interview, is negotiable.

Such stratospheric views and prices are a reminder of the heady days when the tower's superstructure was climbing into the sky and Trump was

riding high on *The Apprentice*, before the recession laid the tower's sales—
and the nation—low. Like many grandiose skyscrapers before it, this one
was conceived in boom times and completed only after the boom went
bust. But the Trump Tower's short-term real estate woes are less important, in the end, than its long-term contributions to the cityscape. In this,
his Chicago apprenticeship, Donald Trump has risen to new heights, even
if he hasn't quite given us architecture with a capital "A."

POSTSCRIPT

*Later in 2009, the Chicago-based Council on Tall Buildings and Urban Habitat,
the global arbiter of height standards, changed its criteria for measuring skyscrapers, which, in turn, changed the Trump Tower's official height measurement.
The old standard was that a skyscraper's height was determined by calculating
the distance from the sidewalk outside the main entrance to the building's spire
or structural top. The new standard is that height is measured from "the lowest,
significant, open-air, pedestrian entrance" to the top. For the Trump Tower, this
meant that the bottom of the skyscraper was no longer considered to be the main
entrance along North Wabash Avenue, but the lower-level shops along the Chicago river walk. The change brought the tower's official height to 1,389 feet.*

Over the Top

THE BURJ DUBAI, THE NEW WORLD'S TALLEST BUILDING,
SHOWS THAT NOTHING SUCCEEDS LIKE EXCESS

JANUARY 4, 2010

If ever a skyscraper was burdened with great expectations, it is the Burj
Dubai, the colossal half-mile-high tower designed by Chicago architects
that is about to open in the Persian Gulf emirate of Dubai. This high-
rise isn't simply meant to shatter height records. It is supposed to be a
national icon, a symbol for a madly exuberant, now debt-ridden, city-state
that mixes the manufactured spectacle of Las Vegas with the helter-skelter
growth of Houston.

In the wrong hands, the 160-story, mixed-use skyscraper—the world's
tallest building and the world's tallest freestanding structure, whose height
is roughly double that of Donald Trump's Chicago tower—could have
been a monstrosity, an extra-extra-large version of the architectural cartoons that blight the skyline here. Yet as designed by the Chicago office of

Skidmore, Owings & Merrill and its former design partner, Adrian Smith, the Burj Dubai represents a great leap forward in height and, especially for Dubai, in design quality.

It is a luminous, light-catching skyscraper that looks like a skyscraper—ridiculously tall but exquisitely sculpted, elegantly detailed, and unapologetically exultant. Nothing so perfectly summarizes the bigger-is-better outlook of Dubai's ruler, Sheikh Mohammed bin Rashid Al Maktoum, and the tower's developer, the state-backed Emaar Properties.

In contrast to Dubai's preposterous collection of architectural cartoons—here, a big-bellied tower that suggests an oversize perfume bottle; there, a paper-thin skyscraper that looks like someone sliced a giant hole in its top with a pair of scissors—the Burj Dubai offers God-is-in-the-details articulation along with its dazzling shape. Fittingly for this waterfront tourist mecca, the shape recalls a giant sand castle in the sky.

Writing from thousands of miles away, some critics have taken note of the tower's empty floors and spiraling shape, branding it an act of hubris—a modern-day version of the biblical Tower of Babel. Yet to be in Dubai is to realize that the building's genius is that it does not stand aloof from the zany, Xanadu-in-the-desert character of the emirate but channels that energy into a work of architecture that is, if not profound or especially adventurous, then at least serious and almost noble.

Rising improbably from what was desert just six years ago and built to house an Armani hotel, about 1,000 condominiums, small offices for jet-setting magnates, and an observatory for the masses, the $1.5 billion Burj Dubai is by no means immune from this emirate's maddening "build now, plan later" mentality. It is far easier to reach by car than by foot, and even the roads leading to it are a maze. A nearby rail stop on Dubai's new transit line will open on the same day as the tower, but that is about as green, or energy-saving, as this project gets. In addition, little effort has been made to have the skyscraper culminate long urban vistas, as the Eiffel Tower does so magnificently in Paris.

Even so, the Burj Dubai succeeds as an Eiffel Tower that people will live in—not a pure symbol but a working icon that anchors an emerging city within a city called (what else?) Downtown Burj Dubai a few miles from the alluring azure waters of the Persian Gulf. Compared with other parts of Dubai, where high-rises are crammed so closely that people in one apartment building can practically reach out the window and shake hands with their neighbors, the district has an appealing openness, a quality accentuated by a shallow man-made lake built to one side of the giant tower. As if the spectacle of the world's tallest building was not enough, the lake flaunts a crowd-pleasing, Las Vegas–style fountain that

shoots dancing jets of water 500 feet into the air (accompanied, naturally, by music). Yet it also sets off the Burj Dubai, allowing the tower to be glimpsed from head to toe.

And what a view it is, at both close range and from afar—a feat that architect Smith, who left SOM in 2006 to start his own firm, and his chief collaborator, SOM's chief structural engineer Bill Baker, accomplished through a classic Chicago synthesis of architecture and engineering.

The tower is remarkably tall and remarkably thin because of its innovative structural system: a six-sided core of concrete buttressed by massive concrete walls that support the three wings of the Y-shaped skyscraper. These cost-efficient, wind-resisting bones are sheathed in a sophisticated skin of double-layered glass and aluminum that strongly resembles the exterior of the SOM-designed Trump International Hotel & Tower in Chicago. At the 156th floor, the concrete is replaced by an inner structure of steel, which carries the glass-sheathed, mostly unoccupied portion of the skyscraper—all 600-plus feet of it—to the summit, which reportedly rises 2,684 feet above the desert floor. (Emaar Properties is expected to reveal the exact height at the tower's opening ceremonies.)

A spire that tall sounds silly, the ultimate folly, yet somehow it works. From a distance, the Burj Dubai looks like a Middle Eastern version of Oz—not oppressive, but beckoning; inevitably, not freakishly, tall. Smith kept reworking the top to get the proportions right and his tweaking paid off. Here, in contrast to the disappointing flagpole-like spire at Chicago's Trump Tower, the skyscraper and its subtly spiraling setbacks mount rhythmically to a thrilling climax. Yet, as at Trump, the silvery Burj Dubai reflects the sky beautifully—only more so because the exterior, its curving contours subtly evoking the pointed arches of Islamic architecture, has so many gem-like facets.

Smith is known for the philosophy of contextualism, which preaches the virtues of adapting a building to its surroundings, so it is no surprise that the Burj Dubai meets the ground equally well—even if it is a little chunky from up close. The foot-like extensions of its Y-shaped floors step down humanely to a surrounding plaza. Three lozenge-shaped entrance pavilions—with precisely detailed, cable-supported glass walls that enclose an air pocket and sunshades—lead to the respective lobbies for the tower's offices, hotel, and condos. In the bargain, the projecting pavilions will prevent wind downdrafts from knocking pedestrians off their feet.

Along with lush gardens that extend the tower's helical geometry into the landscape, these features transform the gargantuan Burj Dubai into a

THE BURJ DUBAI (RENAMED THE BURJ KHALIFA)
More than just a record-breaker, at once elegantly detailed and exquisitely sculpted.

gentle giant—not unlike New York's Empire State Building, whose setback profile has long exemplified how a tall building should meet the ground. Unlike so many high-rises in the emirate, the Burj Dubai seems rooted in its site, not plopped onto it. It simultaneously stands out and looks like it belongs.

The skyscraper's interior remained incomplete before its opening and was therefore impossible to fully evaluate. Yet a brief look at one of the tower's residential floors suggested that SOM's design will likely succeed in function as well as form. The Y-shaped floor plan creates narrow apartment depths that keep interiors close to prized views of the Persian Gulf, the Dubai skyline, and the desert. Widely spaced columns, as opposed to the narrowly clustered piers of Chicago's Aon Center, smartly accentuate those vistas. Why build so high if you can't see to the end of the earth?

Under the leadership of Nada Andric, SOM's interiors department has wisely chosen restrained, elegant finishes to provide relief from Dubai's visual cacophony. In the residential floor's elevator lobby, bands of Brazilian rosewood on the walls create a warm domestic feel—as close to "home sweet home" as one can reasonably expect in a half-mile-high skyscraper. Within the apartments are the usual top-drawer brands (Sub-Zero refrigerators, Miele range hoods). Kitchens are open to living spaces and views, American style.

How many people will actually be living and working in the Burj Dubai? That, along with the tower's exact height, remains a mystery. An Emaar spokeswoman declined to answer whether Dubai's real estate bust and plummeting property values have led some buyers to walk away from their deals. The first residents are scheduled to move in to the Burj Dubai next month. The 124th floor observatory opens the day after the skyscraper's formal unveiling.

The prospect of a partly empty skyscraper invariably opens the Burj Dubai to charges of overbuilding. Surprise: it's happened before. As the history of the Empire State Building reveals—when it opened in 1931, it had so few tenants that it was known as the "Empty State Building"— today's white elephant is often tomorrow's beloved landmark. Like the Empire State, the Burj Dubai reflects the exuberance and overreaching ambition of its age. Thanks to its Chicago-based architects and engineers, it possesses the quality and artistry that will enable it to take its place not only in the record books but also among the pantheon of the world's iconic skyscrapers.

Nothing succeeds, it seems to defiantly declare, like excess.

In a stunning move at the opening ceremony, the Burj Dubai was renamed the Burj Khalifa—an abrupt change that recognized the leader of the neighboring oil-rich emirate of Abu Dhabi, Sheikh Khalifa bin Zayed Al Nahyan, who bailed Dubai out of its 2009 debt crisis. Also at the ceremony, Dubai's leader, Sheikh Mohammed bin Rashid Al Maktoum, revealed the skyscraper's height to be 828 meters, or 2,717 feet—more than 1,000 feet taller than the previous world's tallest building, the 1,667-foot Taipei 101 in Taiwan.

Responding to speculation that much of the Burj Khalifa would remain vacant because of Dubai's real estate collapse and plummeting property values, Emaar Properties executives said the skyscraper's condominiums were 90 percent sold. Substantial amounts of the proceeds from those sales were in hand, the executives said, thereby making the tower profitable. Gradually, the empty tower came to life, though not without missteps. In February 2010, its observatory was forced to shut down after an elevator malfunction and remained closed for nearly two months. But the observatory reopened in April 2010, followed by the debut of the tower's Armani Hotel. Owners were expected to start moving into the skyscraper's condos in May 2010.

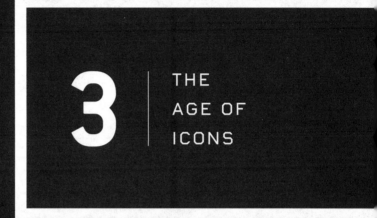

3

THE
AGE OF
ICONS

THE FEVERED POST-MILLENNIUM BUILDING BOOM SPILLED INTO THE ONCE- sedate realm of cultural buildings, which no longer were the sole province of establishment firms turning out solid but unremarkable temples of the arts. Now, seeking to duplicate the success of Frank Gehry's Guggenheim Museum in Bilbao, Spain, museum directors acted like real estate developers and commissioned star architects—or "starchitects," in that ungainly coinage—to design attention-getting, one-of-a-kind buildings that would raise attendance, put their cities on the map, and (almost as an afterthought) serve as a place to display paintings and sculpture. Leaders of colleges, universities, and other cultural institutions followed suit. These buildings were alternately described as works of spectacle or as "icons." While the word "icon" historically had been associated with religious imagery, iconic architecture had little to do with the worship of a deity. It was venerated principally for its striking and easily marketable forms.

For a time, nearly every city and its leading donors, flush with money from the soaring stock market, seemed to be erecting a new cathedral of culture. But unlike the creators of Gothic cathedrals, the "starchitects" were not anonymous master builders. They were celebrities who belonged to a select flying circus, jetting around the globe, competing for prime commissions. They shared no style or structural rationale; each had his or her own visual brand. This bold new approach produced unforgettable masterpieces, such as Frank Gehry's Walt Disney Concert Hall in Los Angeles, yet it also could lapse into irrational exuberance, leaving behind buildings in which the quest for novelty and notoriety superseded all else.

CATHEDRALS OF CULTURE

Winged Victory

SANTIAGO CALATRAVA MARRIES SCULPTURE AND STRUCTURE,
AND MOLDS A NEW IDENTITY FOR THE MILWAUKEE ART MUSEUM

MARCH 2002

Unlike Las Vegas high rollers, art museum directors don't walk around with suitcases full of cash and dice to spill on green felt crap tables. But maybe they should, considering the gambler's mentality it takes to build a great museum today. Anyone wanting to repeat the much-hyped Bilbao effect must forge a partnership with an architectural superstar, raise millions of dollars, then hope that the finished product turns out to be a media megastory that draws critical raves as well as hordes of visitors.

For better or for worse, this is the way the global museum game is played at the beginning of the 21st century, and it certainly describes the high-wire act that the Milwaukee Art Museum has performed with its $122 million addition designed by Zurich-based, Spanish-born architect and engineer Santiago Calatrava. Not only is this Calatrava's first building in the United States and his first museum, but it also represents his most extensive essay in kinetic architecture, sporting a 217-foot-wide sunshade, or *brise-soleil*, set atop the museum's glass-sheathed reception area, that unfurls like the wings of a giant bird.

THE ADDITION TO THE MILWAUKEE ART MUSEUM
An urban event, where spectacle meets art.

Before the addition opened, questions abounded about the feasibility and appropriateness of the daring contraption. A tropical sunshade in frigid Milwaukee? There were concerns, too, about Calatrava: How could he relate his stark white, gravity-defying, steel-and-concrete modernism to a midwestern Rust Belt city best known for its three "B's"—bowling, beer, and brats?

Today, though, it is clear that Milwaukee's gamble has paid off in the form of a striking monument that is at once a strong personal statement and a sensitive essay in the making of place. While visitors may flock to the addition to glimpse the *brise-soleil*, they are likely to come away realizing that the device is not an isolated gimmick. What makes the bird-like building fly is Calatrava's singular fusion of sculpture and structure.

Structure has been off the architectural radar screen for nearly a quarter of a century, ever since the postmodern assault on the formulaic modernist buildings of the 1970s. But Calatrava is at pains to reveal a building's bones, making them the centerpiece of his baroque visual drama. Although his Milwaukee addition is not without faults, it nevertheless has real significance because it reasserts and refreshes the age-old premise that architecture is a building art.

To fully grasp the importance of Calatrava's design, one must understand its spectacular site, just to the east of downtown Milwaukee on the shores of Lake Michigan. In 1957 Milwaukee's civic leaders imported to this setting an earlier star, Eero Saarinen, to design a multipurpose modernist structure that would house a war memorial above and an art museum below. Saarinen's solution, a cruciform concrete mass set atop a heavy, stone-clad base, nobly commanded its environs, but it had limited room for galleries and made the museum visually subservient to the war memorial. The space crunch was temporarily alleviated in 1975, with the museum's first addition, a low-slung brutalist building by Milwaukee architect David Kahler that was wedged between the war memorial and the lake. But the appropriately modest, if unremarkable, addition left the museum without a memorable formal identity.

Calatrava, who won the Milwaukee commission in 1994—besting the Japanese finalists Arata Isozaki and Fumihiko Maki—set out to correct that problem in a composition that grew substantially in cost and scope after it was unveiled in 1996. That shift occurred because Calatrava's design (and his charm on the fund-raising circuit) opened wallets. The budget shot from $38 million to $122 million to include higher-than-expected construction costs and major additions, such as the *brise-soleil*, a 100-space underground parking garage, and gardens by landscape architect Dan Kiley. The Milwaukee firm of Kalher Slater served as architect of record.

THREE DISTINCT ELEMENTS IN A POWERFUL WHOLE

In its finished state, the addition conveys the impression of a powerful whole, even though it is made up of three distinct elements: a low-slung gallery building that extends southward from the Saarinen and Kahler wings; a 250-foot-long, cable-stayed pedestrian bridge that links the museum to downtown Milwaukee; and the *brise-soleil*, which sits atop a steel-framed reception hall and consists of 72 paired steel fins that are wider at their widest point than the wingspan of a Boeing 747-400. Driven by hydraulic motors, the fins ostensibly are there to control the temperature and light in the reception hall, but it is hard to deny that their primary purpose is to endow the museum with a landmark presence it never had underneath the war memorial.

While reaction has been favorable, some critics have observed that by separating the grand reception hall from the more modest gallery building, Calatrava has dodged the conflict between the container and the contained that must be resolved if a building is to rank as a great art museum. Indeed, Calatrava's addition has very little art in it. Just 12,000 of its 142,000 square feet are devoted to galleries, with the rest going to public spaces like the reception hall. But Calatrava's task was less to resolve the ongoing battle between art and architecture than to recast the entire museum's inner workings and identity. He did the former by shifting public areas out of Kahler's wing and turning the space they once occupied into galleries, thus giving the museum 30 percent more room for art display. He did the latter by creating a grand civic space and a new image for both the museum and Milwaukee.

Take, for example, his deft handling of the spectacular shoreline site. He keeps the gallery building low to preserve views of Lake Michigan from the city. Throughout the addition, he abstracts nautical imagery (sails, planks, prows, masts, soaring birds) to link the museum to the lake.

Calatrava is equally good at relating his addition to both its urban setting and to Saarinen's war memorial. The sculptural presence of the *brise-soleil* winningly culminates the axis of Wisconsin Avenue, projecting the museum's presence into downtown Milwaukee's heart. Meanwhile, the addition echoes Saarinen's cross-shaped plan, while Calatrava's building opens up a genuine dialogue with Saarinen's: the old structure still earthbound, the new one using 21st-century technology to realize the floating quality to which its 20th-century predecessor could only aspire.

When the *brise-soleil* unfolds, it is an event, one that beckons museumgoers outside with their video cameras. As the fins move upward, the sunshade suggests the bottom of an hourglass. Then, as the fins reach their apex and transform themselves into softly curving arcs, the resemblance to a bird becomes unmistakable. This is spectacle *and* art, a stunning and skillful transformation of heavyweight steel into lightweight kinetic sculpture.

As the rest of the exterior demonstrates, Calatrava is a master of this kinetic genre. His cable-stayed bridge in Milwaukee is a structural tour de force; its wafer-thin steel deck makes it seem suspended in midair. There are other memorable flourishes, like the gallery building, which culminates, on the addition's south side, in a beautifully sculpted prow that recalls the extended fingers of a human hand.

Calatrava speaks of his design as a series of gestures, which seems appropriate, because the building, like a sculpture, resembles a body moving through space. Yet befitting its role as architecture, the addition shapes space, as when the gallery building frames a stone forecourt and Kiley's gardens on its flanks. The garden's low-slung hedges aptly echo the horizontality of Calatrava's building and the lakefront, but they still have a presence of their own, forming room-like enclaves.

To be sure, the addition has rough spots, especially its unrefined connection to the existing buildings. The base of the reception hall seems cartoonish because its window mullions are larger and less elegant than Calatrava had hoped for. And the hall's proportions are inelegant due to the bulky concrete structure that supports it.

But these problems are quickly forgiven once the visitor moves inside, especially if the point of entry is the 100-space parking garage beneath the galleries. Here, in an inspired departure from the typical heavy-handed, post-and-beam garage, Calatrava uses inclined, steel-reinforced concrete columns that narrow toward a foot-like steel base. Their lyrical, dancing effect recalls the famous "lily pad" concrete columns at Frank Lloyd Wright's SC Johnson & Son Administration Building in nearby Racine, Wisconsin.

There are unmistakable echoes of that building's streamlining in the parking garage's gracefully curving concrete walls. But it seems less important to compare Wright and Calatrava than to observe that, in Milwaukee, as in his earlier works, Calatrava's exposed structure imitates the figural complexity of nature and thus departs from the machine-like regularity of the Miesian mode. This organic quality endows the addition with an inherent human scale. It seems as much a house as a culture palace, though there is no denying its cathedral-like identity, especially in its soaring, sun-washed reception hall and in the gallerias that extend outward from it like the side aisles of a church.

By siting the addition's temporary exhibition gallery just off the hall, Calatrava makes clear that one has entered an art museum rather than a generic mall. Within the exhibition space, his expressed concrete ceiling beams have a palpable presence, yet they are not so strong that they overwhelm the art. Movable wall dividers are low enough to lend the gallery intimacy, but the visitor still feels like he is in an expansive space, one that bears the architect's distinctive imprint.

STRUCTURE IN THE SERVICE OF SCULPTURE

The addition's finest strokes are the twin gallerias that flank the gallery and lead to the original buildings. Far from being mere passageways, the gallerias, which house changing displays of contemporary art, are destinations that are distinguished by the rhythmic, lyrical expression of their arching concrete ribs.

As in the garage, the ribs are grounded in steel joints that at once suggest the human foot and express the steel that reinforces them. Yet here the concrete, painted white, seems otherworldly, dematerialized. Does this

GALLERIAS AT THE MILWAUKEE ART MUSEUM ADDITION
The poetry of structure, revealed by arching concrete ribs.

mean Calatrava isn't being "honest" with materials by failing to express
the heavy lifting the ribs do? No. Again, to great effect, he puts structure
in the service of sculpture, drawing out, as he has said, "the inner potential
for poetic expression that materials possess."

Calatrava's addition handsomely realizes that potential. It takes us in
dazzling new directions even as it reminds us of the traditional importance
of materials and structure. While the addition does not match such masterpieces as Louis Kahn's Kimbell Art Museum in Fort Worth or another
famous bird-like building, Saarinen's TWA Terminal at John F. Kennedy
International Airport in New York City, it superbly serves its complex program while creating an instant landmark. For Calatrava, it represents an
enormously successful American debut—a powerful hint of what he still
may accomplish by embedding structure into sculpture.

Architectural Record

POSTSCRIPT

*The Milwaukee Art Museum addition became a beloved civic icon and a new
symbol of its city. Attendance rose, along with the museum's international profile.*

But in the short term, the addition proved to be a financial albatross as well as a spirit-lifting representation of a bird. The dramatic expansion of its scope saddled the museum with an unprecedented $25 million debt, which was retired only in 2006. As the Milwaukee Journal-Sentinel's *Mary Louise Schumacher reported in 2007, the addition also left the museum with "significantly increased expenses and a stretched-thin staff."*

For Calatrava, the addition would prove to be a launching pad for what was, at least initially, a rocket-like ascent in the United States. He would be tapped to design the proposed Fordham Spire in Chicago (see p. 101), whose original developer, Christopher Carley, was captivated by the Milwaukee building. And the Port Authority of New York & New Jersey would commission him for the new transportation hub at the World Trade Center in New York City, whose above-ground portion, echoing its predecessor in Milwaukee, was designed to resemble a great bird alighted on a plaza..

A Musical Ark for Los Angeles

FRANK GEHRY'S SPECTACULAR DISNEY HALL DRAWS ENERGY FROM THE CITY'S CHAOS AND STEERS IT TOWARD A NEW VISION OF COMMUNITY

OCTOBER 26, 2003

Frank Gehry's brilliant new Walt Disney Concert Hall is a musical ark with silver sails that dance in the bright blue California sky. The $274 million hall channels the chaotic, sprawling forces of modern life and transforms them into an exuberant, exquisite celebration of community, especially a curvaceous, wood-paneled auditorium that is one of the finest rooms in America.

Rising on a hilltop a few blocks from this city's bland patch of downtown office towers, Disney Hall superbly resolves a range of competing agendas: architecture and acoustics, artistry and technology, the urge to create a great stand-alone object and the responsibility to connect such a structure to the city around it.

It is a personal triumph for the Los Angeles–based Gehry, who persisted for 15 years to get it built, and a civic triumph for his city, which now has something other than the sun-bleached white letters of the Hollywood sign to flaunt on postcards.

Even so, Disney Hall is simply a beginning, a way to start making a dense, walkable urban center in a *Blade Runner* downtown that seems to

THE WALT DISNEY CONCERT HALL
A long-delayed triumph for Frank Gehry and a new civic landmark for Los Angeles.

have been planned entirely by traffic engineers. You've seen one too many Disney movies if you think this singular structure can instantly duplicate the so-called Bilbao effect, named for the way Gehry's Guggenheim Museum in Bilbao, Spain, drew tourists by the planeload after it opened in 1997.

Inevitably, some will charge that the concert hall, with its swooping metallic curves, is nothing more than "Bilbao: The Sequel," a cynical attempt to cash in on Gehry's Spanish blockbuster. Yet that's like saying that all of Frank Lloyd Wright's Prairie-style houses are alike because they have overhanging eaves and art glass windows. Design is a language, and Gehry's grammar is constantly evolving and endlessly inventive.

The concert hall confirms his standing as a maestro of metal, one capable of making cold steel seem as warm as a bouquet of red roses. The building's buoyant, festive arcs simultaneously suggest the musical performances inside and celebrate the dynamic flux of urban life.

The origins of Disney Hall reach back to 1987, when the now-deceased Lillian Disney made a $50 million gift for a new concert hall in honor of her late husband, Walt. A year later Gehry won a design competition for the project, which would replace the neighboring Dorothy Chandler Pavilion as the home of the Los Angeles Philharmonic. But a spiraling budget and management problems almost scuttled the effort. A groundbreaking wasn't held until late 1999. Miraculously, Gehry's original design concept survived and actually has gotten better.

Stainless-steel shingles, which were less expensive than the limestone Gehry initially proposed, cover the structural steel frame. Shaped with the aid of CATIA, a computer program used to design the complex curves of French Mirage fighter jets, the cladding looks remarkable—taut and crisp, perfectly accentuating the building's baroque curves. The "body language" of the building, as Gehry calls it, could not be more welcoming—the very opposite of the haughty Chandler Pavilion, a modern temple enclosed with columns and raised on a podium. (The Chandler Pavilion remains the home of the Los Angeles Opera.)

Unfortunately, the hall occupies a boxed-in site, which undercuts its identity as an urban landmark. Gehry's sculptural forms typically look best when they are on an urban "edge," such as the river along the Guggenheim Bilbao, that gives them room to preen. Yet it is hard to see the whole of Disney Hall from the freeways that slice past downtown L.A. You wish the hall could trade places with José Rafael Moneo's nearby cathedral, which presents a forbidding face to the freeway alongside it. That way, it could more easily integrate itself into the city's daily life, as the Sydney Opera House can because of its spectacular waterfront setting.

But Gehry unlocks the hidden potential of his imperfect site. His urban design masterstroke was to place Disney Hall's main auditorium on a diagonal, orienting the building's main entrance to the street corner. This arrangement leaves room for lush public gardens on one side of the building while devoting the other to glassy, sidewalk-level walls that invite pedestrians to enter the hall's skylit, meandering lobby. For those who drive to the hall (which is just about everybody), there is a seven-level underground garage connected to the lobby via a spacious, high-ceilinged escalator.

Gehry cleverly uses his curving forms to disguise the boxy presence of the main auditorium, making Disney Hall seem to rotate gracefully around the corner instead of presenting a blunt edge. Peeling back the mask-like wrapper of the stainless steel, he reveals a glassy entrance to the lobby. He further breaks down the hall's mass with a stunningly baroque pavilion, reserved for major donors, that is clad in a highly reflective stainless steel, as shiny as a newly minted dime.

But to talk simply about Disney Hall's spectacular exterior would be to miss its true three-dimensional beauty. Gehry designed the concert hall from the inside out, wanting it to be, above all, a vessel for great sound.

Working with chief acoustician Yasuhisa Toyota of Nagata Acoustics, he created an extraordinary main auditorium, a great boat of a room that is bereft of such formal trappings as chandeliers, red velvet seats, special boxes for wealthy concertgoers, or a proscenium stage that forms an invisible barrier between audience and performers.

DISTINCT HALLS

What the 2,265-seat hall does have is a completely fresh look that results from the merging of two distinct concert hall types: a traditional shoe box–shaped auditorium, prized for its intimacy and acoustics; and the contemporary "vineyard" approach, which places hill-like tiers of seats around the stage. The latter is exemplified by one of Gehry's favorite buildings, Hans Scharoun's expressionist Berlin Philharmonic Hall of 1963.

As could be seen during a pre-gala performance, his synthesis of these types has produced a multi-tiered auditorium that is both grand and intimate, a big room that feels as small as a chamber music hall. It is a symphony of swelling wooden forms that suggest the hull of a ship, the belly of a whale, and the jolly curves of the building's exterior.

These moves aren't arbitrary; the curves and grooves in them are designed to enhance the listener's experience, bouncing music back to concertgoers so the sound doesn't get swallowed in an acoustical black hole. An exuberant Gehry-designed pipe organ provides an appropriate visual exclamation point.

Offering splendid sight lines to all and concealing social hierarchy rather than accentuating it, the concert hall is a palace of democracy. It ranks with Louis Sullivan and Dankmar Adler's Auditorium Theatre in Chicago as one of the most profound architectural expressions of American culture.

"INDIVIDUALISTIC HEDONISM"

For all of its seemingly uncontrolled energy, Gehry's design maintains a precarious balance, simultaneously evoking Los Angeles' unruly individualism and speaking to the civilized pleasures of the public realm. The concert hall is such an architectural success that it inevitably will raise hopes that this famously center-less city might actually develop a thriving urban

THE INTERIOR OF THE WALT DISNEY CONCERT HALL
A symphony of swelling wooden forms, one of the finest rooms in America.

core, realizing ambitious plans for a vibrant mixed-use district anchored by Disney Hall.

And when might that happen? "Not in my lifetime," says the white-haired, 74-year-old Gehry.

Give him credit for being the ultimate realist—and for designing an American masterwork that draws energy from urban chaos and charts an exuberant course beyond it.

POSTSCRIPT

One of the issues that architecture critics face in assessing a building is that it makes hundreds of small impressions. Which ones make it into the critique and which are left out? In writing this review, I omitted any reference to what seemed to be a very minor flaw of Disney Hall: standing on the sidewalk outside the building, I felt tremendous heat radiating off its steel exterior. It was like being inside a microwave. I assumed it was an isolated problem that would be fixed. Wrong.

In February 2004, four months after Disney Hall's triumphant opening, the Los Angeles Times *reported that searing reflections off the polished steel panels that formed the exterior of the hall's Founders Room were bouncing into the condominiums of people living across the street. Around noon on sunny days, as the* Times *revealed, temperatures would rise by as much as 15 degrees, "forcing residents to get off their patios, draw the blinds and turn on the air conditioners for up to three hours until the sunlight shifts." A consultant's study later concluded that beams of sunlight reflected from the hall were raising sidewalk temperatures to 140 degrees Fahrenheit, high enough to inflict bystanders with serious sunburn.*

Architects for Gehry's firm explained that they took the glare from the steel into account in designing the building, but that an error during construction made the shiny sheets of metal face at a slightly different angle than they had called for, thereby causing the problem. In March 2005, workers began sanding the polished steel of the Founders Room and other portions of the building to dull the steel's gloss and eliminate the glare. Although the episode embarrassed Gehry, it backhandedly drew attention to his achievement, prompting debate about whether it was proper to alter a building that, less than a year and a half after its opening, already had become a landmark.

Rocky Mountain Highs and Lows

DANIEL LIBESKIND'S DENVER ART MUSEUM ADDITION IS A
STRIKING URBAN PRESENCE BUT DOESN'T SOAR AS A SHOWCASE

OCTOBER 8, 2006

With his elfin stature, towering intellect, and aggressive designer eyewear, architect and ground zero planner Daniel Libeskind has been a media fixture for so long that it's hard to believe his shimmering, sharp-edged addition to the Denver Art Museum is his first American building.

The new $110 million project reveals both the strengths and weaknesses of Libeskind's madly exuberant neo-expressionist style, with its knifing prows and peaks, tilting cubes, and ski-slope roofs that seem perfect for the Rockies.

It is a startling, often over-the-top piece of architectural sculpture, a surprisingly sensitive shaper of urban spaces, and a disappointingly spotty art museum in which basic functional problems have not been adequately solved. Perhaps the addition represents a cautionary tale for the era of globe-trotting star architects, a warning against irrational exuberance, in which the knock-your-eyes-out container overwhelms the art it contains.

THE HAMILTON BUILDING OF THE DENVER ART MUSEUM
A startling, over-the-top piece of architectural sculpture.

Officially known as the Frederic C. Hamilton Building after the oilman who is its major benefactor, the addition rises a few blocks from Denver's mediocre asparagus-patch of a downtown skyline. A complex internal network of tilting steel trusses supports its cacophonous collage of crystalline forms, which the New York–based Libeskind designed in cooperation with Denver's Davis Partnership Architects. A taut, silver-gray titanium skin wraps the structure while a prosaic sky bridge links the addition to the museum's original building, a tough-but-alluring castle designed by Italian architect Gio Ponti.

If Ponti's structure implies that an art museum should be a fortress, protecting sacred treasures, Libeskind's comes off as more of a funhouse, a populist palazzo that invites you to partake of its architectural thrill ride.

BREATHTAKING SIGHT

That ride is a "Look, Ma, I can fly" collection of gravity-defying, computer-designed cantilevers, such as a prow-like corner that soars over the heavily traveled street between the Libeskind and Ponti buildings. Alternately threatening and delightful, the edgy gestures make Michael Graves's neighboring Denver Central Library—a postmodern collage of colorful drums, blocks, and pyramids—seem stolid by comparison.

Even if Libeskind's hard-edged forms lack Frank Gehry's suppleness, his building nonetheless captures Denver's youthful energy and speaks to its extraordinary natural landscape, popping up from certain vantage points like a man-made mountain.

While his addition appears to be a self-referential object, it actually succeeds in weaving together disparate parts of the cityscape. Its titanium shingles relate beautifully to the sparkling, tiled skin of the Ponti building.

INSIDE THE DENVER ART MUSEUM'S HAMILTON BUILDING
Awkward display spaces, where function is forced to accommodate form.

And Libeskind's site plan ingeniously places the addition to one side of a closed-off street that has been transformed into an attractive outdoor plaza outfitted with tables, chairs, and large-scale contemporary sculpture. Across the way, also shaping the street, is an aboveground parking garage, its brute concrete walls masked by glass-faced, Libeskind-designed condominiums that serve up more of his signature skewed forms.

The plaza effectively links the museum's gentrifying neighborhood to Denver's Beaux-Arts Civic Center, a sylvan but largely lifeless precinct of government buildings and open spaces laid out by Chicago architect Edward Bennett, Daniel Burnham's coauthor on the great 1909 *Plan of Chicago*. The new museum ensemble even makes Graves's library look better, creating a handsome foreground that replaces the dreary collection of surface parking lots that once occupied the area.

Traditionalists are sure to rant about the show-off architecture, but Libeskind's design succeeds in putting a contemporary spin on the urban context rather than embalming it in architectural formaldehyde. The result is a fragment of his masterful, yet now gutted, ground zero plan, in which culture leavened commerce and his crystalline forms shaped a powerful urban whole.

Inside the museum, the story is considerably more mixed, though it starts dramatically—and well—with a 120-foot atrium that coils through the four-level building. With its boldly sloping white walls, angular stone stairs, stark shafts of natural light, and landings that offer dazzling overlooks, the atrium makes the heart beat faster, and not just because of the altitude. It's a man-made canyon walk, as joyous as Libeskind's 1999 Jewish Museum Berlin is haunting.

But the atrium also reveals an embarrassing gaffe, one that recurs throughout: Libeskind's eccentric design forced the museum to install low wooden barriers to prevent visitors, particularly blind people, from bumping their heads on tilting walls and stairs. The makeshift devices exhibit a jarring lack of refinement.

Libeskind's galleries—which house temporary exhibits as well as a permanent collection strong in American Indian, pre-Columbian, and Spanish colonial art—do not bring honor to the post-minimalist camp of museum design and its revolt against the clinical white-box rooms of the Museum of Modern Art. In some cases, the architect's splaying walls have forced the museum to add flat surfaces for hanging paintings. As if to push back, the museum's curators forced Libeskind (in the interest of preserving light-sensitive works of art) to eliminate windows from his original design.

The outcome is not a model of the art of compromise. A temporary exhibition gallery devoted to Japanese art feels claustrophobic, with Libeskind's ubiquitous off-kilter geometry fighting the serene art instead of forming a subtle counterpoint. Throughout, the galleries lack the soothing natural light and rich range of wall colors that enliven the Ponti building's interiors and enrich the experience of viewing its art.

There are some bright spots, especially in the two-level modern and contemporary galleries, where curators have deftly arranged temporary walls and placed works of art to take full advantage of Libeskind's non-Euclidean geometry. In the building's prow, for example, sculptor Antony Gormley's *Quantum Cloud XXXIII*, an abstract human figure made of sharp-edged metal pieces, looks radiant beside a narrow, diagonal slit of a window.

Here, at least, art and architecture seem in perfect harmony, but all too often in this building the art is forced to accommodate the architecture rather than the other way around. Might the Denver Art Museum have achieved a better balance by hiring an architect such as Renzo Piano, whose designs are less earthshakingly dramatic but more sympathetic to displaying art? Perhaps, but then the museum wouldn't have the most striking object of all in its collection—a visually spellbinding new home that brings new life to the city around it.

POSTSCRIPT

Controversy continued to swirl around Libeskind's addition to the Denver Art Museum. Shortly after the opening, the building's sharply angled roof sprung a leak, causing water to drip into its dramatic atrium. In April 2007, the museum announced that 30 employees had taken a buyout and that 8 positions had been eliminated, reducing the museum's staff by 14 percent. As Mary Voelz Chander reported in the now-defunct Rocky Mountain News, *the eliminated positions came from departments, such as visitor services, whose staff size had increased in anticipation of the opening. In addition, the museum sliced its projected attendance for the Hamilton Building's first 12 months from 1 million visitors to between 750,000 and 1 million.*

By 2009 the leaking roof was finally fixed and the museum opened a show, titled Embrace, *which featured 17 site-specific works by international artists inside the Libeskind building. As* Architectural Record *noted, the show appeared to be an attempt to refute the criticism that the building's unconventional galleries were ill-suited for displaying art.*

Blades of Glass

THE NEW SPERTUS INSTITUTE AND ITS GEMLIKE WALL FORM
A WELCOME COUNTERPOINT TO CHICAGO'S MICHIGAN AVENUE
HISTORIC DISTRICT

NOVEMBER 25, 2007

Chicago's rough-hewn cityscape, already studded with architectural jewels, has a sparkling new gem. It resembles an exquisitely cut diamond dropped into the great wall of stone that rises like a cliff across from Grant Park.

With its faceted, folded facade of glass glinting softly in the sun, the new Spertus Institute of Jewish Studies at 618 South Michigan Avenue is a beguiling expression of light, both actual and metaphoric. It is at once novel and neighborly, a building whose spectacularly sculptural, computer-

THE SPERTUS INSTITUTE
Where a folding, faceted wall of glass engages in a rich and respectful dialogue with its historic neighbors.

aided design is truly of our era even as it engages in a dialogue across time with the masterpieces that put Chicago on the architectural map.

The 10-story, $55 million structure, which was paid for almost entirely with private funds, represents the finest cultural project in Chicago since the 2004 completion of Millennium Park—and a welcome sign that the park's bold embrace of the new was no one-shot deal.

Designed by Chicago architects Ron Krueck and Mark Sexton—whose portfolio includes award-winning modernist houses and a supporting role in the design of Millennium Park's Crown Fountain—the new Spertus forms an object lesson in how the past should engage the present: through sophisticated counterpoint rather than violent contrast or facile imitation.

There is no tacked-on brick and limestone here to "blend in" with the mighty row of historic buildings across from Grant Park. Nor are there Stars of David or other overt religious symbols.

Instead, the building's facade stands, like so much glass origami, for the power of lifelong learning in Jewish culture and the rich complexity of that culture. If there is overt symbolism in this building, it can only be seen in what is not present: no concrete barricades, no off-putting walls of stone, no barbed wire. Howard Sulkin, the institute's ebullient president, had the courage and foresight not to turn this building into a fortress after the calamitous events of September 11.

Set on a former vacant lot just north of the institute's old home, a mediocre glass-faced structure at 610 South Michigan, the new Spertus provides more space for each of the institute's three main divisions: Spertus College, the Spertus Museum, and the Asher Library. It adds such attractions as a 400-seat theater and a kosher café, said to be the only one in downtown Chicago.

WELL CONNECTED

In the old building, these uses were stacked like flapjacks on separate floors. The new one offers a spatial surprise: the architects punched a soaring lobby and a meandering atrium through the building's steel frame, symbolically connecting its functions in a series of grandly scaled rooms that borrow light, space, and vitality from one another.

True, the new Spertus is neither faultless nor wholly original. Modernist architects have for years been playing with the idea of folded facades as an alternative to the postmodern custom of slathering buildings with decoration. The Pritzker Prize–winning Paris architect Christian de Portzamparc completed a much-praised facade of folded glass in his slender 23-story LVMH Tower in Manhattan all the way back in 1999.

But this is the first time such a treatment has been pulled off in any significant way in Chicago, and it truly occupies center stage. It marks the first insertion of a contemporary design into the cliff-like wall of buildings that extends along the western edge of Grant Park since Mayor Richard M. Daley pushed through city landmark status for the area in 2002.

At the time, architects fumed that giving city bureaucrats tight rein over this so-called Historic Michigan Boulevard District, which includes such masterpieces as Adler & Sullivan's muscular Auditorium Building, would put a crimp on their creativity. But Krueck + Sexton have shown that accepting constraints, as opposed to unbridled freedom, is an essential part of the creative process.

Like the other buildings in the Michigan Avenue historic district, theirs has a bottom, a middle, and a top. And it's deeply three-dimensional, not simply a flat plane. Yet its startling wall of glass is every bit a product of the computer age and the freedom new technologies have given architects to customize forms rather than standardize them, as in the industrial age. The new Spertus facade is composed of 726 pieces of glass, formed in 556 different shapes, including parallelograms that tilt in two ways, not one. The glass pieces are clipped onto extruded aluminum frames whose three-legged, twisting profile resembles a human femur bone. The pieces project outward over the sidewalk by as much as five feet and inward toward the center of the building by as much as two feet.

Far too often these days, such technical wizardry seeks only to produce "wow" buildings, as if architecture's job was to make us yelp. But in the capable hands of Krueck + Sexton, the new Spertus is no one-liner.

The building's crystalline forms are dramatic enough to stand up to the heft of such muscle-bound neighbors as the Chicago Hilton. Yet they do not seem jagged and aggressive, as can the silvery, sharp-pointed buildings of Daniel Libeskind. Rather, they appear soft and billowy, like folds of drapery or a woman's body. The building even has a "skirt," a sheltering projection of glass that playfully sweeps over the sidewalk and lets you discover the structural girdle that makes the skirt stand up.

MIRRORS ITS SURROUNDINGS

To the architects' credit, they have extended such elegance down to the smallest details, such as the thickness and low-iron content of the building's glass. This ensures that the glass handsomely mirrors its surroundings and the sky rather than reflecting them in the jittery manner of conventional glass. The overall result is that the design thrillingly but nobly transports the Michigan Avenue wall into the 21st century.

Yet the beauty of the new Spertus runs deeper than its voluptuous glass facade. The building's transparency communicates far more effectively than the opaque glass of Spertus's former home that this is a public place, a cleft in the wall of stone buildings along Michigan Avenue. Here, the architecture democratically invites passersby to venture in and glimpse the over-the-treetops views of Grant Park, which Sulkin romantically refers to as "Eden."

After visitors pass through metal detectors—these and non-shattering laminated exterior glass are among the few visible responses to post–September 11 security concerns—they will find themselves in a striking three-story lobby. It is dominated by a folded, fragmented wall of white plaster that somewhat heavy-handedly reprises the glass exterior.

There's still much to like here, starting with the mix of uses that pin-wheel around the lobby—a gift shop, the kosher café, classrooms, and the theater—and the way the architects have threaded them together with an elegant steel-and-glass switchback stair. As in a good city, one activity promises to energize the other.

Even so, it's disappointing that the lobby's burst of open space stops at the third floor instead of extending all the way up the building's north side, as Krueck + Sexton had originally proposed. Soaring prices for steel and other materials foiled that grand design, which, if realized, would have raised the building's interior to a whole new level.

Krueck + Sexton have nonetheless delivered some superb spaces that retain the core of their original idea, most notably on the four upper floors. There, the skylit atrium meanders marvelously downward, from changing exhibition galleries on the 10th floor to a grand, multipurpose hall on the 9th floor to a soaring reading room on the 8th floor and finally to a student lounge on the 7th floor. These spaces, some of the most powerful and magical interiors in Chicago, make vertiginous hotel atriums seem like barns by comparison.

NATURALLY BRIGHT

The architects use skylights, light wells, and open floor plans to make the building, just 80 feet wide, seem far more spacious than its constrained site would seem to allow. Natural light even reaches to the back of the build-ing, where, on the 9th floor, a monumental horseshoe-shaped wall of glass

INSIDE THE SPERTUS INSTITUTE
A wandering atrium of grandly scaled rooms that borrow light, space, and vitality from one another.

encloses what promises to be a memorable open-storage display of meno-rahs, holy arks, and more than 1,000 other objects of Judaica. In short, the building enhances its contents rather than overwhelming them.

The architects have quietly excelled at handling the hidden structural and planning moves that should make the steel-framed building a well-functioning vertical village. As visitors sit in the column-free theater, which is made intimate by an unusual partitioned balcony, they will likely be unaware that 14-foot-deep trusses are bearing the weight above them and transferring the loads down to the foundations.

Such uses will help the new Spertus to extend the cultural vitality of Michigan Avenue farther southward, creating a new anchor of activity between Millennium Park and the Museum Campus. More broadly, the design can be understood as an expression of the cultural confidence now felt by once-marginalized American Jews, "a certain people," as the author Charles Silberman once called them. Significantly, this bold building faces directly onto Chicago's front yard rather than being shunted to the shadows. An uncertain people could not have pulled that off. The new Spertus is a triumph of architecture and—ironically, coming from a people who have borne witness to so much darkness—a gift of light.

POSTSCRIPT

At first, the new Spertus Institute was celebrated as a cultural icon on a budget, its $55 million price tag a bargain compared to the recent crop of museums that cost in excess of $100 million. With the onset of the recession, however, the picture looked very different. As the Chicago Tribune *reported in 2009, the institute's endowment had dropped precipitously, and Spertus owed $43.6 million of the $51.6 million it borrowed for its new home. To survive, Spertus cut costs, laying off more than a quarter of its full-time staff, reducing the hours of its museum, and closing its kosher café. Inevitably, these changes had an impact on the building's architecture. Fewer people funneled through its atrium, diminishing the space's vitality.*

FROM SPECTACULAR TO SUBTLE

THE PUSH FOR INSTANT ICONS WAS SO PERVASIVE THAT IT INEVITABLY LED TO A countermovement, which prized subtlety over spectacle and reasserted the role of function as a determinant of architectural form without lapsing into the arid functionalism that represented the worst of International Style modernism. Indeed, in such exemplary projects as Steven Holl's Bloch Building addition to the Nelson-Atkins Museum of Art in Kansas City, Missouri, function and spirit were melded into a remarkable synthesis, which emphasized a gradually unfolding discovery of space rather than an eye-popping form.

A Brighter Idea

STEVEN HOLL'S BLOCH BUILDING AT THE NELSON-ATKINS MUSEUM OF ART IN KANSAS CITY REDEFINES THE MUSEUM ADDITION

MAY 27, 2007

Far too many recent museum buildings have all the subtlety of a frying pan whacking you over the head. They shake. They shimmy. Their geometric gyrations overshadow the very art they're supposed to showcase. New York architect Steven Holl's quietly brilliant new addition to the already distinguished Nelson-Atkins Museum of Art in Kansas City, Missouri, wisely departs from this self-indulgent norm. It is a work of subtlety, not spectacle, though, in truth, it packs some unexpected "wow."

Holl breaks the paradigm of the "look at me" building with a partly underground structure, 840 feet long, that tumbles down a slope alongside the Nelson-Atkins' original neoclassical temple. The most visible feature isn't one big eye-grabbing shape, but a string of smaller, elegant ones. Five irregularly shaped glass pavilions (Holl calls them "lenses") pop out of the earth, engaging the sylvan landscape of the adjoining Kansas City Sculpture Park and energizing the addition's spatially fluid interior with softly diffused daylight.

By day, the lenses are veiled in mystery, alternately brooding and iridescent. But as the sun sets and soft white light glows outward from them, they become magical, ethereal, and seemingly weightless, like something from the moon. Not since Frank Gehry's startling eruption of metal—the Guggenheim Museum in Bilbao, Spain—made its smashing debut 10 years ago has a museum been this enchanting.

The happy twist is that the package doesn't overwhelm the contents. Inside are some of the finest museum galleries completed in recent years, at once architecturally assertive with their flaring ceiling vaults and deeply respectful of the Nelson-Atkins' fine collection of contemporary art, photography, and African art. It's a very different story from Daniel Libeskind's madly exuberant Denver Art Museum addition, where tilting titanium walls create both a spectacular image and a less-than-ideal setting for art.

Along with last year's exquisite Glass Pavilion of the Toledo Museum of Art, designed by the Tokyo-based firm of SANAA, the Bloch Building is everything that its flashier counterparts in Denver and elsewhere are not: serene but lively; modest but by no means mousy.

These buildings demand to be seen—no, the better word is experienced. For the camera cannot fully capture their spirit-refreshing shifts of light and scale, as well as their deft interaction with their surroundings, both natural and man-made.

Known as the Bloch Building (after H&R Block magnate Henry Bloch and his wife, Marion), the addition sits in an arts district five miles south of downtown and was co-designed by Chris McVoy, a partner at Holl's firm. The Kansas City firm BNIM served as architects of record.

The Bloch Building represents the largest part of a $196 million civic undertaking that has renovated the 1933 museum building and expanded the sculpture park, a magnificent public space to the museum's south that is dotted with sensuous bronzes by Henry Moore and playful, oversize shuttlecocks by Claes Oldenburg and Coosje van Bruggen.

THE BLOCH BUILDING OF THE NELSON-ATKINS MUSEUM OF ART
A reaction against iconic architecture that became an icon itself.

For the 59-year-old Holl, who has shown a willingness to break the rules in such acclaimed recent projects as the University of Iowa's School of Art and Art History, the key decision was to make the sculpture park an integral part of his design rather than a mere adornment.

"A REAL IDEA"

When he went up against five other finalists for the job (including Pritzker Architecture Prize winners Tadao Ando of Japan and Christian de Portzamparc of France) in 1999, he was the lone contestant to ditch the museum's preferred option of putting the addition in front of the museum's north side. Instead, he placed the addition on the old building's flanks and conceived it as an exercise in "complementary contrast": light, not heavy; looking out to the landscape, not turning inward; a fusion of landscape and architecture, not an object in a field.

"He was the only one with a real idea," said the museum's director, Marc Wilson.

The wisdom of Holl's gambit instantly becomes apparent as you approach, most likely by car (Kansas City is a driving city, not a walking city). The north side of the old building remains fully visible (the other plans would have covered it), and it looks better than ever in its new setting. Two old surface parking lots are gone, replaced by a serene but lively reflecting pool, co-designed by Holl and artist Walter De Maria, which portrays a symbolic gold-leafed "sun" surrounded by 34 porthole-shaped "moons."

The moons double as neon-ringed skylights for an underground parking garage with vaulted concrete ceilings. It tries hard to be a fitting automotive gateway for the museum but falls short because natural light fails to wash its outer walls.

Yet things improve markedly as you come upon the Bloch Building's lenses, which are clad in 6,000 vertical glass planks, custom-made with low iron so they can transmit clear (rather than green-tinted) light. Holl has used this translucent, U-shaped "channel glass" before, but never so extensively. And, frankly, it takes some getting used to. Early critics likened the lenses to Butler buildings, those graceless, standing-seam metal structures that often serve as warehouses in industrial parks.

A JEWEL-LIKE PRESENCE

As the day goes on, however, the lenses change as the light reflecting on them changes, morphing from pale blue and green to bright iridescence to fiery red to softly glowing white. As you move around them, you grasp how they are both jewel-like objects and definers of the grassy new sculpture courts between them. The courts not only extend the sculpture park over the Bloch Building's roofs. They also serve as energy-saving green roofs that insulate the galleries below and control storm water in the bargain.

This gradually unfolding sense of discovery, which emphasizes the movement of the viewer through space rather than a single "wow" image, stems from an axiom Holl learned as a student: A building should be a lot more when you go into it than when you first look at it.

Measured by that self-imposed standard, the Bloch Building strongly delivers. Once you step inside, teased by glass-sheathed revolving doors just off the reflecting pool, the building's initial off-putting muteness gives way to an enthralling, ever-shifting drama of space and light. It begins in the long lobby of the first lens, a grand ceremonial space with polished plaster walls, sloping ramps, a super-long steel staircase, and ceilings that are as neatly creased as pressed pants.

The ramps lead to a well-handled junction, where you can head outside to the sculpture park, descend again into the new building, or enter the old one. Then the galleries take over, and they reflect Holl's years of experience with art—he is an accomplished watercolorist and has completed several museums, including the acclaimed Kiasma Museum of Contemporary Art in Helsinki, Finland—as well as his enlightened philosophy of museum design.

GOING WITH THE FLOW

"How can you do a museum that at once respects the art and isn't a bunch of white boxes that sucks the life out of the art?" he said, referring to the architecturally neutral galleries long preferred by New York's Museum of Modern Art. "You can't just be sitting there like a bump on a log. You've got to do something."

He does it with fluid, dynamic spaces that make the Bloch Building a continuous experience, not unlike a river, rather than a series of discrete rooms. In the galleries, ceilings and floors tilt, but not walls, which allows the curators to create lively but contemplative spaces that are ideally suited for the display of art.

The diffuse light seeping down from the lenses, for example, enlivens Donald Judd's *Large Stack*, a work of stacked, stainless-steel shelves and amber Plexiglas. Holl uses an ingenious structural invention—covered steel columns that flare outward at the top, carrying the roofs of the lenses and drawing daylight into the galleries with their curving undersides—to carve out oases of space and light in what easily could have felt like a grotto.

Some of these spaces are as spiritual as chapels. Others mix cool northern light with warm southern light. Such variety is the point: Holl rejects the standardized for the customized, which is one reason why this very long building shouldn't induce museum fatigue. In case it does, a walkway that runs between the galleries and the sculpture park allows you to make an easy exit.

INSIDE THE BLOCH BUILDING
Carving out oases of space and light in what could have been a grotto.

The journey culminates in the Isamu Noguchi Sculpture Court, a glass-walled gallery where a bed of Japanese river rocks begins inside the museum and reappears outside in the sculpture park, making the border between interior and exterior appear to disappear.

This elegant ending powerfully accentuates Holl's achievement in navigating a middle way between over-the-top neo-expressionism and the bland neutrality of the "white box." That outcome is as important for the broader direction it suggests as for the Bloch Building itself: a move beyond spectacle and toward an artful—and sustainable—merging of architecture and the landscape.

POSTSCRIPT

Repeating a familiar pattern of expansion and retrenchment, the Nelson-Atkins Museum of Art announced in 2009 that it would cut its 175-person staff by at least 20 positions. The job cuts, the Kansas City Star *reported, were meant to trim operating expenses. As at the Denver Art Museum, the costs associated with an ambitious museum expansion and overblown attendance projections contributed to the dire picture.*

The Bloch Building resulted in higher lighting, heating, and staff costs, the Star *noted. With attendance below projected levels, income from parking and other fees also was less than anticipated. The museum already had made its most symbolic cutback in 2008, cutting back the lighting of the Bloch Building's signature lenses by 14 hours per week.*

Temple of Light

MUCH MORE THAN A CONTAINER FOR ART, RENZO PIANO'S
REFINED MODERN WING OPENS TO NATURE AND THE CITY

MAY 3, 2009

In architecture, as in love and the stock market, timing is everything. As America extricates itself from an age of excess, when flashy new museums started to resemble exploded Coke cans, along comes the Art Institute of Chicago with a splendid new wing of restraint and refinement. Against the backdrop of self-indulgence, this self-confident box looks fresh.

As shaped by Italian architect Renzo Piano, the $294 million, 264,000-square-foot Modern Wing does more than expand the museum's space by a third and make the Art Institute the nation's second-largest art museum after New York's Metropolitan Museum of Art. Boldly planned and exquisitely crafted, it is a temple of light, in which carefully filtered sunlight will be as central to the visitor's experience as steel, aluminum, and Indiana limestone.

True, the long-awaited wing breaks no new conceptual ground and will require tweaking if it is to resolve the conflict between the introverted act of looking at art and its extroverted views of the skyline and Millennium Park.

Yet the Modern Wing ultimately meets the challenge Piano set for himself: to write a new chapter in the story of Chicago's gravity-defying quest for lightness and transparency. That story began in the 1880s when Chicago architects invented the steel-framed skyscraper, liberating buildings from the shackles of load-bearing masonry and enabling thick, stone walls to become thin, light-admitting curtains of glass.

An art museum is not a skyscraper, of course, but it does tend to be an inward-turning treasure box. Curators want to protect precious objects from the damage done by direct sunlight. And they typically are not fans of slanting walls or other assertive architectural moves that threaten to disturb the contemplative act of engaging with a piece of art.

Piano, however, has long believed that museumgoers have their most satisfying experience when museums offer a connection to nature and their surroundings. That way, people are less likely to get disoriented, as they tend to do in a vast museum like the Art Institute. A familiar painting or sculpture may seem fresh when it is seen under different light conditions.

In such celebrated works as the Menil Collection in Houston, the Nasher Sculpture Center in Dallas, and the Beyeler Foundation Art Museum in Basel, Switzerland, Piano has put this philosophy into practice—and he has done it so well that he has won a near monopoly on American art museum commissions. Yet his ubiquitousness has spawned a backlash, with some critics charging that his work has become formulaic.

At first glance, the Modern Wing would seem unlikely to silence those critics. For it has all the familiar elements of Piano's art museums: strong axes slicing confidently across the site, parallel earthbound walls that telegraph the layout of its interior, and a "flying carpet" roof outfitted with curving metal blades designed to transform harsh sunlight into a softly diffused light that seeps into the galleries below.

Yet the wing turns out to be anything but generic, and the roots of its success can be traced to the Art Institute's bold decision (announced in 2001, two years after it had hired Piano) to shift the addition from the museum's south end to the north, where it would face Millennium Park, then three years from opening. This was an urban design masterstroke—good for the Modern Wing and good for the park.

The wing benefits because it sits across the street from a cultural powerhouse that drew more than 4 million people last year. The park benefits because the wing creates a wall-like sense of enclosure along its southern flank, joining with nearby skyscrapers to frame what increasingly feels like a new town square.

THE MODERN WING OF THE ART INSTITUTE OF CHICAGO
Boldly planned and exquisitely crafted, a superb example of classicizing modernism.

As if to underscore the synergy between the wing and the park, Piano joins them with a still-under-construction, 620-foot-long pedestrian bridge that shoots over Monroe Street and leads to a rooftop restaurant and sculpture terrace, as well as stairs that take you down to the museum proper.

The shift from south to north also had dramatic—and altogether positive—consequences for the Modern Wing's architecture. Because north light is not harsh, the move enabled Piano to design the building with a wall of enormous windows facing north toward Millennium Park. Yet the shift also challenged him because architect Frank Gehry's Pritzker Pavilion, an outdoor concert venue with explosive petals of stainless steel and a dome-like trellis, sat across Monroe Street in the park.

Instead of trying to one-up Gehry, Piano engaged him, designing his flying carpet sunshade as an "umbrella for sight" that would converse, as it were, with Gehry's "umbrella for sound."

Working with the wing's architect of record, the Chicago firm of Interactive Design, Piano more than holds up his end of the conversation. He sculpts the flying carpet's support beams so they look remarkably light and holds them up with pencil-shaped steel columns that enhance the impression of weightlessness.

Further defying gravity, Piano gives the north facade an energy-saving double layer of glass. The outer layer consists of a "flying facade" of tall, super-thin pieces of glass that hang from an invisible steel beam. This is the art of levitation, and Piano is a master at it.

Not unmindful of the Art Institute's past, Piano endows the wing with a reassuring, temple-like symmetry and clads its parallel walls in the same Indiana limestone that covers the rest of the museum, including its 1893 building at Michigan Avenue and Adams Street. In doing so, he creates a vivid tension between past and present, earthbound masonry and floating metal. All this accomplishes the Art Institute's aim that the wing form a second, but hardly secondary, entrance.

In addressing the wing's large and potentially intimidating interior, Piano devised the following strategy: he would break it into discrete parts and give each part its own character, introducing surprise and visual delight whenever possible. He succeeds, though not without flaws.

As you make your way to the museum's rooftop restaurant, for example, you encounter dramatic views of the downtown skyline and the white prow-like end of the pedestrian bridge, hanging like a surreal object over the railroad tracks that bisect the museum's east and west halves. Similarly, the light-filled, orange-floored education center on the first floor has an appropriate playfulness—and is infinitely more attractive than its basement-confined predecessor.

INSIDE THE MODERN WING
Striking an ideal balance between naturally lit, contemplative spaces and urban vitality.

But Griffin Court, the skylit, 300-foot-long north–south "main street" that leads from the Monroe Street entrance toward the museum's Rice Building, is, at least in its present state, a disappointment. Despite its resemblance to a European galleria and the presence of an elegantly suspended steel-and-glass staircase that pays homage to the "floating" Mies van der Rohe staircase in the Arts Club of Chicago, this street seems lifeless. It needs art on its walls as well as the color, motion, and scale of people to enliven it.

Upstairs in the galleries, however, Piano's magic is back. The third-floor galleries devoted to European modern art display works by Picasso, Brancusi, and other masters who have long needed a showcase of their own at the Art Institute. More important, the galleries exhibit a dazzling airiness. The visitor can see through taut vellum ceilings to the underside of the flying carpet and, through it, to the sky and the clouds.

The light that descends is soft, calm, and even, but never monotonous. It changes with the weather and the rhythms of the day. Computerized sensors on the roof are supposed to adjust the artificial light in the galleries accordingly. Above the vellum, a glass skylight keeps out the rain. Here, Piano doesn't upstage the art but puts flesh on the idea that superb art demands superb settings.

Though less riveting, the second-floor galleries for contemporary art are quite handsome—well proportioned and topped by a ceiling of thin, precast concrete beams into which artificial lighting is deftly integrated.

It is only when the visitor arrives at the galleries along the wing's north-facing windows, expecting to see works of art displayed alongside dramatic views of Millennium Park and the skyline, that there may be a tinge of regret. In daylight hours, the views are screened behind fabric sunshades that protect the art. The views are still there; they're just calmer—and not so spectacular—with the sunshades. "We're erring on the side of caution right now," said Meredith Mack, the museum's chief operating officer.

Piano elaborates that museums need tuning, as musical instruments do. He predicts that curators and conservators eventually will figure out when they can open the shades without fearing damage to the art: "I think they will probably find a reasonable balance between two extremes—on one side, concentration on the piece of art; on the other side, enjoying the view."

In crucial ways, then, the Modern Wing isn't a finished building, but one that will require the most sophisticated stewardship to achieve its full potential. And that potential is rich indeed, given the way the building engages our eyes and our emotions—not by stunning us with a single "iconic" image, but with an architecture that unfolds with great skill and subtlety. Even if the Modern Wing is not blazingly experimental, even if it does not knock our socks off, it can be counted upon, much like the original Art Institute building, to delight us for decades, even centuries.

Architectural fashions come and go. Quality like this endures.

POSTSCRIPT

Piano's prediction that the Modern Wing would need tuning proved prescient. Following the addition's opening, some museumgoers complained that finding their way through the wing was not easy. The building's atrium served as a moat, for example, forcing visitors in the principal galleries to go downstairs, cross the atrium, and then take an elevator back upstairs to reach the building's restaurant. On the other hand, the presence of people made the atrium a far more appealing space.

The quality of light in the Modern Wing also required ongoing attention. Achieving an ideal mix of natural and artificial light was expected to take months. Yet as subsequent visits revealed, the decision to deploy the sunshades in the galleries facing Millennium Park was sound, enabling Piano and his clients to strike a proper balance between looking inward at the art and looking outward at the city.

Like other cultural institutions that expanded their facilities during the boom years, the Art Institute was shaken when the recession hit. One month after the Modern Wing opened, the museum announced it was laying off 22 people, 3 percent of its staff. Museum spokeswoman Erin Hogan insisted that the layoffs would have been worse without the Modern Wing, which she said had increased revenue by driving up attendance and memberships.

A Sidewalk through the Sky

WITH NAUTICAL FLOURISH, THE NICHOLS BRIDGEWAY CONNECTS THE MODERN WING OF THE ART INSTITUTE TO MILLENNIUM PARK

MAY 14, 2009

Chicago, get ready for your latest joy ride.

A new pedestrian bridge linking Millennium Park and the Art Institute of Chicago's Modern Wing is a walk through the treetops, a sidewalk soaring through the sky. Climb the Nichols Bridgeway, as this sloping 620-foot-long span is called, and you're hovering over Monroe Street, as though you are in a helicopter.

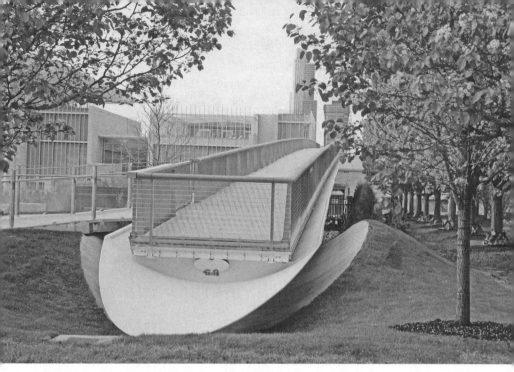

THE NICHOLS BRIDGEWAY IN MILLENNIUM PARK
A playful sidekick to the regal Modern Wing, joining the disparate worlds of popular and high culture.

The soon-to-be-opened bridge delivers fun with a capital *F*, even if it doesn't rise to the level of architecture with a capital *A*. It will also make its debut burdened by two questions: Will a small but perceptible wobble in its midsection need to be stabilized? And will people who skip the bridge and instead cross Monroe at street level get smacked by speeding cars?

Designed by Italy's Renzo Piano, the same architect responsible for the Modern Wing, the span endows Millennium Park with its second pedestrian bridge by a winner of the Pritzker Architecture Prize. The first, Frank Gehry's 960-foot-long BP Bridge, is a delightfully snaking piece of sculpture, sheathed in stainless-steel shingles, that curves like a lazy river over intimidating Columbus Drive.

Piano's bridge is far more sober than Gehry's. It's a straight shot consisting of curving steel sections that are welded together to resemble the hull of a racing yacht. Sealing the nautical metaphor, Piano, who like many architects is an avid sailor, gave the bridge delicate, prow-shaped ends. The bridge begins its ascent well inside in the park, near the southwest corner of Gehry's Pritzker Pavilion, and climbs to the Modern Wing's third-floor restaurant and sculpture terrace.

It's a fabulous journey. The bridge lifts you above the park, giving you a chance to look down on it. You see the Pritzker Pavilion's silvery steel shells and Lurie Garden's big green "shoulder hedge." From above Monroe, you can gaze out at the blue waters of Lake Michigan or through the skyscraper canyons of the Loop. At the end, you survey the sunken commuter railroad tracks that bisect the Art Institute. They are a vertiginous 50 feet below.

Ever sensitive to human experience, Piano details the bridge to calm fears and promote interaction. The deck, 8 to 12 feet wide, is big enough to allow people to cluster while others pass by. The wood handrail is an extra-wide 10 inches, giving it the feel of a substantial barrier.

Less reassuringly, the portion of the bridge over Monroe oscillated slightly during my test walk. It made me think of London's famously wobbly Millennium Bridge, which was forced to close three days after being unveiled with great fanfare in 2000. That bridge didn't reopen until 2002, after an engineering retrofit. An Art Institute official said the museum would test the span with a group of people before it opens.

And what of the view *of* the bridge, as opposed to the view *from* the bridge?

From some vantage points, it appears thin and elegant, because of Piano's sleight of hand in dealing with its four pairs of supporting piers in Millennium Park. The architect, who famously wants his buildings to seem as if they are defying gravity, largely hides the piers behind evergreen trees. Seen from Michigan Avenue, the bridge appears to be floating across the sky, like something out of a surrealist painting. From below, its hull-like underside is infinitely more graceful than the exposed beams on the bottom of a typical highway span.

But the bridge can also appear a bit tubby, a result of the eternal conflict between physics and aesthetics. As it makes its leap across Monroe, its midsection has a deeper curve, with thicker steel, than its elegantly thin ends. Bridge designers are always trying to resolve the tension between strength and beauty. Here, Piano doesn't get the shallowness he wanted.

He and the Art Institute also haven't figured out how to deal with pedestrians who want to head directly to the wing from the south end of Millennium Park. Surely they're not going to walk all the way north to the bridge's entrance and then double back to the Modern Wing. Many pedestrians, as I observed, jaywalk across heavily trafficked Monroe, jogging, if necessary, to outrace approaching cars. This is an accident waiting to happen. The city needs to either approve the midblock crosswalk the museum wants or require the Art Institute to post signs directing pedestrians to the nearest street corners.

Despite these faults, the bridge seems destined to become a hit with the public. It reaches out like a welcoming arm to the throngs in Millennium Park, many of whom have never set foot inside the Art Institute. If the Modern Wing is regally self-assured, the span is its playful sidekick, largely succeeding in its quest to join the disparate worlds of popular and high culture. Both take a once-stodgy institution and make it more accessible and inviting.

POSTSCRIPT

The wobble in the Nichols Bridgeway did not require correction, but the absence of a midblock crosswalk linking Millennium Park and the Modern Wing proved to be a genuine public safety hazard, endangering the jaywalkers. In late 2009, the Chicago Department of Transportation announced that it would install a painted crosswalk on Monroe Street, along with push button–activated warning signs. The Art Institute agreed to pay about $100,000 for the improvements.

BIG STARS ON CAMPUS

COLLEGES AND UNIVERSITIES WERE NOT IMMUNE TO THE ICON CONTAGION. THEY, too, imported "starchitects," intent upon changing their images or luring students, faculty, or donors who would write checks for splashy projects. The outcomes were as mixed as the aesthetic approaches that the stars brought to the commissions. While campuses are often thought of as enclaves from everyday life, the new college and university buildings mirrored the culture's shifting lifestyles and, at least in the pre-crash days, its rising affluence.

The New School of College Design

CAN SEXY, SIGNATURE BUILDINGS SUCCESSFULLY FUSE FORM AND FUNCTION?

JANUARY 14, 2007

For the architects of today's college campuses, the question isn't "To be or not to be?" It's "To icon or not to icon?"

With colleges and universities spending billions of dollars to upgrade facilities and to attract students, faculty, and major donors in a hyper-competitive academic marketplace, the pressure to produce iconic "look at me" architecture is more intense than ever. Yet there is no guarantee that a sexy, signature building will successfully fuse form and function.

Consider New York architect Steven Holl's Simmons Hall at the Massachusetts Institute of Technology, a spectacular, sponge-like structure with thousands of two-foot-square windows. A typical single room in the five-year-old dorm has nine windows, each of which has its own tiny curtain. At night, students have complained, it can take five minutes to close the curtains.

On the other hand, there's the happier saga of the University of Iowa's new art and art history building, a striking, reddish-brown collage of oxidizing steel that soars over an old quarry pond. Students genuinely seem to like the building, and the American Institute of Architects has named it the winner of a prestigious national Honor Award. The architect? The same Steven Holl who designed MIT's controversial Simmons Hall.

That a single architect could provoke such different reactions reveals the high-stakes gamble that campus administrators and building committees are making these days when they bring in high-priced, high-profile designers: Which will you get—Dr. Jekyll or Mr. Hyde?

That tension is equally evident in two Chicago campus commissions that have attracted the interest of some of the profession's brightest stars: a proposed creative and performing arts center at the University of Chicago, along with a planned media production center at Columbia College Chicago in the South Loop. In each case, campus planners are acutely aware of the conflict between attention-getting forms and the prospect that such designs will turn out to be functional flops and isolated objects that fail to connect to their surroundings.

"I would say we're trying to find a way to use that tension productively," said David Thompson, the University of Chicago's associate dean for planning and programs in the humanities.

To many Americans, the image of the campus remains an architecturally harmonious place set apart from the hurly-burly of the marketplace. The serene, neo-Gothic quadrangles of the University of Chicago form one paradigm. The well-mannered neoclassical pavilions that flank the rolling lawn of the University of Virginia are another. "An academical village," the campus's architect, Thomas Jefferson, called it.

Increasingly, however, that image seems quaint. Many colleges and universities, including Columbia and others that have breathed life into Chicago's downtown, don't consist of traditional campuses at all. They're grown piecemeal, their classrooms wedged into a variety of older buildings. There is no gateway into their campus, no revered "Old Main" building that says tradition with a capital *T*. Above all, there is no lawn.

The architecture has also changed. Old-fashioned harmony? It's mostly gone. A more fitting metaphor is the jazz ensemble, where different players

THE MCCORMICK TRIBUNE CAMPUS CENTER AT IIT
A symbol of the new architecture on campus, forgoing the old harmony for the new heterogeneity.

riff off each other's solos. Once meant to communicate eternal values, architecture—for better and for worse—has become a commodity that helps campuses sell themselves. It's all part of the mind-set that makes the student a consumer and the university a business. And many of the students formed their lifestyle expectations in the pampered age of Starbucks.

DON'T CALL THEM DORMS

These students don't just eat. They graze, which explains the new profusion of on-campus food courts, delis, and coffee shops. As for living quarters, "We tend to say apartment-style living. We don't even use the word 'dormitory,'" said Nancy Zimpher, president of the University of Cincinnati, which has spent roughly $2 billion since 1992 transforming a once-scruffy commuter school into an architectural showplace by importing such star architects as Thom Mayne, Frank Gehry, and Michael Graves.

Good planning matters just as much, as you see by comparing the University of Cincinnati's Campus Recreation Center with its new counterpart at the University of Illinois at Chicago.

The UIC building—designed by Christopher Frye of the Chicago office of PSA-Dewberry and located on Halsted Street, just west of the Dan Ryan Expressway—works well enough. Its sculptural composition of folding planes, such as an aggressively V-shaped roof above the swimming pool, enlivens the bleak tableau of the university's cavernous, concrete hulks. The interior is also nicely handled, with racquetball courts, pools, and other facilities ringing a skylit, easy-to-navigate central atrium.

The building is conveniently located near UIC's campus center and dorms, but it's nonetheless a stand-alone object at the university's edge. Mayne's piano-shaped Cincinnati recreation center, in contrast, is artfully wedged into the campus's center, right between the football stadium and a redesigned quad. And it's not just a cathedral of sweat.

Mayne packed classrooms, dorms, and a food court into the building, creating a lively urban mix. The chockablock rec center is less an icon than a connector, drawing energy from the activities it houses and the people coursing through it.

For universities that sponsor such adventurous work, the payoffs can be immediate, though, in truth, the architecture doesn't deserve all the credit. After the Illinois Institute of Technology opened its Rem Koolhaas–designed campus center and an adjacent dorm by Helmut Jahn in 2003, enrollment at the architecture school zoomed (by fall 2006) to 747 students, more than doubling what it had been before the new buildings appeared.

The IIT campus center exemplifies the new direction of campus architecture, with its brash orange walls and a sound-baffling tube that shushes the roar of CTA elevated trains. Its interior—with slashing diagonal pathways and a cinematic collection of visual vignettes, like a hot-red trench lined with computer screens—has been likened (favorably) to being in a pinball machine.

"It's actually made for the students," marveled Chakrapani Duggirala, a 25-year-old graduate student from India, as he shot pool with a friend beneath the underside of the tube.

Speaking of IIT's collection of techies, Donna Robertson, dean of the university's architecture school, said: "My joke is that the engineers and scientists are never happier than when they are looking down the lens of a microscope. But the building gives them a reason to lift their gaze up and out and commune with each other."

Still, there are pitfalls associated with the new school of campus design. Innovative architecture often requires extra time to build; Koolhaas's tube proved so difficult to construct, for example, that IIT's campus center opened more than three years late. Sometimes experimental work can go over the top, as in Gehry's business school building at Case Western Reserve University in Cleveland, a mountain of metal with too much architectural firepower for its tight site.

"LEGO BRICKS"

Then there is the difficult-to-anticipate human factor, which the MIT magazine *Technology Review* captures in a story about Holl's Simmons Hall. Like the Iowa art building, Simmons Hall won a national Honor Award from the American Institute of Architects. But the building has forced students to adapt to it, rather than the other way around.

The Holl-designed furniture for the dorm includes "beds and drawers that stack like Lego bricks—or would, if they weren't too heavy to lift," the magazine story says. "Movers hired by MIT helped freshmen settle in; eventually an underground trade developed in wrenches to unbolt the furniture. Senior Aron Zingman doled them out with a warning: 'The beds weigh 250 pounds. You can get crushed to death by them.'"

These are the poles—no-holds-barred expressionism and prosaic functionalism—that campus planners must navigate as they reshape the nation's colleges and universities. Today's fresh icons, they must be aware, are often tomorrow's out-of-date period pieces. And the duds aren't easily discarded. You can throw an old textbook in the attic. Architecture doesn't go away.

POSTSCRIPT

As the recession hit with full force in 2008, many colleges and universities began reconsidering planned construction and renovation projects. The same credit crunch that was hobbling real estate developers also hampered the schools. Another restricting factor: concern over how the crisis would affect state and federal budgets, fund-raising, and enrollment.

Nevertheless, some projects moved forward. In early 2010, for example, Columbia College Chicago opened its vibrant, cinema-inspired media production center, designed by Chicago architect Jeanne Gang and her firm, Studio Gang Architects. And the University of Chicago announced in 2009 that it would proceed with a pared-down version of its creative and performing arts center, designed by New York architects Tod Williams and Billie Tsien. The opening was set for 2012.

Triumphant Homecoming

HELMUT JAHN DESIGNS AN ILLINOIS INSTITUTE OF TECHNOLOGY
DORM THAT LOOKS ELEGANTLY AT HOME

JULY 27, 2003

He's back. And I don't mean that Bulls superstar Michael Jordan is making another return to the team.

We're talking about Chicago's top architect, Helmut Jahn, who has just finished a bracingly innovative new dorm at that citadel of modernism, the Illinois Institute of Technology. Called State Street Village and located just west of the elevated tracks at 33rd and State Streets, it is (a) Jahn's first building in Chicago in more than a decade; (b) the first new building at IIT in more than 30 years; and (c) the first of a one-two architectural punch that the school will finish delivering in September when it opens its long-delayed campus center by Dutch architect Rem Koolhaas.

Because students won't move into the 367-bed facility for a few weeks, the jury is still out on whether it's livable as well as eye-catching—and that is a major hedge, because no building, no matter how beautiful, can be fully judged without assessing its impact on the people who use it.

Even so, one still can say at this stage that Jahn has struck the perfect balance between respecting Ludwig Mies van der Rohe's epoch-defining temple of steel and glass, Crown Hall, across State Street and making his own, more sensuous statement. His dorm expertly quiets the racket of Chicago Transit Authority trains even as it turns them into sculptural objects that can be glimpsed behind its wonderfully transparent walls of glass.

For Jahn, now 63 and long past his Flash Gordon days of posing in gangster hats on the cover of *GQ*, the dorm is likely to go down as a triumphant homecoming, provided students accept his notion that the interior, which has lots of exposed concrete, is an exercise in "comfortable coolness" instead of cold and stark.

After emigrating to Chicago from his native Germany, Jahn studied at IIT in the 1960s but never graduated before embarking on a career marked by such structures as the garish State of Illinois Center (now the Thompson Center), the remarkable United Airlines Terminal at O'Hare International Airport, and the bustling Sony Center in Berlin.

Lately, the vast majority of his work has been in Germany and Asia, where adventurous clients are more willing to let him push the aesthetic envelope than their conservative counterparts in Chicago. His last project in the city—the handsome stone-clad 120 North LaSalle Street office building—was finished in 1992. Even his lone Chicago-area success

STATE STREET VILLAGE AT IIT
Respecting the architecture of a modernist master while making a statement of its own.

story of recent years, which came in the suburbs rather than the city, was bittersweet.

In 2001, after Jahn completed an award-winning, seven-story corporate headquarters for Ha-Lo Industries, Inc., a promotional products company in north suburban Niles, the company went bankrupt. The building—now occupied by Shure, Inc., a professional audio electronics manufacturer— was quickly labeled a steel-and-glass monument to corporate excess.

HARDLY EXCESSIVE

By contrast, the IIT dorm, which Jahn shaped with his associate John Dur- brow, is hardly excessive, especially when measured by the yardsticks of time and money.

The concrete-framed, five-story structure has taken just 15 months to build—lightning-fast compared with Koolhaas's McCormick Tribune

Campus Center, which will open more than three years behind schedule due to delays associated with its unusual design. And the dorm's $28 million price tag is bargain basement next to the $68 million MIT shelled out for a comparable structure by New York architect Steven Holl, especially because Holl's dorm has 17 fewer beds. Such constraints have a way of enforcing discipline.

The IIT project banishes the overwrought Jahn, who turned structural members into massive, even threatening forms, earning him the nickname "Baron von High Tech." Instead, it reveals a more subtle, self-assured hand, that of an architect who wisely chooses to engage rather than upstage Mies's Crown Hall, the legendary, girder-topped glass pavilion across State Street. Flash Gordon, as Jahn-watchers have known for a while now, has grown up.

While State Street Village is 550 feet long, not unlike a skyscraper laid on its side, it's quietly assertive, even covertly traditional. Three U-shaped residence halls, each comparable to a conventional courtyard building, face toward State Street. Curving screens of perforated steel sweep over their courtyards and two broad pedestrian passageways between them. Jahn draws these parts into a singular whole with State Street Village's leaning facade of corrugated stainless steel. The building clearly belongs to the 21st century even as it resembles a streamlined railroad car of the 1930s.

As urban design, the dorm is highly effective, especially in concert with Koolhaas's adjoining campus center, whose signature flourish is a 531-foot-long tube that sits atop its roof and wraps around the elevated tracks. Together, the long, low-slung structures and their curving, corrugated steel profiles do precisely what Chicago architect (and Mies's grandson) Dirk Lohan envisioned in his fine campus master plan. They fill the former no-man's-land of surface parking lots around the "L," restoring the lost "urban edge" of low-rise commercial and residential buildings that once framed Mies's steel-and-glass pavilions and their park-like setting.

The key is that Jahn's urban edge manages to be both sharp and permeable. The dorm has enough presence to act as a space-defining wall for the grassy quadrangle-like space to the north of Crown Hall. Yet its passageways allow pedestrians to walk through State Street Village rather than around it. That encourages interaction between IIT's dorms to the east of the elevated tracks and its academic buildings to the west.

A LITTLE LUXURY

State Street Village is equally successful as architecture, possessing a striking linearity that represents a marked improvement on the prosaic group of apartment buildings pictured in Lohan's master plan. Yet it is not a scaleless mega-building.

Jahn uses the openings in the dorm's curving profile to create pleasing rhythms of solids and voids while his corrugated stainless-steel cladding gives the exterior a rich presence that belies the building's tight budget. There is further visual pleasure in the perforated steel screens, which appear transparent or opaque depending on the direction of the sunlight, and in the glass "wing walls" that the architect has attached to the building's ends. Along with a thick concrete wall that faces the elevated tracks, the wing walls shield the interior from noise and provide a finishing accent like the crown of a great skyscraper.

But the greatest visual pleasure comes from the way Jahn elevates the courtyards and passageways into visual poetry—not by hiding the "L," but by celebrating it. By wrapping the backsides of the openings with huge walls of sound-blocking glass, he transforms a negative into a positive. No longer does the ear-splitting roar of the trains render the core of the IIT campus uninhabitable. Now the trains are shushed—and turned into kinetic sculpture.

With handsome plantings by Chicago landscape architect Peter Schaudt, the courtyards and passageways extend the park-like setting of the campus into the barren area along the "L." They also draw daylight into the interior and endow students' rooms with views onto the green spaces. In Jahn's view, a dorm is essentially a no-frills project, and an architect has to take whatever steps he can to lend it a little luxury.

He's right, but I still wonder how students are going to react to his interior, which houses four-bedroom suites that share a common bathroom, as well as apartments with as many as six bedrooms. It's possible that students won't like the interior's exposed concrete floors and ceilings, the tight quarters of the suites, and some hallways, which are bereft of natural light and heavy on exposed concrete. The interior also lacks dramatic architectural features that will promote interaction among students, such as the blob-shaped, multi-story lounges that rise through Holl's MIT dorm.

In other words, will State Street Village be a village in name only?

Probably not. Within the constraints of a budget that was far tighter than Holl's, Jahn has been attentive to the students' needs. He's provided them with lounges and kitchens at the back of most floors, as well as fifth-floor gathering spaces with plasma TV screens, plus rooftop decks with striking views of the downtown skyline. The interior also extends the Miesian principles of technology and flexibility into the 21st century, boasting movable furniture and such user-friendly features as a computer service that can alert students when their laundry is done. I just wish there were more of the six-bedroom units, which have a large social room and broad expanses of windows that take full advantage of the building's linearity. They provide views and a quality of spaciousness that the other apartments lack.

In its present state, then, Jahn's building answers one question and begs another. It's a terrific piece of architecture and urban design, a worthy extension of IIT's Miesian heritage, and a possible prototype for future residential buildings along the "L." But we won't know if it's truly designed for living until students start banging it around and testing it in ways that the architect probably never anticipated.

Let's take another look in the future. For now, be glad that Helmut's back.

POSTSCRIPT

State Street Village proved popular with students, who dreamed up ingenious ways to reconfigure its loft-like suites and apartments to their liking. Revisiting the dorm a year after it opened, for example, the Chicago Tribune *encountered a sophomore electrical engineering major who raised her bed off the floor to make way for her desk below. "I like to take naps," the student said, "so if my bed is out of view, that's a good thing." Other students used their wardrobes as space-dividing screens and placed them so they did not block the prime downtown view afforded by the dorm's floor-to-ceiling windows. In short, the flexibility of the spaces and the adaptability of the furniture enabled the students to tailor their surroundings.*

Elsewhere within State Street Village, students warmed up Jahn's cool, exposed-concrete corridors by chalking the dorm's sterile walls with a rainbow of colors. Birds, however, found it more difficult to adapt. Many killed themselves running into the dorm's remarkably transparent glass walls. In response, IIT installed protective netting at one of the courtyards. "Please do not touch netting," a sign cautioned. "Bird Safety Experiment in Progress."

Standing Out While Fitting In

THOM MAYNE'S CAMPUS RECREATION CENTER AT THE
UNIVERSITY OF CINCINNATI IS THE LATEST PIECE OF AN
EXEMPLARY PUZZLE

JANUARY 29, 2006

Every once in a while, a building comes along that fulfills your faith that architecture can be a noble profession, not just a parade of street-walking "starchitects" who strut their signature styles around the globe. The new

Campus Recreation Center at the University of Cincinnati, by Thom Mayne, the 2005 winner of the Pritzker Architecture Prize, richly deserves such praise.

What might have been a mere collection of gyms and pools, a typical college sweatshop, instead offers an extraordinary synthesis of place—sensitive urban design, cutting-edge architecture, and bold interiors.

It is ironic that Mayne's triumph comes at the University of Cincinnati, which for years has sought to remake both its sprawling campus and its middling commuter-school reputation with buildings by architectural superstars—a Peter Eisenman here, a Frank Gehry there, and so on. But what this really produced was a lot of publicity and a kind of architectural petting zoo, in which a variety of eye-catching structures were plopped down incoherently.

Mayne's $113 million building—which includes dorms, lecture halls, a restaurant, a dining hall, and even bleacher seats for the adjoining university football stadium—is the latest piece of a puzzle that departs from that shortsighted attitude.

Following a brilliant master plan by the landscape architect George Hargreaves, a former utilitarian road through the hilly campus has become a winding, picturesque brick street, free of cars, which the university calls "Main Street." The street and the carefully coordinated ensemble of buildings around it suggest an Italian hill town, a sort of San Gimignano on the Ohio River. The spectacular revamp is one of the most significant acts of campus planning since Thomas Jefferson laid out his "academic village" at the University of Virginia, a rolling lawn framed by neoclassical temples, in the early 19th century.

Unfortunately, the Campus Recreation Center is not entirely free from "starchitect" tics. Repeating a familiar design motif from Mayne and his Santa Monica, California, firm, Morphosis, the building's dorm rooms have prison-like, slit windows that diabolically block views. But you can forgive Mayne that trespass because the rest of the building, for which KZF Design of Cincinnati served as the architect of record, is so good.

Located near the south end of the hilltop campus, not far from the handsome, neo-Georgian buildings that face the surrounding neighborhood, the rec center resembles, at least from the air, a grand piano that slides beneath a bent bar.

The piano-shaped part of the building houses, among other things, a lap pool, a leisure pool with a meandering "lazy river," and a giant multipurpose space with room for six basketball courts and a suspended running track. The bent bar, raised above the piano on concrete-encased stilts, includes four floors of student housing. It is one of the non-athletic

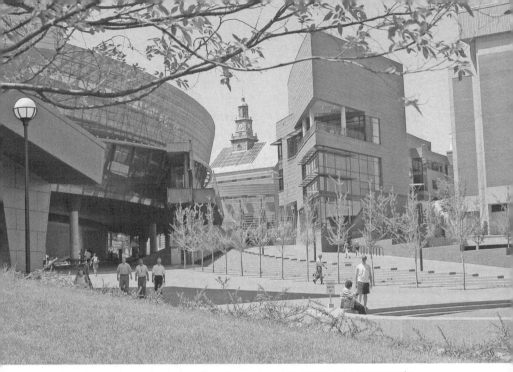

THE CAMPUS RECREATION CENTER (*LEFT*) ON THE UNIVERSITY OF CINCINNATI'S
"MAIN STREET"
Going beyond the "starchitect" mentality to form a vibrant center of campus life.

uses the university added to the building in midstream, a classic example
of what KZF's Dale Beeler jokingly refers to as "mission creep."

Far from leading to an unwieldy mess, these uses have made the rec
center more in sympathy with the densely urban character of two neighboring buildings along Main Street. One, the Tangeman University Center
by Gwathmey Siegel & Associates Architects of New York, took an old,
dimly lit neo-Georgian building and transformed it into a bustling, skylit
student union that retains its historic clock tower.

The other, the Steger Student Life Center by Moore Ruble Yudell Architects of Santa Monica, houses student activities offices and is wedged
onto a narrow site along Main Street. Roughly 500 feet long and 45 feet
wide, it is the perfect street-shaper, resembling a giant parenthesis.

In a notable departure from the diva "starchitect" norm, Mayne and
the other architects agreed on common geometry (curves) and common
materials (zinc exterior walls, though Mayne wound up using steel and
aluminum to save money).

Hargreaves further drew things together with an urbane, brown brick-
paved plaza that spills like a gorge between the boldly curving walls of the

recreation and student life buildings. At the bottom of the hill, where there used to be a giant surface parking lot, the plaza becomes a series of grassy mounds where students sun themselves.

Mayne's building at once responds to these disparate external conditions and has its own persuasive internal logic. Seven massive steel roof trusses, 100 to 450 feet long, run beneath the smoothly sculptural roof of the piano-shaped building and make possible its grandly scaled, clear-span interiors. But the rec center is not a structural monolith, like Chicago's McCormick Place.

BROKEN UP INTO PARTS

Recognizing that the rec center, which is more than 1,000 feet long, could seem oppressive, Mayne wisely broke it into parts. The parts reflect what he calls, sounding like an archaeologist, "the found conditions of the site." The most obvious example is the rec center's curving lecture-hall wing, which deftly continues the bowl of the university's U-shaped Nippert Stadium. The wing's graceful, fluid form is topped by an elegant, tiara-like sunscreen of steel and perforated aluminum, a signature Mayne touch.

While the housing bar and its gun-turret windows could be the headquarters of the old KGB, the building's sharply cut rectilinearity sets up an effective tension with the classroom wing's curves. The housing bar also manages to frame the plaza in front of the nearby Engineering Research Center, a handsome postmodern building by University of Cincinnati alum Michael Graves.

But the rec center really soars because Mayne deals with more than just the buildings around it. He's integrating campus pathways and the movement of students through the building.

"It's like a network you find in the infrastructure of a freeway," said the Southern Californian, though his design serves pedestrians rather than cars. "The building is produced to support the connection of things through the campus. That turned into the idea of transparency. Everything is open to everything else. That's one of the major ideas of the university— of forming relationships and making connections."

This is not empty rhetoric. As you walk by the rec center or through it, you quickly notice that its functions— a swimming pool, a climbing wall, and others—aren't buried behind blank walls. Nor do you need signs to find them. They are, instead, showcased under glass.

Mayne lends further drama to the see-through experience by placing these activities well above or below the pedestrian's eye. The pools, for example, are well below street level, so they come off as mini-canyons. Porthole-shaped roof openings and skylights bring in welcome shafts of light.

While the interior can be brooding and battleship-like because of its restrained palette of black, gray, and white, it is nonetheless enlivened by the bright colors of its furniture and students' clothes, as well as a power-ful sense of order. That order comes from the trusses, which are sheathed in aluminum panels and soar with athleticism over two grand spaces, the swimming pool and the multipurpose space.

None of the trusses are the same. Mayne is no fan of the structurally expressive regularity of Ludwig Mies van der Rohe. Instead, the trusses create a dynamic, ever-shifting sequence of low and high spaces, compres-sion and release. The effect depends upon that essential tool of our time, the computer, to imitate the infinitely complex, timeless order of nature.

Because all this is so deeply humane, you want to slap Mayne for outfit-ting the dormitory bedrooms with two or three tiers of windows, including one just six inches high. Mayne explains that, in contrast to the lightness and liveliness present elsewhere in the rec center, he sought to create a darkened, meditative environment, comparable to the architect Le Cor-busier's La Tourette Monastery near Lyon, France. But the slit windows are a maddening self-indulgence. Why lift students up where they might reasonably expect a view, then cut it off?

Despite this juvenile detail, the vast majority of this extraordinary build-ing is the work of a mature master. Here aesthetic power is wedded to social promise, and the result is not an icon preening in solitary splendor, but a building that both expresses social connections and elevates them to the level of art.

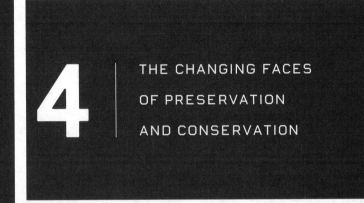

4 | THE CHANGING FACES
OF PRESERVATION
AND CONSERVATION

AS THE HISTORIAN WILLIAM CRONON HAS OBSERVED, THE MOVEMENT TO preserve old buildings and the movement to conserve the landscape have common cause, especially in the United States. In this country, which often seems hell-bent on sweeping away the old in favor of the new, historic landmarks and the grand sweep of nature present a necessary counterbalance: they represent where we came from, an essential link to the past that enriches our present and informs our future. In the early 21st century, these associations took on fresh meaning in light of new threats to the environment, both natural and man-made.

With a surge of construction changing the face of neighborhoods as well as downtowns, and with major examples of mid-20th-century modernism approaching an age that made them vulnerable as well as venerable, historic preservationists faced challenges on new geographic and intellectual terrain. Which potential landmarks should be spared from demolition and why? And how to react to the partial preservation of historic structures like Chicago's Soldier Field or the brand of architectural surgery known as the "facade-ectomy"?

Many preservationists had marched in their first picket lines to stop the spread of steel-and-glass boxes. Now, ironically, they were trying to save those very buildings. And there was another twist of fate: as concerns about climate change put the movement for energy-saving "green" buildings in the ascent, new and nettlesome conflicts arose over how to carry out historic preservation: Which was more important, saving buildings or saving the planet? Preservation and conservation thus embarked upon a new chapter in their long-standing, typically harmonious relationship—a simmering, sibling rivalry.

NEW CHALLENGES FOR
HISTORIC PRESERVATION

The Danger of Becoming Skin-Deep

CHICAGO HISTORIC BUILDINGS BECOME SHELLS AS NEW RULES
OF PRESERVATION ARE LETTING THE CITY'S HISTORY SLIP AWAY

APRIL 8, 2007

Back in the 1960s, the pioneers of historic preservation faced stark choices
as they battled to protect such renowned structures as McKim, Mead and
White's Pennsylvania Station in New York City, or Louis Sullivan and
Dankmar Adler's Garrick Theater in Chicago: Either save the building or
watch the wrecker's ball smash it to smithereens.

But today developers across the nation have devised a fiendishly clever
way to confuse the issue: instead of preserving an entire building, they
retain only the building's facade, destroy everything behind it, and graft
the retained exterior onto a new internal structure, as though it were the
skin of a dead animal.

This radical form of architectural surgery, which preservationists
justifiably have labeled a "facade-ectomy," has surfaced with rising fre-
quency in recent years, gutting historic structures across the nation, from
cast-iron buildings in Baltimore to red-brick warehouses in San Diego.
And now, with the complicity of the Daley administration, it is making
its debilitating presence felt in the heart of the nation's most important
architectural city, Chicago.

THE NEW MAXWELL STREET
A saccharine stage set that reveals the risk of saving mere slices of history.

Better to save something than nothing, say the developers, who are surely more interested in getting their projects through prickly landmark review boards and clearing historic sites for big construction cranes. And while it's true that such projects typically possess the human scale and eye-pleasing decoration rarely found in bland condominium towers, they still rankle. The reason: they create a stage-set city that treats buildings like two-dimensional wallpaper, not three-dimensional artistry. That destroys a building's essence and, at worst, makes a mockery of the very history that these exercises in architectural taxidermy purport to respect.

To sample the damage that facade-ectomies do, go to the corner of Halsted and Maxwell Streets, where the University of Illinois at Chicago has completed its redevelopment of the old Maxwell Street Market, the once-raucous bazaar where generations of peddlers hawked their wares along the sidewalk. There, historic facades are clipped onto the front of a new parking garage, complete with curtains and blinds in the upper-story windows, as if real people really lived inside. With their medallions, fluted columns, and ornamental brickwork, the facades form a sanitized streetscape populated by saccharine life-size sculptures, like one that portrays a peddler selling tomatoes. The old Maxwell Street Market was dirty, messy, and infused with a singular sense of place. It was not, like this facile tribute, clean, ordered, and bordering on generic.

"When does [Chicago] cease to be known for broad shoulders, to be seen instead for its paper-thin facades? At what point will Chicago not be Chicago, but merely a commercially based parody of itself?" asked David Bahlman, president of the nonprofit Landmarks Preservation Council of Illinois (now Landmarks Illinois), at a recent hearing of the City Council's Committee on Historical Landmark Preservation.

During the hearing, aldermen unanimously approved the latest architectural skin job, a plan by Chicago-based Prism Development Co. to dismantle, demolish, repair, and reconstruct the 11-story Farwell Building, a classical and art deco gem at 664 North Michigan Avenue, as part of a 40-story condominium development.

IDEALS AND REALITY OF BUILDING REUSE

Ideally, the adaptive reuse of a historic building retains the structure's bones as well as its skin. Think of the Hotel Burnham at the corner of State and Washington Streets. There, in 1999, a team of architects gorgeously transformed the old Reliance Building into a boutique hotel while simultaneously enhancing every aspect of its revolutionary late 19th-century design. Step inside and you can see old offices turned into hotel rooms, the room numbers on the doors precisely replicating the typefaces of a century ago.

With Chicago in a development boom that has put historic buildings in the path of new ones that generate property and sales tax dollars, however, it is becoming far more difficult to uphold the standard set by such exemplary examples of adaptive reuse. "Now we're in this great gray zone of preservation. It's not fully saved. It's not fully lost," Jim Peters, the Illinois preservation council's director of planning, said. "I think that's the slippery slope we've gotten into."

Shaving away everything but the facade of a historic building has been done before, of course. In 1989, at 10 South LaSalle Street, architects Moriyama & Teshima jammed a modern office building with blue and lime green walls between the temple-like base of the 1912 Otis Building by the legendary Chicago firm of Holabird & Roche. Even now that project remains an astonishing visual mismatch.

What's different today is that such selective shavings of history are far more widespread—not a last resort, but a first option. That much is evident a block west of Michigan Avenue and the cliff-like ensemble of historic, masonry-covered buildings that face Millennium Park.

HISTORIC FACADES ON CHICAGO'S WABASH AVENUE
Saving a streetscape, but wreaking havoc on architectural integrity.

After Chicago granted landmark protection in 2002 to the so-called Michigan Avenue cliff, the barons of real estate picked up their spreadsheets and infiltrated Wabash Avenue, where the obstacles to profit were less daunting. There, they could erect huge new condo towers that would seize upon Millennium Park's allure. To make way for the towers, as well as the parking garages that would serve them and the construction equipment that would build them, all but a sliver of seven historic structures were demolished. Some even belonged to the Jewelers Row District, an official city landmark district along Wabash that recognizes the rich history of Chicago's jewelry makers.

At 21 to 29 South Wabash, a massive steel scaffold holds in place a trio of five- to six-story facades that provide a tangible record of the construction boom that followed the Chicago Fire of 1871, including a Victorian with huge keystones above its windows. Someday these facades will camouflage a parking garage that forms the back of the Legacy at Millennium Park, a 72-story glass condo tower. But their present state reveals them for what they really are: a slice of history no thicker than prosciutto.

The same ambiguity pervades the restored facades of four historic buildings that line the parking garage and street-level shops of the Heritage at Millennium Park, a 59-story condo tower that rises behind the Chicago Cultural Center at Michigan and Randolph. It was designed by the firm responsible for the Legacy at Millennium Park, Chicago architects Solomon Cordwell Buenz, along with historic preservation consultants McGuire Igleski & Associates of Evanston.

Walking on the east side of Wabash Avenue, it is hard not to be seduced by the facades, with their green urns, white sea horses, and other ornamental grace notes. But look more closely, and the skillful illusion is revealed. The upper floors don't have people living or working in them. Their windows are dark and lifeless. These aren't the facades of freestanding buildings. They've been stuck onto the parking garage. The outcome is gray, not black and white: The facade-ectomy saves a streetscape, but not a building. The streetscape retains its human scale. Yet the building loses any semblance of integrity.

A LIVING MUSEUM

As much as preservationists denounce such compromises, the deals are unlikely to disappear. Too much money is at stake. The city is a living museum of architecture, not one frozen in time. The question is how to adapt to this daunting new reality. Are some partial preservation jobs better than others? Yes, it turns out.

At one end of the spectrum—the wrong end—is the Maxwell Street redevelopment, planned by Darien-based Wight & Co. with help from historic preservation consultants Hasbrouck Peterson Zimoch Sirirattumrong of Chicago. The facades papering the parking garage and new buildings across the street were taken off other buildings in the area, restored, and reassembled. As handsome as they are, they make this a Maxwell Street that never was. This is not the preservation of history. This is the editing and eradication of history.

At the other end of the spectrum is the redevelopment of the Oliver Building, an official Chicago landmark that graces the city's burgeoning theater district. Located at 159 North Dearborn Street and originally the headquarters of the Oliver Typewriter Co., the structurally expressive 1907 building was designed by the same firm, Holabird & Roche, responsible for the marred Otis Building at 10 South LaSalle.

In the late 1990s, the Oliver stood in the way of the expansion of the Oriental Theatre (now the Ford Center for the Performing Arts), just to the east at 24 East Randolph Street. To make way for an expanded backstage at the Oriental, Chicago architect Daniel P. Coffey designed a plan that gutted the Oliver but preserved one-third of its original steel structure, along with the building's Dearborn Street facade and part of its alley facade.

A perfect historic preservation solution? No. But it's far better than a complete "facade-ectomy." At least it retained a semblance of the building's structure and three-dimensional identity.

In the tight quarters of downtown, of course, such solutions cannot be carried out everywhere. Which raises vexing questions: Would Chicago be better off by simply allowing developers to demolish landmark designs, such as the Farwell Building, that will be skinned and rebuilt on new internal structures? How much can you strip from a landmark building until it ceases to be a landmark?

There are no easy answers, but there is a need for new standards that recognize the integrity of architecture as well as the necessity of economics. As things stand now, the rise of the "facade-ectomy" is producing beguiling but sliver-thin vestiges of the past. As we stroll by on the sidewalk, they present a comforting masquerade, offering the impression that we're saving the style and meaning of history when, in fact, we're destroying all but a fraction of it.

Healing Process

IT'S UNCLEAR WHETHER COOK COUNTY HOSPITAL CAN OR SHOULD BE SAVED, BUT THERE HASN'T BEEN A FULL AIRING OF THE QUESTION

MAY 15, 2003

As Cook County Board president John Stroger forges ahead with his controversial plan to demolish Cook County Hospital, it is worth remembering a similar battle fought more than 30 years ago—and decided after the late Eleanor "Sis" Daley put her foot down.

The year was 1972. The building in the crosshairs was the Chicago Public Library on Michigan Avenue, beloved for its Beaux-Arts exterior and Tiffany-designed stained-glass dome. Developers wanted to tear down the old library and erect a modern office tower. Richard J. Daley, then Chicago's mayor, was about to let them have their way.

His wife said no. "I don't think that would be nice," she told a *Tribune* reporter about the plan to destroy the building she had used as a child.

"That's a beautiful site where it is. I'm for restoring and keeping all these beautiful buildings in Chicago." Soon after, a special mayoral committee voted unanimously against demolition.

Today the former library, renamed the Chicago Cultural Center, is one of downtown's most vibrant structures, teeming with people attending lectures, exhibitions, performances, and other activities. But two miles to the west, Stroger is readying to tear down Cook County Hospital, and no person in power, no "Sis" Daley, has materialized to shout, "Wait a minute!"

The old hospital, a sumptuous classical monument that symbolizes compassionate care for the poor, embedded itself in the public consciousness as the basis for the popular television series *ER*. Now it is about to be destroyed with virtually no public debate. And at a cost to taxpayers of as much as $30 million.

It's unclear whether Cook County Hospital can or should be saved. What is certain, however, is that there hasn't been a full airing of the question of demolition versus preservation.

Time is short. Stroger is expected to ask the County Board to authorize a demolition contract in two months. And county officials are turning a deaf ear to those, including real estate developers, who want to breathe new life into the now-vacant structure.

As Michael LaMont, the county's director of capital planning and policy, said: "From an artistic point of view, yes, it looks artistic. But it's not the solid great structure [preservationists] are making it out to be. . . . It is not in good shape."

Yet it also can be argued that his comment represents a self-fulfilling prophecy, one based on an outdated consultant's study as well as outdated attitudes about the vital role historic buildings play in the life of a city. If such an approach had prevailed in 1972, the old public library would be long gone and downtown would be the poorer for its loss.

The stand that "Sis" Daley took came at the dawn of a new age, when Chicagoans and Americans—jolted into awareness a decade earlier by the destruction of such landmarks as Pennsylvania Station in New York City—realized that they needed to fight to preserve the nation's architectural treasures.

Now a new crisis looms. Chicagoans are discovering that the unofficial neighborhood landmarks that once lent character to their communities—churches, social clubs, corner commercial buildings, graystones, and three-flats—are being razed by the hundreds.

As this year's "A Squandered Heritage" series in the *Tribune* has documented, more than 700 buildings identified by the city as potential landmarks already have come down. And Cook County Hospital, which stands on the Near West Side, not far from scores of vacant lots once filled by potential landmarks, is the next big target. The hospital closed in late 2002 after a new county medical center, named for Stroger, opened nearby.

In response to the *Tribune*'s accounts of the destruction of hundreds of potential landmarks, some city officials have questioned the worthiness of many of the demolished buildings. But the architectural quality of Cook County Hospital can't be dismissed as easily.

SOURCE OF STRENGTH

Completed in 1914 and designed by Cook County architect Paul Gerhardt, the two-block-long building is a West Side cousin of the Chicago City Hall that predated it by three years. The monumental presence and ornate decoration of its Harrison Street facade—which features pairs of three-story, fluted Ionic columns as well as faces of lions and cherubs— powerfully communicates the idea that the building represented a source of strength and succor to the poor and sick.

That idea is touchingly reinforced by a 1920s art deco monument to the French medical researcher Louis Pasteur in the public park across the street from the hospital. Inscribed in its stone walls is this quote from Pasteur: "One doesn't ask of one who suffers: What is your country and what is your religion? One merely says, You suffer. That is enough for me. You belong to me and I shall help you."

Though Cook County Hospital had a reputation as a bedlam-filled warren where patients were dumped in old-fashioned wards, it also had an illustrious medical history. Not only was the hospital recognized nationally for its innovative burn treatment unit, but it also broke ground in the diagnosis of sickle cell anemia and had one of the best emergency rooms in the country.

All that would seem to qualify the shuttered institution for city landmark status. But city officials are sitting on the sidelines. Pete Scales, spokesman for the Department of Planning and Development, said of county officials: "It's their property, and in deference to the County Board, we're not reviewing it at this time."

County officials have said there is no need for further discussion about tearing down the hospital because a 1988 study found that the structure could not be saved. But preservationists argue that the study is out-of-date because it was conducted 15 years ago—well before gentrification swept over the Near West Side and led to an astonishing rise in land values. In addition, they assert, the study never looked at any possible use of the building except as a hospital or medical facility.

OLD COOK COUNTY HOSPITAL
An emblem of compassionate care for the poor—and the need to preserve landmarks outside downtowns.

Developers are "champing at the bit" to convert the hospital to a new use, said David Bahlman, president of the Chicago-based Landmarks Preservation Council of Illinois (LPCI), a statewide advocacy group.

One of the developers, Preferred Real Estate Investments Inc. of Philadelphia, is converting a former, coal-fired power plant in Chester, Pennsylvania, into offices. The reuse of the plant, a massive 1918 neo-classical structure, is pumping new life into Chester, a small, economically depressed city about 20 miles southwest of Philadelphia. The company wants to perform the same kind of transformation in Chicago.

The controversy over the hospital's future is "unbelievably similar" to the arguments over the fate of the power plant, said Ira Saligman, acquisitions manager for Preferred Real Estate Investments. "Once the building is torn down, they will never build another building like this again."

The implications of the plan to raze Cook County Hospital extend far beyond its granite, terra-cotta, and brick walls. The case is a test of Chicago's resolve to protect its neighborhood treasures.

Indeed, a decision to save Cook County Hospital could represent the same sort of decisive turn that occurred in 1972 when "Sis" Daley entered the already-brewing controversy over the old public library. Along with the widespread revulsion to the demolition of Louis Sullivan and Dankmar Adler's Chicago Stock Exchange Building in the same year, the reclamation of the public library helped set the stage for a downtown preservation movement that of late has been able to save everything from the old Reliance Building to the cliff-like wall of buildings along Michigan Avenue.

IS IT STRUCTURALLY SOUND?

Any reuse proposal for the hospital inevitably will face the question of whether the building is structurally sound and whether the cost of fixing it would be prohibitive. Stroger says the 1988 study found problems with the hospital's structural, mechanical, ventilation, and electrical systems. But most of those systems would be replaced or significantly upgrades in a major rehabilitation, according to Preservation Chicago, a city advocacy group. "I can't imagine any structural problems with it," said LPCI's Bahlman, who toured the hospital last year before it closed. "There weren't any yellow tapes in front of doors saying 'Danger, don't enter.'"

Another key issue is cost. The county has to remove the asbestos in Cook County Hospital whether the building is torn down or reused. Should the county spend up to $30 million to clean the building and tear it down? Or should it clean the building and turn it over to a developer for a nominal price?

In addition to saving millions of dollars in demolition costs, redeveloping the hospital would put the property back on the tax rolls and could accelerate the Near West Side's economic revival.

"I think there has to be a discussion before we enter into the contract," said first-term Cook County commissioner Larry Suffredin, one of a new group of board members. "The older board members feel that that's already occurred. For the newer board members—we have a right to find that out, to be part of a hearing before we vote on a demolition contract."

The hospital's fate is not yet sealed. That leaves time for a citizen outcry, such as the one that recently saved the onion-domed Medinah Temple (now a handsomely restored Bloomingdale's store) and, decades ago, the old Chicago Public Library.

The library wouldn't have been spared and brilliantly reinvented if it weren't for debate—at least within the Richard J. Daley household.

CO-AUTHORED WITH PATRICK T. REARDON

A debate did happen about the future of Cook County Hospital, and it produced a surprising outcome: the very government body that had sought to tear down the building wound up proposing its renovation and reuse. First, in 2006 the National Park Service listed the hospital in the National Register of Historic Places, a step that made its potential redevelopment eligible for tax credits. Then, in 2007 Todd Stroger, who had replaced his father as Cook County Board president, floated a plan to preserve and renovate the building as office space. In the proposal, the county's Office of Capital Planning and Policy said the project would "restore the detailed Beaux-Arts style facade that makes the building unique, thereby retaining the building as a testimonial to the significant contributions Cook County [Hospital] has made to the medical profession, care of the indigent and as an architectural treasure." In March 2010, the Cook County Board unanimously approved a proposal to spend $108 million to transform the old hospital into a medical office building.

Why Losing Solider Field's Landmark Status Matters

UNCLE SAM DRAWS A LINE, SAVING AVANT-GARDE ARCHITECTURE FROM ITS WORST EXCESSES

JULY 25, 2004

Avant-garde architecture has been on a spectacular roll in recent years, as the recent opening of the Frank Gehry–designed band shell at Millennium Park attests. But a nagging question has always lurked in the background: When would bold modernism become too bold? Now we know, courtesy of that legendary architecture critic, Uncle Sam: at Chicago's Soldier Field, the Eyesore on Lake Shore.

When the federal government took the first step to strip Soldier Field of its National Historic Landmark status last week, it sent a message that resounds far beyond Chicago's aesthetically mangled lakefront football stadium: The government will react—and strongly—if avant-garde architects and arrogant politicians sack the nation's most extraordinary places.

The point is not to stop avant-garde architecture, but to save it from its worst excesses. In the last decade, cutting-edge designs such as Gehry's Guggenheim Museum Bilbao have won both critical praise and popular acclaim. Yet the public inevitably will sour on the avant-garde if it destroys cherished historic buildings and districts, just as people came to abhor the soulless public housing projects and sterile towers on plazas they were force-fed in the 1960s.

There are better examples of how bold modernism can bring together the old and the new. Despite its chaotic curves, Gehry's band shell actually respects the Beaux-Arts symmetry of Chicago's Grant Park. And projects like the rebuilding of Germany's parliament building, the Reichstag, by Britain's Norman Foster demonstrate with extraordinary skill and sensitivity the idea of respectful (rather than violent) contrast: the new should strike up a pointed dialogue with the old rather than outshout it.

If that distinction is ignored, we can only expect the chasm between politicians and the public—and between architects and those for whom they design—to grow. And that is precisely what is happening in Chicago.

After the news broke that the National Park Service had recommended that Soldier Field be removed from the federal landmark list, the *Tribune*'s website posted a poll on the stadium's controversial Klingon-meets-Parthenon design. Sixty-seven percent of the 7,188 people who responded agreed that the design is the "Eyesore on Lake Shore," a reference to the stadium's location on Lake Shore Drive, while 15.6 percent characterized it as a "superb synthesis of old and new." The remaining 17.4 percent, presumably all Chicago Bears fans, said the stadium is "a pigskin palace and nothing else matters."

THE NEW SOLDIER FIELD
A Klingon-meets-Parthenon mismatch that destroys proportions and a sense of place.

Compared to this admittedly unscientific, snapshot of public disapproval, the reaction of Mayor Richard M. Daley, Soldier Field's prime political sponsor, was remarkably pallid. The mayor blithely told reporters he was unconcerned about the recommended de-designation. That suggests that either Daley wants the story to go away, or he's clueless about the significance of National Historic Landmarks (NHLs) and the public's furor over what has happened to this one.

Well, here's a short course, Your Honor, in the NHLs: There are 2,364 of them, and they include such structures as the White House, the Empire State Building, the Brooklyn Bridge, Abraham Lincoln's home in Springfield, and Louis Sullivan's masterful Carson Pirie Scott & Co. store at State and Madison Streets. Underscoring the gravity of last week's recommendation, the government rarely removes properties from the list.

"EXCEPTIONAL PLACES"

As the keeper of the list, the National Park Service says on its website that NHLs are "exceptional places" that "form a common bond between all Americans." In contrast, the better-known but less selective National Register of Historic Places has 77,951 listings, including both the NHLs and properties that are of state and local significance.

The use of the word "place" in the Park Service website is telling. Architecture is about construction—it is about columns and beams and cantilevers—but it is fundamentally about constructing cultural identity: Buildings both reflect and affect who we are.

In the vastness of a sprawling continent, the best buildings become landmarks—places that literally (and beautifully) mark the land. Matching the authenticity of the spot where history actually occurred with the three-dimensional power of architecture, they tell stories about our common past that no theme park, with its stage-set artifice, can match.

Before its $660 million renovation was completed last September, Soldier Field (which opened in 1924 as Municipal Grant Park Stadium) fully lived up to the exacting standards of this exclusive list. Its rows of paired Doric columns—one on the stadium's east side, the other on the west—created a powerful presence along the lakefront. They enclosed a multipurpose interior that hosted such events as the legendary 1927 Jack Dempsey vs. Gene Tunney boxing match (won by Tunney after the infamous "long count"), a 1944 wartime speech by Franklin Delano Roosevelt, a 1964 speech by Martin Luther King Jr. at a racial justice rally, and the

1926 ceremonies that formally dedicated the stadium as a memorial to the 120,144 American soldiers killed in World War I.

To be sure, Soldier Field was a deteriorating hulk before the rehab, which was spearheaded by the Bears and the Chicago Park District, the stadium's owner. But it was, at least, recognizable. Today, if former vice president Charles Dawes, who attended the 1926 dedication ceremonies, were to rise from the grave and return to Soldier Field, he would undoubtedly gaze at its colossal mismatch and say: "Huh?"

DO NO HARM

As the nation's historical treasures adapt to changing circumstances, they should be altered in a way that does not do violence to the very qualities that made them special. Yet that balance has not been struck at Soldier Field, which was principally designed by Ben Wood and Carlos Zapata of Boston, with help from Chicago's Dirk Lohan. These are highly talented architects, and what makes evaluating their stadium so difficult is that the new structure—at least when considered in a vacuum from the old one—is in many respects outstanding.

With its dynamic diagonal supports, sweeping lines, and angled planes, the new seating bowl possesses a superb stylized athleticism. Its cantilevered seating tiers afford a remarkably intimate view of the action on the field. But in the end, the power of place is more important than virtuoso architectural star turns. As the strongly worded, three-page recommendation from National Park Service architectural historians makes clear, the stadium "no longer retains its historic integrity." A final decision by the U.S. Department of Interior, of which the Park Service is a part, is expected in 2005.

DOMINATION, NOT INTEGRATION

No longer do Soldier Field's once-proud colonnades etch a shape against the sky, as if they were the Acropolis of the lakefront. No longer does the stadium have a low-slung profile that harmonizes with the shoreline's horizontal sweep. No longer do the colonnades enclose a space in the tradition of the Coliseum and the great Roman architecture. Bears fans can't even see the old columns from their seats.

Beguiling as Wood and Zapata's sweeping modern shapes are, they make the colonnades look like toys—cute bookends on either side of the sweepingly monumental modern forms. The new doesn't exist independently of the old, as the architects insist. It dominates and interrupts it, as if former Bears' defensive lineman William "the Refrigerator" Perry had plunked his ample haunches atop a picket fence.

The bottom line: parts of Soldier Field remain—not the whole.

Perhaps that's why so many people have wondered aloud whether it would have been more honest to simply tear down the colonnades rather than go through the political charade, as Daley and the architects did, of saying that they were saving one of Chicago's great landmarks.

Of course, we'll never know about alternatives because the all-powerful mayor and his allies steamrolled the project through the Illinois legislature. Not surprisingly, his own landmarks commission never attempted to give Soldier Field the city landmark status—and thus, the official protection—it deserved. Because no federal funds were used in the project, the federal government was powerless to stop it.

FINDING ARCHITECTURAL HARMONY

Foster's Reichstag reconstruction, completed in 1999, reveals that there is a better way: he restored the classical German parliament building, yet he also made such bold steps as placing a glass dome atop the building and its legislative chamber. And he inserted within the dome a helical ramp that winds its way up to an observation platform.

Based on a visit to the site, I can say that the juxtaposition is at once spectacular and successful: not only do the old and the new retain their integrity; they inform each other, both formally and symbolically. The helical ramps allow the people to rise above their political representatives in the chamber below, providing a powerful symbol of Germany's revived democracy.

There is no better example of how avant-garde architecture can avoid the carnage it has created in Chicago. To show it will not tolerate a repeat of Chicago's "Mistake by the Lake," the government needs to put its stamp of approval on the courageous and carefully reasoned recommendation it just received: it should give Soldier Field the boot.

POSTSCRIPT

In 2006 the National Park Service announced that U.S. Interior Department secretary Gale Norton had signed an order removing Soldier Field from the roster of National Historic Landmarks.

Love It? Hate It? Or Both?

AN ARCHITECTURE CRITIC REVISITS THE BUILDING HE DESPISED
AS A STUDENT AND HAS A REVELATION

NOVEMBER 2008

"Just one thing I want you to know up front," I replied when the editors of Yale's alumni magazine asked if I would come back to New Haven to review the restored Art & Architecture Building. "As a student, I hated it."

In the early 1980s, some two decades after the building's opening, it was easy to hate the A&A, as everyone called it. Those years represented a high-water mark for postmodernism and its nostalgia for historic architecture. As a result, in the cruel way that the tides of architectural taste are wont to turn, the reputation of the building's daring modern architect, Paul Rudolph, was at a low ebb. Many of us nonetheless appreciated Rudolph's poured-in-place concrete castle and how it magnificently culminated the march of Yale's arts buildings up Chapel Street. Living with it—and, especially, inside of it, as a graduate student struggling to wrap my arms around a vast body of architectural knowledge—was another matter.

The jagged edges of Rudolph's signature walls of corrugated concrete, which threatened to cut clothes and skin, were only the beginning. At any given time, a third of the lights were burned out. The original bright orange carpets had turned a sickly green. Everywhere, partitions sliced up Rudolph's flowing, vertiginous interior spaces. Raw concrete was ubiquitous—on the walls, the ceilings, the floors. The place, in short, was parking-garage tough.

My dehumanizing experience there was hardly unique. Rarely have soaring architectural ambition and the simple quotidian needs of users clashed as violently as they have at the corner of York and Chapel Streets. There is a famous story about a client of Frank Lloyd Wright's furiously telephoning the master from the middle of a dinner party as water from a leaking roof drip-dropped down on his bald head. Wright's cavalier reply: "Move your chair." The trouble was that we art and architecture students couldn't move our chairs, our models, or our canvases, at least not out of the A&A. We were trapped in this unforgiving structure.

An architecture school building is supposed to be a model, inspiring students and offering them something to emulate. For me, at least, the reverse was true. I would emerge from Yale seeing the A&A as a tyrannical object lesson in what architecture *shouldn't* be—an exercise in willful, self-indulgent form-making that elevated the ego of the architect above the spirits of a building's users.

YALE'S RESTORED ART & ARCHITECTURE BUILDING
Even the most notorious modern landmarks can have second lives.

So, this September, as I stood across York Street from the A&A at 10
p.m., I couldn't believe my eyes. Light poured outward from the building's vast windows and illuminated its grand interior spaces and the plaster
casts of architectural decoration that hang on their walls. I had made a
point of visiting the building late at night because that was when its gloom
had weighed most heavily on me as a student. But what I found was a light
box, perfectly revealing Rudolph's desire to create a captivating spatial
drama.

I had never seen this before.

Now called Paul Rudolph Hall, the freshly restored A&A is no longer
a freestanding building but part of a single interconnected structure with
two other main parts, a new history of art building and a new library that
joins the lower levels of the two structures. It is an enormously complicated $126 million undertaking, energetically directed by New York City
architect Charles Gwathmey, and it has achieved mixed results.

Gwathmey's masterful restoration of the A&A, skillfully and lovingly
done, fully recaptures the lost glory of this modernist icon. His banal addition, the Jeffrey Loria Center for the History of Art, doesn't come close

to matching the muscular presence of its predecessor. But it is at least commodious, and, in truth, the triumph of the restored A&A would have been impossible without it.

Gwathmey cleverly shifted elevators, mechanical systems, a reception area, and some faculty offices out of the A&A and into the new building, where they serve both structures. He thus freed the A&A to be what I suspect Rudolph always wanted it to be—a dazzling piece of architectural sculpture, unfettered by niggling everyday concerns.

The brilliant son of a Kentucky minister, Rudolph was a charismatic wunderkind who was appointed chair of Yale's architecture department in 1958, before he'd reached his 40th birthday. Under his direction, Yale led a revolt against the very less-is-more modernism that the Bauhaus master Walter Gropius had taught Rudolph at Harvard. The A&A, dedicated on November 9, 1963, exemplified the shift from sober functionalism to bold expressionism.

Instead of a simple steel-and-glass box with flexible modules of "universal space," Rudolph designed a powerfully sculpted structure, in which a dazzling variety of interior spaces pinwheeled around four principal interior columns. Their centrifugal energy carried through to the exterior, where towers at the building's corners seemed to explode onto the street.

Inside, Rudolph packed 37 levels into the A&A's ten floors (two below-ground). Steps, balconies, and bridges helped create an ever-shifting internal topography that sensible Bauhaus buildings, with their endlessly repeating floors, conspicuously lacked. His spatial theatricality reached its climax in the building's heart, the two-story drafting room, presided over by a marble Roman statue of the goddess Minerva.

Further thumbing his nose at the ahistorical inclinations of the Bauhaus, Rudolph playfully decorated the A&A with bits and pieces of history—Assyrian reliefs in the stairwells, Ionic capitals perched on metal poles in the lecture hall. The whole amounted to an extraordinary synthesis that reflected the influence of the atrium-like "great workroom" of Frank Lloyd Wright's Larkin Building, as well as the heavy concrete brutalism of the Swiss-born modern master Le Corbusier. Hordes of people visited. The building won awards, and architectural magazines around the world splashed its images on their pages. "It was the Bilbao of its time," said the current architecture dean, Robert A. M. Stern, referring to Frank Gehry's critically acclaimed and enormously popular Guggenheim Museum in Bilbao, Spain.

But the glory proved short-lived. The dazzling forms often did not function. On the seventh floor, where Rudolph followed the cues of an art department slow to adapt to shifting styles, painters were outraged that the ceilings were too low for their large canvases. Sculptors and graphic designers were consigned to the grim subbasement, where the ceilings were just seven feet high. Acoustical problems were pervasive. Music played upstairs would travel down the building's four main columns, which served as ventilation shafts, upsetting readers in the library. The jagged concrete walls proved difficult to clean. There was no air-conditioning, so the air was stultifyingly still.

If Rudolph had successfully asserted that architecture can be a stirring art, rather than a bloodless collection of spaces assembled by technocrats, he had failed miserably in coming to terms with the field's more prosaic demands. Architecture is above all a social art, the art with which we live. Yet his building was, in crucial respects, unlivable.

Over time, the once-revolutionary building became the target of a counter-revolt, which deemed its spatial gymnastics and hard-edged materials oppressive—even a symbol of the national hubris associated with the war in Vietnam. By June 14, 1969, when a fire of suspicious origin severely damaged the A&A, the blaze was widely interpreted as a violent form of architectural critique. "I just said that the building was so guilty that it burst into flames all by itself," said Yale alumnus and adjunct architecture professor Turner Brooks. A year later, during New Haven's infamous Black Panther trial, Brooks watched as the National Guard cordoned off the streets in front of the building. "Looming behind them," Brooks recalled, "was the great charred hulk of the A&A, which represented everything that was wrong about everything."

The chair who followed Rudolph, postmodernist Charles Moore, was no fan of his predecessor's heroic vision—and he was even less inclined to preserve it. In the years after the fire, partitions carved up the once-open studio spaces. The growing art and architecture schools condoned other unsympathetic changes in order to squeeze usable space out of the building. The Yale University Art Gallery took back the statue of Minerva after the fire (and after students painted her toenails). By the time I arrived in 1982, the A&A was a ruin before its time, though it possessed none of the romantic aura of a decaying monument in the English countryside.

During the deanship of Chicago architect Thomas Beeby, however, a reaction set in against postmodernism and its superficial decorative effects. "When I got there, the students actually loved the building," said Beeby, who headed the school of architecture from 1985 to 1992. With money flowing freely after the boom years of the late 1990s, and with the School of Art moving to a home of its own across Chapel Street in 2000, the stage was set to remake the A&A. It had managed to last long enough for people to appreciate it again.

In restoring Rudolph's troubled masterpiece, Gwathmey was performing a far more complicated task than remaking a single building. He and the architects at his firm, Gwathmey Siegel & Associates, were wrestling with an extremely difficult design issue: How do you preserve a singular landmark and add on to it at the same time? The question had a special master-student tension, because Gwathmey worked for Rudolph when he was a student.

Rudolph, who died in 1997, had always envisioned expanding the A&A. Though he left no precise instructions, Gwathmey and Stern said, his idea was to break through the stair tower on the building's north side and form a courtyard framed by the A&A on one side and the new building on the other. That is essentially what Gwathmey has done, though his "courtyard" is not an outdoor space but a portion of the new Robert B. Haas Family Arts Library, which brings together Yale's collections in art, architecture, and drama. The library's Great Hall is topped by domed skylights that draw natural light into the multilevel atrium, where students curl up in bright orange Womb chairs designed by Eero Saarinen.

Yet for all its fidelity to Rudolph's plan, the seven-story history of art building—which houses lecture halls, classrooms, and faculty offices—is hardly self-effacing. Instead of quietly taking its place alongside the A&A, it seeks to strike up a conversation with Rudolph's building, echoing it in some ways while departing from it in others. The height and mass of the new building appear to match the old one. But its diagonal and curving geometry departs from Rudolph's right angles, as do its exterior materials, which are panels of zinc and limestone instead of corrugated concrete. Like just about every client these days, the history of art department wanted its new quarters to be an icon.

For the A&A, at least, the project has yielded superb results. It was no accident that I found the building's exterior so wonderfully transparent. Gwathmey specified large new windows to restore Rudolph's original see-through look, which had been compromised by previous renovation. (The windows are insulated, and the project is expected to qualify for a Leadership in Energy and Environmental Design silver rating.) Gwathmey also attended to critical details, bringing back a new version of the concrete spandrels below the windows. Their sleek forms re-create a vivid counterpoint with Rudolph's rough-edged concrete. The concrete itself, cleaned with water and bleach, even looks less menacing.

The recaptured spatial drama of the vertiginous interior is extraordinary, suggesting that Rudolph would have made his atrium cut through the entire building—if only the fire marshal had let him. In the fourth- and fifth-floor drafting area, the partitions that chopped up Rudolph's grand expanses have been removed, and two U-shaped concrete bridges boldly span the drafting area. The bridges restore a key element of the original design and provide a bracing lookout point from which to admire a replica of the long-gone Minerva. Here, space flows in completely unexpected ways—up, down, in, out, sideways. Light entering through skylights bathes the muscular concrete columns, making this cathedral of work the perfect distillation of the modernist trinity of space, light, and structure.

This time around, though, God is in both the big picture and the details. Bright lights and orange carpets are everywhere, allaying the toughness of the concrete. New ventilation equipment makes the air move instead of being deadly still. "It definitely feels different," said Steve Ybarra, a second-year master of architecture student.

The building seems sure to remain in good order as long as Stern is in charge. He's a detail fanatic. Even though he was dressed in a custom-tailored English suit on the day he took me around the building, he was pulling weeds out of planter boxes on the A&A's roof. "I take care of this joint," he cracked.

While the would-be icon of the history of art building has some memorable moments, particularly a dramatically raked main lecture hall, it simply can't match the punch of the restored A&A. Taking a break from his drafting table, junior Russell LeStourgeon observed that the brutalist monument no longer seemed so brutal. "Before it was like a cave, like ruins," he said. "Now it's preserved ruins. We pulled our first all-nighter and at sunrise we went out on the roof. We felt very in touch with Rudolph."

I felt the same way as I left the A&A. It seemed tragic that Rudolph's masterwork had led to his fall from grace. He deserved better than to be marginalized at the end of his career. It is fitting that the restoration at once celebrates him and sends the broader signal that, no matter how disheveled they appear, masterpieces of mid-twentieth-century modernism can and should be preserved. Before, I hated this building. Now I love/hate it. Surely its exemplary restoration will inspire new generations of students—and serve as a cautionary tale against the brilliant but arrogant form-making that got the A&A into the terrible bind from which it has now escaped.

Yale Alumni Magazine

This Mies Building at IIT Can Go

SQUAT BRICK STRUCTURE ISN'T THE ARCHITECT'S BEST WORK,
AND THE METRA EXPANSION MERITS ITS RAZING

MAY 7, 2009

You'd never suspect that a great architect shaped the clunky brick box at the corner of 35th and Federal Streets on Chicago's South Side. But the master of the steel-and-glass box, Ludwig Mies van der Rohe, designed this humble brick hut at the southwest edge of the Illinois Institute of Technology. It was called "the Test Cell" or "the Gunnery," names that hinted at the building's covert purpose. Built during the Cold War in the early 1950s, it reportedly led to an underground testing facility for explosives.

Get a good look at this building now. It soon will be demolished to make way for an $11.7 million Metra station, backed with $6.8 million in federal stimulus funds, which will bring riders to U.S. Cellular Field, the Bronzeville neighborhood, and IIT's resurgent campus. And you know what? That's perfectly fine. Mediocre buildings by world-class architects sometimes have to make way for pieces of civic infrastructure that uplift the community as a whole.

As you might suspect, a cadre of historic preservationists doesn't see it that way. While they acknowledge that the little Mies building is no masterpiece, they argue that it has real architectural merit. The scruffy structure originally had a handsome facade of pure beige brick, they insist, and it holds the corner well.

"A lot of people have said it's nothing more than a box. One wonders if these critics have ever heard the statement 'less is more,'" said Grahm Balkany, an IIT student, referring to a signature Mies epigram.

"If you had even a minor doodle by Rembrandt, and you weren't forced to throw it in a fire, why would you?" another proponent of saving the building, Chicago architecture critic Edward Lifson, wrote on his *Hello Beautiful!* blog.

These advocates are vastly overstating the merits of a building that is utterly dispensable. They are engaging in hero worship when they ought to be thinking dispassionately about what, if anything, this building means in the broader arc of Mies's career and the very real consequences that would result from stopping or significantly slowing construction of the Metra station. Historic preservation should not occur in an urban planning vacuum.

The German-born Mies, who fled Hitler's Germany and came to Chicago in 1938, planned the IIT campus not as a conventional series

THE TEST CELL AT IIT
Not worth saving, despite its association with the master of steel and glass.

of history-inspired buildings ringing a quadrangle, but as a "campus in a park." Flowing green space would envelop sleek, modernist structures of steel, brick, and glass. The campus would serve as a large-scale illustration of St. Augustine's maxim, which Mies was fond of quoting: "Beauty is the splendor of truth."

Know-nothing naysayers, like the *Princeton Review* college rating survey, have lambasted the outcome as sterile and ugly. Yet four years ago, the revolutionary campus was named to the National Register of Historic Places, a crucial step because the designation required state historic preservation officials to review the use of federal funds to tear down its buildings.

Once Balkany informed the Illinois Historic Preservation Agency that his research demonstrated Mies's role on the Test Cell, the agency properly slowed the project and asked Metra to consider alternative locations and designs for the station. But Anne Haaker, a respected deputy state historic preservation officer, said she eventually green-lighted the demolition because the Test Cell wasn't built to Mies's original design, had been altered significantly, and didn't contribute to the National Register district.

It was the right call, and not just on the narrow question of judging the building's merits.

If the Test Cell were an "A" building or even a "B+" building, Metra would be justified in ordering Chicago architects Skidmore, Owings & Merrill to redesign the station to accommodate it. But the Test Cell isn't close to top-drawer, so the alternatives being floated by the preservationists, such as shifting the station to an empty parcel south of 35th, simply aren't worth the cost, delay, or inconvenience.

On the other hand, the benefits of the station—which has the political sponsorship of U.S. representative Bobby Rush (D-IL) and is scheduled to be complete in July 2010—are clear.

By providing a new stop along Metra's Rock Island District Line, which courses through Chicago's southwest suburbs and the city's South and Southwest Sides, the station can be counted upon to get scores of drivers off the congested Dan Ryan Expressway. They won't only be White Sox fans going to and from U.S. Cellular Field. They will include IIT faculty, students, and staff; people who work at the university's technology park; cops based at Chicago's 35th Street Police Department Headquarters; and residents of the Bronzeville neighborhood.

All this will save energy, spread the benefits of the stimulus plan to poor and middle-class neighborhoods that most need them, and further boost the resurgence of an urban campus that was once so forlorn that its trustees actually contemplated moving to the suburbs.

What's good for the campus will be good for its truly significant Mies buildings (and there are 19 of them). Zealous historic preservationists have got to learn this lesson: It often makes sense to save the best and let go of the rest.

POSTSCRIPT

This story prompted a telephone call from Mies's grandson, Chicago architect Dirk Lohan, who designed the master plan that helped bring about the revival of the IIT campus. Lohan was explicit: The Test Cell building was not worth saving. "Mies probably told some junior member [of his office] to do this thing. I'm sure he wasn't very interested in it at all," Lohan said. "It was like an outlying little shed. . . . You can't write architectural history with that building." The Test Cell building was demolished in late 2009.

Historic Preservation and Green Architecture

FRIENDS OR FOES?

MARCH 2010

Whenever I hear people talking about tension between green architecture and historic preservation, I am taken aback. What tension? Choosing between conservation and preservation, it would seem, is like choosing between a Volvo and a Saab. More unites them than divides them.

Both movements cut their teeth in the 1960s, challenging the prevailing value system of postwar American culture and its unbridled faith in anything "new." And both camps drew inspiration from brilliant women who wrote brilliant books—Jane Jacobs, whose *The Death and Life of Great American Cities* assaulted the conventional wisdom about "urban renewal," and Rachel Carson, whose *Silent Spring* helped give birth to the environmental movement by documenting the harmful effects of pesticides.

Preservationists and conservationists are close relatives—sisters or brothers—not strangers. Yet if you scratch the surface of their relationship, it is possible to find evidence of a simmering sibling rivalry.

Take the tension that surfaced in Chicago last year, when the owners of the Sears (now Willis) Tower revealed plans to make the nation's tallest skyscraper more energy efficient. Among the measures they considered: splashing a coat of heat-reflecting silver paint on the tower's heat-attracting black facade. Although the 37-year-old high-rise is not an officially protected landmark, the idea that it could be radically altered in the name of saving BTUs sent shock waves coursing through Chicago's architectural community. Fortunately, the owners backed off their glittery idea, but not before my colleagues at the *Chicago Tribune* floated some fanciful alternatives for "greening" the tower, including encasing it in an environmentally friendly hemp shopping bag.

All joking aside, the Sears Tower saga begs some fundamental questions: Should preservationists place a new and unremitting emphasis on saving energy, or should retaining the integrity of architectural masterworks remain paramount? To what extent, if at all, should preservationists be guided by the U.S. Green Building Council's standards for Leadership in Energy and Environmental Design (LEED) certification?

In other words, should the green movement and the threat of climate change prompt a rethinking of what it means to be a historic preservationist at the dawn of the 21st century?

The answer, in a word, is yes, but in truth, things are considerably more complicated than that. A close look at three projects in the Midwest reveals the need for a broad spectrum of approaches, based on the recognition that different circumstances demand different responses—and a healthy dose of innovation.

THE SETH PETERSON COTTAGE

Like Frank Lloyd Wright's Taliesin in Spring Green, Wisconsin, the tiny Seth Peterson Cottage near Lake Delton, Wisconsin, has a tragedy-laced history. Its namesake owner died before the 880-square-foot cottage was completed in 1960. Another owner then finished the house, but it fell into disrepair after 1966, when the state of Wisconsin bought the property to enlarge a state park. Only in the late 1980s, when local activists conceived the idea of restoring the cottage and renting it out to visitors, did things look up.

Enter Chicago architect John Eifler, who was hired for the restoration. Eifler's mechanical engineer determined that the existing house, with single-pane glazing covering 60 percent of the facade, would burn up money on winter heating bills. So Eifler proposed double-glazing and ran his radical idea by the state historic preservation officer. The response was predictable: Rather than set a possibly dangerous precedent, the State Historic Preservation Office refused to approve the request.

But someone on the nonprofit's board knew the governor of Wisconsin and got his ear. And before you know it, Eifler said, the governor called

THE SETH PETERSON COTTAGE
How new green priorities lead to new methods of historic preservation.

the head of the state historical division and asked, in effect: "Why are you giving those good people in Lake Delton such a hard time?" And that, remembered Eifler, is how he got his double-glazing. By adding appropriate Usonian-style furniture and by retaining single glazing in other areas, the architect went on to restore this Wright gem to its former glory.

But when work on the Seth Peterson Cottage finished in 1992 (the 125th anniversary of Wright's birth), the clock hadn't just been turned back. It had been turned forward, anticipating today's energy concerns. Eifler put a radiant heating system in the floor, a feature the original client could not afford, and he installed insulation below it, ensuring that heat would rise into the house rather than seep into the earth below. He even designed pockets in the ceiling for electronic roller shades (still on the cottage's wish list) that would drop down on winter nights and further insulate the glass.

As a result of his foresight, the cottage stays warm in winter and cool in summer. This isn't just good for the environment, it's good for preservation. Because the Seth Peterson Cottage Conservancy isn't spending thousands of dollars heating the property, it has sufficient funds to maintain it.

The broader lesson is that a restoration should not only reinstate the past; it should also prepare a building for the future. If a building cannot meet tomorrow's standards, in Eifler's view, it is doomed to become obsolete. And that will lead the public and policymakers to wonder why they should devote precious resources to the very cause preservationists hold dear. Eifler's radical mantra: Preservationists have to reinvent themselves— or they will become dinosaurs.

S. R. CROWN HALL

Clearly, that approach will not work on every project. Take the recent restoration of Ludwig Mies van der Rohe's S. R. Crown Hall at the Illinois Institute of Technology. Because this 54-year-old icon of International Style modernism is a Miesian masterwork, it demanded an entirely different response from the one used on Wright's modest cottage.

By 2003, time and deferred maintenance had taken their toll on Crown Hall, which is home to IIT's College of Architecture and represents Mies's greatest achievement at the university's South Side campus. The elegant travertine stairs had cracked, and the once-crisp black Mies facade had turned a faint shade of gray. The restoration team—Chicago architects Krueck + Sexton and preservation architect T. Gunny Harboe—faced the enormously difficult challenge of modernizing the steel-and-glass temple

S. R. CROWN HALL
Where restoring an icon took precedence over saving the planet.

while also making it look as if they had never touched it. And that meant standing up for the icon, even at the expense of saving energy.

Wisely, for example, the architects rejected a consultant's suggestion to insulate Crown Hall's huge upper-level sheets of glass, also known as lights, with low-emissivity coating. Although the low-E coating would have improved insulation, it also would have made the lights noticeably darker than Mies had intended. Instead, the architects specified a highly transparent low-iron glass. This thoughtful decision formed just one part of an aesthetic triumph, in which the bone-beautiful clarity and revolutionary transparency of the masterly original were fully restored.

So, did the architects simply shove aside green design? Not at all. As part of the restoration, they replaced the landmark's lower lights, a series of translucent laminated-glass windows left over from a previous renovation. These windows had trapped heat, reflecting it inward. Bringing back Mies's original sandblasted glass restored the cool elegance of the lower lights *and* provided green benefits, letting in more natural light and cutting down on heat gain. In addition, the architects crafted a strategy for future greening. Opening Crown Hall's bottom-hinged hopper windows and roof vents on a systematic basis, for example, would allow the building to naturally vent itself in warmer months.

At Crown Hall, then, the restoration team achieved a very different balance than Eifler did at the Seth Peterson Cottage. Because the architects were restoring an icon, retaining the authenticity of the original outweighed energy concerns. Krueck + Sexton, along with Harboe, did what greening they could—and put off the rest for another day. To Harboe, the essence of sustainability is cultural, not simply scientific. It means prolonging the life of buildings that attain the highest level of artistry and express our highest cultural ideals. Why save civilization, he asked, if it means compromising the integrity of civilization's greatest achievements?

SEARS, ROEBUCK & CO. POWER PLANT

So we have two restoration approaches that are polar opposites, one privileging energy, the other iconic status. But I know of another, exemplified by the just-completed restoration of a muscular 105-year-old power plant that supplied steam and electricity to Sears, Roebuck & Co.'s once-thriving catalog operation on Chicago's West Side. It shows that a hybrid approach can work within the envelope of a single building.

Designed in 1905 by Chicago architects Nimmons & Fellows, the power plant combined Chicago School efficiency with classical decoration, exhibiting such flourishes as terra-cotta rondelles that depicted bolts of electricity. When Sears left the West Side in 1973 for its 110-story tower downtown, the power plant seemed like a white elephant. Yet after a skillful adaptive use led by Chicago architects Farr Associates, who worked with the Midwest office of MacRostie Historic Advisors, this former palace of steam has been transformed into a palace of learning. It's called the Charles H. Shaw Technology and Learning Center, and it includes a public charter high school known as Power House High. Landmarks Illinois honored the project in 2009, and in 2010 the Shaw center is expected to win LEED platinum certification from the U.S. Green Building Council. The two recognitions reveal how it deftly walks a tightrope between preservation and green design.

That balancing act is especially evident in the power plant's old engine room, a striking space with soaring arched windows and glistening, glazed brick walls. It is now used for school assemblies, a cafeteria, and community events. Originally, with superheated steam coursing through the room, its thick walls did not require insulation. But with the heat provided by engines long gone, the walls were sure to turn cold in the winter—and stay that way. During early phases of the design, the architects actually discussed covering, or "furring out," the original glazed brick walls with studs, insulation, and drywall. Then, in a bit of Disney fakery, they would have covered the drywall with a new layer of glazed tile to simulate the original glazed brick.

THE CHARLES H. SHAW TECHNOLOGY AND LEARNING CENTER
Successfully combining the agendas of conservation and preservation.

"We said, what the hell are we doing?" Farr Associates' president, Doug Farr, remembered. "Yes, it solves this problem. But it creates new problems. And it's incredibly expensive."

Instead, Farr and his team, led by principal Jonathan Boyer and project manager Rose Grayson, decided to keep the glazed brick. They compensated for the lack of insulation with huge new exhaust fans that vent heat in the summer and a plenum, or air chamber, that slowly releases heated air during winter months. Mindful of how the plenum, if left visible, could mar the historic interior, they cleverly tucked it beneath a bench for students.

To fully achieve their green aims, the architects concentrated on the building's other half, where giant boilers once turned water into steam. There, in addition to removing a thicket of machinery and inserting floors, stairwells, and corridors into the towering vertical space, they insulated brick walls and reglazed an existing skylight with more energy-efficient glass.

The results are inspired as well as inspiring, engaging students with distinctive surroundings that preserve the power plant's past and chart an ecology-minded course for the future. Farr Associates' flexible, pragmatic approach made this triumph possible. By carefully picking opportunities for preservation and conservation, the architects achieved both aims in the same historic structure.

FALSE RESOLUTIONS AND COMMON GROUND

So where does that leave us? Not, I hope, with a false sense of comfort that the agendas of preservationists and conservationists will always be in sync. As these examples demonstrate, that is sometimes (but certainly not always) so.

The real common ground between preservationists and conservationists is evident in cities like Chicago and Grand Rapids, Michigan, which promote mass transit, walkable streets, vibrant cultural attractions, and with them the density that makes urban areas hum. *Density* is what it's all about. If we live densely and don't sprawl, we'll save on energy. And if we save cities, we'll create a demand for the historic buildings in them. The LEED rating system is finally coming around to this understanding. Thanks to recent changes, it now awards more credits to projects in urban settings and to projects close to mass transit. Preservationists continue to press for additional changes that would better recognize the value of building reuse.

This shift in the LEED standards suggests that the key to resolving the conflict between preservation and conservation is not technical but cultural. It's about how we live and how we ought to navigate between perilous extremes: not with overzealous ideology but with an enlightened pragmatism that reshapes and reinvigorates old ideals in response to new realities. By virtue of their common heritage and their common values, preservation and conservation can be friends, not foes. But like good friends or rival siblings, they may need, occasionally, to agree to disagree.

Preservation
(originally a 2009 keynote speech to the Michigan Historic Preservation Network)

THE BLOOMING OF GREEN
ARCHITECTURE

THE ASCENT OF GREEN ARCHITECTURE WAS ONE OF THE GREAT SURPRISES OF the early years of the 21st century, but in retrospect it was hardly shocking, given the significant role that buildings play in causing climate change. When the millennium dawned, green buildings were rare in the United States. By the decade's end, while energy-saving construction was not exactly pervasive, more and more buildings were designed with an eye toward curbing their carbon footprint. Indeed, in the surest signs that environmental values were making their way into the mainstream, developers advertised their buildings as green and critics railed against the practice of "greenwashing," in which companies falsely portrayed their practices as good for the environment. Chicago's mayor, Richard M. Daley, personified the shift toward the sustainable agenda, with his unlikely push to make his once-polluted city "the greenest in America."

Chicago, My Kind of Green

THE WINDY CITY PRESENTS A SNAPSHOT OF THE SUSTAINABILITY
MOVEMENT'S STRENGTHS AND SHORTCOMINGS

OCTOBER 2007

Having lunch the other day with Chicago architect Doug Farr, who has made green design a hallmark of his practice, I got a mind-opening shock.

THE GREEN ROOF AT CHICAGO'S CITY HALL
A much-photographed symbol of Mayor Richard M. Daley's desire to make Chicago "the greenest city in America."

As we sat in the Cliff Dwellers Club, the Michigan Avenue aerie with the stunning views of Grant Park, Farr laid this statistic on me: in Chicago, which Mayor Richard M. Daley famously wants to make "the greenest city in America," only 27 buildings have earned Leadership in Energy and Environmental Design (LEED) status. That's more than in any other American city except Portland, Oregon, and Seattle, but still, only a tiny fraction of Chicago's total of more than half a million buildings. Nationally, as I found out with a phone call to the U.S. Green Building Council (USGBC), the picture is every bit as bleak—with only about 1,100 LEED-certified structures. I left the lunch reeling. After all the hoopla about green design, this was the state of our progress in combating the scourge of global warming?

Well, not entirely, but that snapshot offers a cautionary note as the council prepares for Greenbuild, its annual convention, to be held this year in Chicago. With pathbreaking early skyscrapers, the legendary "White City" of the 1893 World's Fair, and scores of other design innovations, Chicago has long served as "the great American exaggeration," a boisterous, make-no-little-plans town that has expressed in bold relief the best and worst of American architecture. Today the city has reprised that role, representing the green movement's strengths and shortcomings.

Certainly, the movement's strengths are personified by Daley, the tree-hugging, democratically elected monarch who was born on Arbor Day and who has remade (or, more accurately, has re-layered) the city's face since he took office in 1989. If a latter-day Rip Van Winkle had fallen into a deep slumber in that year and awoken today, he would notice an astonishing change in the city's once-harsh landscape: 500,000 trees planted, more than 80 miles of landscaped medians constructed, and 2 million square feet of green roofs built or negotiated—more green roofs than all other American cities combined. Among them are the green roof atop Daley's City Hall; another one at Millennium Park, the post-industrial playground that sparkles with contemporary art and architecture; and a less flashy counterpart at the McCormick Place West Building, one of the nation's largest certified structures, which will serve as the Greenbuild convention site.

I once got a rise out of Daley by calling his penchant for trees, shrubs, and flowers the "Martha Stewartizing of this tough-guy town." But the more I see of his greening push, the more I think it goes beyond literal greening; it's conceptual greening that civilizes the urban jungle, encouraging high-density living and saving energy in the bargain.

Since 1998 developers have completed—or started construction on—more than 200 condominium and apartment buildings containing more than 35,000 units in Chicago's greater downtown area, according to Gail Lissner, Appraisal Research Counselors' vice president. All this makes the Loop, still girdled by the famous elevated structure and its rumbling trains, a kind of giant transit-oriented development. And green is part of this boom. While Chicago trails New York in its number of planned green skyscrapers and lacks a green monument on the order of Foster + Partner's Hearst Tower, it is making strides, as evidenced by the opening of its first green all-residential skyscraper—the handsome 64-story 340 on the Park by Solomon Cordwell Buenz's Martin Wolf.

Meanwhile, Chicago has been in the vanguard of constructing sustainable public and nonprofit buildings, mostly because Daley's iron fist/green thumb has led to the creation of green schools, green police stations, green libraries, even green single-room occupancy housing (SROs) for the poor. The city requires all new public buildings to achieve at least LEED-certified status. In addition, public and private projects receiving city assistance must either have a green roof or pursue green building certification. The city has matched such sticks with carrots. It expedites permits for green buildings and offers a density bonus for downtown buildings that install green roofs. Sometimes the results can be incongruous. A flagship McDonald's, exemplar of the car culture, has a green roof, which is like putting a thin leaf of lettuce atop a bacon double cheeseburger and declaring it "healthy." Yet the overall picture is bright, and it extends beyond downtown to the city's neighborhoods and to some of its poorest citizens.

Helmut Jahn's Near North Apartments, which rise alongside the infamous Cabrini-Green housing project, are a smaller, greener version of his acclaimed State Street Village dormitories at the Illinois Institute of Technology. The apartments offer such eye-catching green features as rooftop wind turbines, which take full advantage of Chicago's dependable breezes. While the story is still out on whether the SRO will help rebuild the lives of its troubled residents, the benefits of green design already are apparent at Chicago's first LEED-certified public school, the Tarkington Elementary School by OWP/P Architects and Warman Olsen Warman. The pluses include better indoor air quality, more natural light, and lower land acquisition costs because the school's play facilities are shared with the local park district. Chicago also claims to be the only city in the world with three LEED platinum buildings, including Farr's Chicago Center for Green Technology, a recycled factory on the city's gritty West Side, where the elevators run on canola oil instead of environmentally toxic hydraulic fluid.

Needless to say, this visible greening makes both the city and the mayor look good. But the benefits are not merely cosmetic. The green mandates have helped weave ecological building practices into the fabric of Chicago's design culture, giving architects the practice they need to design green private buildings. The sustainable standards also have uplifted the public realm.

"We calculate that we are removing the air pollution from 40,000 cars a year," said Sadhu Johnston, Daley's deputy chief of staff and former commissioner of the Department of Environment. Referring to the view of City Hall's green roof from adjacent skyscrapers, he explained: "You're looking down at a prairie with dragonflies, butterflies, and birds. You're seeing the wind blowing the grass instead of a black roof with heat waves on it."

Johnston pointed to other benefits of green roofs, such as a reduction of the urban heat island effect, which makes cities hotter than suburbs and rural areas because a great proportion of the urban land has been developed with hard-surfaced, heat-retaining materials. "We estimate that if we can bring the temperature of the city down by one degree, the public and private sector will save $150 million a year in cooling costs," Johnston said. More people could be out on the streets instead of being holed up in air-conditioned apartments.

Despite its impressive achievements, Chicago's environmental record is hardly spotless. The *Chicago Tribune* recently reported that the city's emissions of pollution have soared since 2001, when Daley vowed to make Chicago a leader in the battle against global warming. Officials of the Chicago Climate Exchange, the financial institution that seeks to cut greenhouse gases through its cap-and-trade system, respond that the city is meeting its emission reduction commitments. Daley also has faced criticism over his failed "blue bag" recycling program, which calls for residents to buy plastic bags and put recyclables in them. Only about one of every ten Chicago households participates in the program, and the city recycles less than 8 percent of the garbage it collects.

Even Johnston acknowledged that the 27 LEED buildings in Chicago constitute a tiny fraction of the green buildings needed to make the city more sustainable. The number is even less significant when viewed within the framework of the energy-wasting sprawl that continues to transform the Chicago region. Suburban subdivisions now reach all the way out to Ludwig Mies van der Rohe's Farnsworth House, built as a rural retreat about 60 miles southwest of the city. "You can live in a wonderful green mansion and work in a wonderful green office," Johnston said, "but if you're driving two hours between the two, it doesn't really matter."

To battle sprawl, Daley has joined with other mayors from the region to form the "Greenest Region Compact," but it is unlikely that fledgling alliance will have the sort of legislative teeth that has given regional planning in Portland its bite. Within the city's limits, Johnston speaks of the need to focus on greening existing buildings, such as Hartshorne Plunkard Architecture's recent recycling of the 24-story, Daniel Burnham Jr.–designed Medical Dental Arts building into a LEED-certified apartment high-rise. While such conversions are far less sexy than new buildings like New York City's Hearst Tower, they will do far more, given the sheer numbers of older buildings, to conserve energy.

Given Daley's passion for green architecture, it should surprise no one that Chicago is not waiting for a lagging Bush administration to take action. One example: targeted greening, which plants trees in industrial areas to combat the urban heat island effect. It also uses green roofs to reduce storm water runoff and prevent flooded basements. Such efforts, which unite the local with the global, offer a pragmatic path toward the essential shift that the green movement still has to make: from green buildings and green infrastructure to a green way of life.

GreenSource

By the fall of 2009, Chicago had jumped ahead of Portland and Seattle to become the U.S. city with the most LEED-certified buildings—88 in all, compared to Portland's 73 and Seattle's 63. The city's more than threefold increase from 2007 reflected a broadening of LEED's reach nationwide, with the number of certified structures rising above 3,100. But critics argued that LEED, which uses a checklist system that awards points for a broad variety of energy-saving features, is not an adequate standard for future environmental challenges and the coming "carbon-neutral" era.

Writing in Metropolis *magazine in 2007, architecture critic James Russell attacked the practice of "point mongering," which he called "the cherry picking of low-effort strategies—some bamboo flooring, a couple of never-used bike racks—that raise the score without doing much of real environmental significance." Underscoring such concerns, the* New York Times *reported in 2009 that some LEED-rated buildings had been outfitted with inefficient mechanical systems and did not live up to their green laurels. In response, the U.S. Green Building Council announced it would start to collect energy-use information from all LEED-certified buildings.*

Starting from "Net Zero"

FIRST-OF-ITS-KIND HOME IN CHICAGO WILL PRODUCE AS MUCH ENERGY AS IT USES

JULY 22, 2009

Michael Yannell's ComEd bill is almost surely less than yours. The 44-year-old Yannell lives in a new Chicago home that is designed to be "net zero," which means it will produce as much energy as it consumes—or more. The $1.6 million, 2,675-square-foot house is the first of its kind in Chicago, a city that already has won blue ribbons for green architecture with energy-saving public buildings and scores of planted roofs.

Yet the Yannell House—which has four bedrooms, two bathrooms, and three occupants (the owner and his two cats)—is more than a mere technical feat. Clean-lined outside and light-filled within, it issues an elegant rebuttal to the supersize, decoration-slathered McMansions that exemplify the pre-crash age of excess.

THE YANNELL HOUSE
Chicago's first "net zero" home, designed to enhance its environs and the environment.

"I wanted to make a big, splashy statement to the city that that was the wrong direction," said Yannell, standing next to a kitchen countertop partly made of recycled newspapers.

It can be argued, of course, that there's something supremely excessive about a man spending so much money on an extra-large home for himself and his cats. But in taking aim at the custom-home market, Yannell is posing an iconoclastic challenge—saying, in effect, to the architects and developers of McMansions: My big house is greener than your big house.

If nothing else, his house shatters stereotypes, proving that hyper-green construction is as possible in frequently cloudy Chicago as in sun-drenched Colorado. "It can be done in pretty much any climate," said Ren Anderson of the National Renewable Energy Laboratory in Golden, Colorado.

In truth, though, it is more challenging in cloudy Chicago, and defining exactly what constitutes net zero can be elusive. Further complicating things, net zero houses tend to require net zero occupants. Forget it if you're going to flood your trees in outdoor lights or stick energy-sucking plasma TVs on walls. Yannell, for his part, has two energy-saving LCD

TVs. "They have kill switches, so they draw no power in the off mode," he said proudly.

A pharmacist at Rush University Medical Center, he is the ideal client for this sort of thing, possessing both ample funds and a zealous level of commitment. By his own calculation, he spent 40 hours researching energy-saving appliances. At first, he simply wanted to build an energy-efficient house. So he went to Farr Associates, one of the city's top green firms. When the architects introduced him to the more ambitious net zero concept, he said "yes" to the upgrade.

"We thought this was a gift from God," Jonathan Boyer, a Farr principal and the house's chief designer, said with a laugh.

Lining the Metra tracks in the Ravenswood neighborhood, the house signals that a well-designed net zero home should be about more than slapping a huge array of photovoltaic panels on a roof. All the elements of good architecture, from the site plan to the details, have to do what they normally do while simultaneously helping to keep the utility bill down. This is integrated green, not superficial green.

The floor plan—a U shape consisting of two non-identical wings joined by a foyer—nicely breaks down the house's mass and helps save energy in the bargain. Each wing has broad bands of triple-paned windows that face southward, drawing in lots of natural light. The roof's broad overhangs, their angle calculated by computer modeling, block the high summer sun. The south wing, which houses the kitchen as well as living and dining areas, is about 10 feet shorter than the north wing, home to bedrooms, an office, and a music room. That lets light filter into the second-story bedrooms and doesn't disrupt views.

The house is equally good at projecting its green identity outward. Its exuberant "butterfly" roof folds upward with sculptural verve, even as it cleverly hides the house's 48 photovoltaic panels and doubles as a rainwater collector. Coming closer, you encounter a delicate "rain screen" facade that deftly combines warm cedar panels and cool fiber-cement board panels. The facade, which screens out the rain while an inner layer provides insulation, seems to breathe like a skin. "Environmental expressionism," Boyer calls it.

The interior is remarkably light-filled and airy, fully taking advantage of the house's unencumbered views to the south.

In the expansive south wing, the underside of the butterfly roof seems to alight on a long steel beam that creates column-free spaces in the combined kitchen, living, and dining area. Tactile details, like the wall tiles made of recycled green-glass bottles, further the impression that the home is handcrafted, not an impersonal machine. Only the passing Metra trains interrupt the serenity, and their sound is muffled by triple-paned glass. The north wing offers pleasures of its own: views back across the courtyard, plus a master bedroom and guest bedroom that feel like tree houses.

The equally green basement has geothermal heating and cooling machines linked to three wells dug 250 feet down. It also features a Rube Goldberg contraption of pipes and filters for the house's gray-water system, which converts spent water from the house's washing machine to clean water that can be used in its toilets. It is believed to be the first gray-water system in a Chicago single-family home.

Boyer projects that the array of photovoltaic and solar-thermal panels will generate 18,000 kilowatt hours a year, exceeding the house's projected energy use by 40 percent. To date, Yannell has paid one ComEd bill of $29.57, despite feeding his surplus energy into the grid. (He gets some electricity from the power company at night.) "ComEd hasn't set up my meter to credit me," he groused.

Net zero houses like his offer the tantalizing prospect of off-the-grid living, where each house serves as its own power plant. Just don't expect a net zero revolution any time soon. The Yannell House's green features added 10 to 15 percent in upfront costs, and it could take years for the owner to recoup that premium. That helps explain why there are only about 100 net zero houses scattered around the United States. Nonetheless, Yannell's eye-catching experiment reveals that a net zero house can do more than just generate surplus energy. It can offer a model, as this house does, for a new way of building—and living.

POSTSCRIPT

By late 2009, the Yannell House had achieved the highest level of recognition from the U.S. Green Building Council, a LEED (Leadership in Energy and Environmental Design) platinum rating. And it was well on its way to attaining net zero energy status. According to Boyer, the house's photovoltaic panels surpassed 80 percent of their expected annual energy production in little more than half a year of operation. Yannell's low-energy usage increased the likelihood that the house would prove its net zero credentials after being lived in for a full year. "We expect to exceed our own model by a sizable margin," Boyer said.

Temple of Green

IN THE GRAND RAPIDS ART MUSEUM, A MEASURED APPROACH
TO DESIGN REVEALS THAT ELEGANCE AND ENVIRONMENTALISM
ARE NOT INCOMPATIBLE

APRIL 2008

For years, trying to duplicate the Bilbao effect, museums have competed to be more spectacular. Now, it seems, they're vying to be more virtuous—virtuous as in green. In San Francisco, Renzo Piano's soon-to-open California Academy of Sciences aims to be the nation's first museum to achieve the highest Leadership in Energy and Environmental Design (LEED) rating—platinum. In Denver, David Adjaye's Museum of Contemporary Art seeks the next highest level of LEED certification, gold. Then there is the new LEED gold-status Grand Rapids Art Museum (GRAM), which claims to be the world's first all-new green art museum. That superlative matters less than the building's achievements, which are considerable.

This handsome temple of art is, in many respects, a myth-buster. Art museums are widely believed to be "sustainability-proof" because they expend enormous amounts of energy maintaining constant temperature and humidity levels to protect their precious contents. Yet this building reveals that a balance between art and environmentalism is possible—if and only if architects, clients, and contractors factor energy savings into every aspect of the design equation. That means borrowing green strategies from conventional structures as well as devising new techniques to satisfy the needs of this demanding building type. "Typical green solutions are often not best," said the LEED case study of the museum, prepared by the design and construction team and sent to the U.S. Green Building Council as part of the museum's successful green submission.

Designed by Thai-born architect Kulapat Yantrasast of Los Angeles–based wHY Architecture, the $75 million, 125,000-square-foot art museum fronts on a vibrant, Maya Lin–designed public plaza in the heart of downtown Grand Rapids, western Michigan's largest city. Home to renowned furniture makers Steelcase, Herman Miller, Knoll, and Haworth, the region already has a rich lode of LEED projects. This one owes its green streak to former Steelcase executive Peter Wege. In 2001 he pledged $20 million to the project, with one string attached: The building would have to be LEED-certified.

Yantrasast, who replaced the museum's initial pick of London-based Munkenbeck + Marshall, turned out to be an ideal choice—a team player who brought Wege's vision to life without resorting to the obvious. The mu-

THE GRAND RAPIDS ART MUSEUM
Achieving a balance between elegance and environmentalism.

seum has no solar panels and no green roof. It is not partly buried in the earth, as is Steven Holl's acclaimed addition to the Nelson-Atkins Museum of Art in Kansas City, Missouri. Instead, the design shows that a museum—or any building, for that matter—doesn't have to look green to be green.

Roughly E-shaped in plan, the museum faces Lin's plaza like a modern version of an ancient temple, the concrete canopy of its entrance pavilion soaring powerfully over thin supporting slabs. Three stacked gallery towers and their sober, squared-off skylights rise to the rear. At night they are transformed into glowing lanterns that memorably advertise the museum's presence. Water is one of the principal themes of Lin's plaza, where a sunken, oval-shaped outdoor room becomes a skating rink in the winter months. The museum picks up on that gesture with its own reflecting pool and water wall.

The urban design subtly reinforces the building's green goals, so subtly that a lot of what it does is literally invisible. Grand Rapids gets a lot of lake-effect snow because it is near the eastern rim of Lake Michigan. To encourage walking, the museum put snowmelt coils underneath sidewalks on surrounding streets. While the coils consume some energy, it is thought they will save far more by getting people out of their cars. In auto-obsessed Michigan, this constitutes radical behavior. The same goes for the museum's public parking lot: it didn't build one. There were already five parking structures within the block.

The green features aren't one-dimensional; they serve broader humanistic aims. The canopy, which shields the interior from the hot summer sun, also shelters an outdoor dining area where museumgoers observe the goings-on in the adjoining plaza. (Well, at least they watch in the warm months; they still duck inside to avoid the bitter winter cold.)

Yantrasast's architecture has more in common with the restrained minimalism of Japanese master Tadao Ando than the explosive baroque modernism of Frank Gehry—no surprise since he is an Ando protégé, having served as project architect on Ando's Modern Art Museum in Fort Worth, Texas. While his building can't match Ando's silky-smooth concrete, it compensates by being far more approachable than a typical Ando fortress.

The E-shaped footprint nicely opens the museum to natural light while Yantrasast skillfully articulates the exterior envelope, enhancing the impression of permeability. On every elevation, he leavens the concrete's massiveness with broad expanses of glass or screen-like aluminum louvers. One facade, in particular, strikes up an effective dialogue with a row of nearby Victorian commercial buildings that resemble the scene in Edward Hopper's *Early Sunday Morning*. Such context-sensitive architecture matters. If you want people to walk and save energy, you'd better give them attractive streetscapes.

Yet the museum's very openness raises the issue of how it can protect its collection from damage wrought by natural light. In public areas, such as the serene entry hall, the answer is a light-filtering system consisting of fixed aluminum louvers as well as energy-saving glass. In the handsomely proportioned upstairs galleries, which are topped by the cube-shaped skylights, light seeps in through multiple layers of glass and, sandwiched in between, operable louvers. For the museum-going public, the solution offers the best of both worlds: the art is protected, yet visitors can see it in filtered natural light.

As on the exterior, many of the most significant sustainable elements are deftly hidden to gallery-goers. The green mandate eliminated toxic substances like carpet glues that can damage art through off-gassing. Behind the gallery walls is marine plywood rather than interior-grade plywood, which is made with toxic urea-formaldehyde glues.

The HVAC system is similarly sophisticated. Galleries and public spaces are equipped with carbon-dioxide sensors that pump more fresh air into a room if it gets crowded with people. In a conventional building, an empty room is an empty room. Not in a museum. "The works of art don't go home at the end of the day," said director Celeste Adams. "At night," she explained, "everything stays at 70 degrees, but the airflow lessens, so the engineers are not pushing as much air through the building." Large energy-recovery wheels, frequently used in research laboratories, condition incoming fresh air, overcoming the hurdle that museums can't use natural ventilation as readily as other buildings.

Two other green features deserve mention. Cisterns tucked beneath the museum collect rainwater for the building's non-potable water system, which is used to flush toilets, irrigate outdoor plants, and provide water for the reflecting pool and water wall. The system is supposed to cut the museum's demand for city-treated water by 20 percent. In addition, gallery mock-ups revealed that 75- to 100-watt halogen lamps would suffice in the art display spaces even though the fittings could take up to 250 watts. Using the lower-wattage lamps is expected to reduce electricity bills as well as cooling loads in summer.

"You can't set goals that are too precise," said Thomas Calmeau, project manager for the owner's representative, the RISE Group, based in Chicago and Anchorage, Alaska. "You have to see where the decision takes you and where the aesthetic takes you."

Admittedly, none of this is very sexy, but the LEED case study projects that the HVAC and light-system measures will reduce energy costs by a sizable 34 percent compared to a typical building. How is it working? "The systems are stabilizing. We think it probably takes at least a year of operating results to say, 'Yes, everything is performing the way it was intended,'" said George Bourassa, national director of commissioning for Jacobs Carter Burgess, the museum's commissioning authority.

Even with its green scorecard incomplete, the Grand Rapids Art Museum points in a new direction, one in which art and environment are viewed as partners, not antagonists. That is as it should be, Adams observed, because museums are about prolonging the life of works of art and the green movement seeks to extend the life of the planet. "That," she said, "should make for a very happy marriage."

GreenSource

POSTSCRIPT

Exceeding its energy goals, the Grand Rapids Art Museum was using 36 percent less energy per square foot than in its previous building, museum officials reported in the fall of 2009. According to figures provided by the U.S. Green Building Council, the museum was one of 44 LEED-certified buildings in Grand Rapids, ranking the small midwestern city eighth among all U.S. cities in the number of LEED buildings—ahead of much-larger cities such as Los Angeles, Boston, and Houston. Rated on a per-capita basis, Grand Rapids was surely near—or at—the very top.

5 | A NEW ERA AND NEW CHALLENGES

ON THE NIGHT OF NOVEMBER 4, 2008, WHEN BARACK OBAMA WAS ELECTED to the presidency, a very different sort of spectacle played out than the ones the nation had witnessed on September 11 and in the aftermath of Hurricane Katrina. That night showcased Chicago in all its splendor, with flag-waving crowds gathering in Grant Park and brightly lit skyscrapers soaring behind them. Yet the scene of hope took place against a broader, far more sobering backdrop—the near-collapse of the nation's financial system, rising unemployment that would only get worse, and the end of years of lavish spending in all realms of American life. A year later, the euphoria of that night in Grant Park had vanished, replaced by bitter controversy over several of Obama's initiatives, including his chief economic recovery measure, the $787 billion federal stimulus package.

The ongoing financial crisis coincided closely with the 100th anniversary of Daniel Burnham and Edward Bennett's visionary *Plan of Chicago*, and thus provided an opportunity to ponder how the future of America's sprawling urban regions might be different from—and greener than—the present. In the years proceeding Obama's election, the drive to redevelop the hurricane-ravaged Mississippi Gulf Coast and New Orleans forcefully demonstrated how housing was back on the architectural agenda—and how architects needed to look beyond their narrow ideological agendas if they were to serve the needs of an ever more diverse society.

The charged debate over Obama's stimulus package would shine a spotlight on the often-overlooked networks of transportation, water, and power that typically come to the public's attention only when they fail to work. Chicago's experience under Mayor Richard M. Daley revealed how these unheralded networks of infrastructure had enormous potential to either uplift or drag down the quality of life for all citizens.

REIMAGINING REGIONS
AND HOUSING

Going Forward

PLANNING FOR CHICAGO'S FUTURE REQUIRES BURNHAM-STYLE
VISION—AND A BIG PAIR OF GREEN-TINTED GLASSES

JANUARY 11, 2009

This could be a smashing year for Chicago, but not only for the reasons—including Barack Obama's inauguration—that probably come to mind. Specifically, 2009 could make a historic mark because it will give the residents of Chicago and its vast metropolitan area a chance to start a civic conversation about how we live, how we grow, and whether the mass suburban sprawl of the last few decades still makes sense in the era of declining fossil fuel supplies and global warming. There's a marvelous excuse to have this conversation. The region will be celebrating the 100th anniversary of one of the greatest city plans in history.

The Burnham Plan—named for its principal author, the Chicago architect and urban planner Daniel Burnham—was formally unveiled in 1909. Officially known as the *Plan of Chicago*, it proceeded to transform Chicago, then one of the ugliest cities in the world, into one of the most beautiful. Published as a book and filled with seductive renderings by artists such as Jules Guerin, it endowed the city with its renowned, nearly continuous chain of lakefront parks as well as a host of marquee public works, from Navy Pier to double-decked Wacker Drive. More important, it permanently encoded in Chicago's DNA the notion that change of any sort is possible, as long as it is backed by sufficient architectural vision, political muscle, and piles of money (think Millennium Park).

The plan's centennial, then, all but invites new forms of visionary thinking, even if the document and the extraordinary results it achieved set a daunting standard. And what sort of thinking is bubbling around? In a word, it's green—a color-coded vision that, like Burnham's utopian "White City" of the 1893 World's Columbian Exposition in Chicago, thoroughly reflects the urban aspirations of its time.

If the ideal in 1893 was to bring order to the chaotic industrial city through the creation of monumentally scaled, classically inspired, and rationally organized urban centers, the goal of many of today's planners, architects, and business and political leaders is tinged with an environmental sensibility borne of frustration with the relentless, low-density spread of homes—sprawl—ever farther from Chicago. This frustration is not the result of snobbery, as sprawl's defenders argue. Rather, it is the product of a conservation ethic that characterizes sprawl as wasteful, particularly at a time of economic crisis.

Sprawl forces the building of new streets, roads, sewers, and schools when much of our existing infrastructure is crumbling. It helps lead to traffic congestion that fouls the air and costs each Chicago-area commuter hundreds of dollars each year in wasted gas and time. It chews up acres of precious midwestern farmland. And it has human costs, separating people instead of building social bonds.

Planners of the new generation prefer compact, walkable communities to sprawling, auto-dependent suburbs. They want to use rail lines, both new and existing, to get people out of their cars, not only for local trips but for long-distance ones. They see wisdom in developing new forms of transit that reflect how jobs are scattered across metropolitan areas, no longer concentrated in downtowns. And they want to protect the open space the region already has while adding new parkland and trails in both the city and the suburbs.

Their aim is not a White City, but a Green Region.

To be sure, well-meaning planners have advocated such goals for decades but failed to stop sprawl's outward march. The lure of getting more house for the buck—coupled with cheap gas that allows people to traverse vast distances at little expense—has proved a potent foe. For decades, revenue-hungry suburbs have approved office buildings, factories, and shopping malls as if each community were an island, ignoring the regional consequences of their actions. But this time there's a change in the air and in the halls of power.

The green movement has infiltrated mass culture. Think of all those hybrid electric cars, energy-saving lightbulbs, and green roofs, like the one atop Chicago's City Hall. Within the suburbs, communities like Naperville, Evanston, and Arlington Heights have been carving out mixed-use hubs that combine restaurants, shops, entertainment, and in-town living. Urban analyst Joel Kotkin calls this trend "the new localism" and predicts that hard economic times may accelerate it as people tighten belts and look to Main Street, not the global stage, for a sense of connection.

And then there's this: Obama comes to the White House at least talking the talk of the "smart growth" advocates who oppose sprawl. He supports neighborhoods with sidewalks, for instance, so people will be encouraged to walk and lead healthier lifestyles. More important, he's pushing the idea that the traditional divide between cities and suburbs is Old Think. His New Think is that economies are regional and what's good for a city is also good for suburbs, and vice versa.

America needs "to stop seeing our cities as the problem and start seeing them as the solution," Obama told the U.S. Conference of Mayors last June, "because strong cities are the building blocks of strong regions, and strong regions are essential for a strong America. That is the new metropolitan reality and we need a new strategy that reflects it."

Which is all very nice, except smart-growth advocates already are taking shots at Obama's proposed, multibillion-dollar infrastructure program, saying it will merely repair the roads and bridges that undergird metropolitan areas rather than transforming sprawl. They're all but calling him "President Pothole."

A GLOBAL CITY

No one disputes that today's Chicago is a vastly different place than Burnham's Chicago. In 1909 the booming region was like an adolescent—gangly, full of energy, still taking shape. Today, by comparison, Chicago is mature, its bones (the expressways and commuter railroad lines) essentially set in place and unlikely to change. And yet, it would be foolish to say that Chicago has stopped growing or that we lack opportunities to shape—and reshape—its growth.

The city presides over a region of bewildering size and complexity. It sweeps in an arc along Lake Michigan from southeast Wisconsin to northwest Indiana and reaches outward to rich farmland some 60 miles from the black stalk of Sears Tower. In Illinois alone, this territory encompasses 7 counties, 283 municipalities, and 8.5 million people—9.3 million, counting southeast Wisconsin and northwest Indiana. Planners expect the region to add another 2.8 million people by 2040, which would bring its total population to more than 11.3 million. That leap would move Chicago into the league of what planners call a "mega-city region," a galactic collection of cities, suburbs, and suburbs of suburbs. In concept, if not in quantity, it already may be there.

Within the region, the old clichés of city and suburb no longer apply. Poor people live only in Chicago? Wrong. The suburbs now have more than 40 percent of the region's poor, nearly double their share in 1980, according to the Heartland Alliance Mid-America Institute on Poverty. The suburbs are just bedroom communities? Wrong. More people commute to work each day in DuPage County, just west of Cook County, than leave the county for jobs. The suburbs are boring? Wrong. Stand in downtown Naperville at the bustling corner of Washington and Chicago Avenues. You're within blocks of about 50 restaurants, every chain store you can imagine, a handsome river walk, the DuPage Children's Museum, one of the world's largest carillons, and a new concert hall at North Central College.

The combined population of Naperville and Aurora, its even larger neighbor to the west, is a staggering 318,000 people—nearly as large as such major-league midwestern cities as Cincinnati (330,000) and St. Louis (350,000). "Around here, 'the city' is Naperville," not Chicago, said Christine Jeffries, president of Naperville's Convention and Visitors Bureau.

THE RIVER WALK IN DOWNTOWN NAPERVILLE
A symbol of how suburbs and urban regions have changed.

Chicago itself, with 2.8 million people, is no longer a decaying Rust Belt city, as during the 1970s, but an ascendant global city, its multicultural flavor encapsulated by the mirrored, stainless-steel wonder of Millennium Park's *Cloud Gate*, designed by the London-based, Indian-born artist Anish Kapoor. The city's diverse economy has shielded it from the steep downturn of one-industry towns like Detroit, while its history of butchering hogs, making tools, and stacking wheat has propelled it to preeminence in the futures markets and a "knowledge economy," where its specialized law and accounting firms excel.

"A knowledge economy doesn't fall from the sky," explained Columbia University sociologist Saskia Sassen, an expert on the phenomenon of the global city. "It actually has its origins in material practice. If you are a steel firm in Utah and you want to go global, you don't go to New York. You go to Chicago. They know how to do it."

But, looking ahead, how can Chicago press its advantages as a global city and create a better quality of life in the bargain?

"BURNHAM 2.0": BIG PLANS, LITTLE CLOUT

One way, it seems, is to draw inspiration from the Burnham Plan and its emphasis on infrastructure as a multifaceted tool for building more beautiful, humane cities. This sort of thinking underlies a forward-looking exhibit at the Chicago History Museum, "Burnham 2.0: A Composite Plan for the High Speed Rail City." The show, shaped by guest curators David Goodman and Romina Canna of the Chicago Architectural Club, is based on the sound idea that a related series of small plans, rather than a single overarching vision, offers the most realistic strategy for channeling growth in this era. It suggests that Chicago should again position itself as a center of infrastructure, this time as a hub for a high-speed trains that run throughout the Midwest.

The show's green aspirations are captured by one of its most arresting images, prepared by Chicago architects Michael Wilkinson and Richard Blender, portraying the transformation of the infamous Circle interchange west of the Loop into a vital landscape where people, not cars, would rule. A new park would be built over the highway with terrarium-like scoops admitting light to the drivers below. Rail travelers would take public transit to an office/hotel center near the University of Illinois at Chicago campus. The architects cleverly call their plan "Circle Square," evoking the urbane public squares of Europe. It's a dazzling vision of the future. Just one problem: the park looks vast and un-enclosed, more *Blade Runner* than St. Peter's Square.

That same frustrating combination—a high-flying concept untethered from everyday reality—characterizes the show's competition-winning design for a high-speed rail hub on the block east of Union Station. The plan—by Michael Cady, Elba Gil, David Lillie, and Andrés Montaña of the Chicago office of tvsdesign—envisions a mostly underground station with a folded green roof that forms a kind of riverfront park. The scheme winningly makes the point that infrastructure can be more than anonymous urban machinery. Trouble is, there are two buildings on the block right now, including the 35-story 222 South Riverside Plaza office building.

But other proposals in the show are both visionary and achievable, like the landscape architect Peter Schaudt's vision for a "Mid-City Transitway" along 8.5 miles of Cicero Avenue. It calls for a new mass transit line that would link the CTA's Orange and Blue Lines, factories for green technology, and new open space. Solar panels on the roofs of the CTA stations would help power the trains. Here is a sustainable, 21st-century alternative to the 20th-century, car-centric vision of the late Mayor Richard J. Daley, who in the 1960s and 1970s unsuccessfully tried to ram a Crosstown Expressway down the Cicero corridor. "We looked at it as a working landscape that could give something back both in terms of sustainability and the economy," Schaudt said.

Like the Burnham Plan, the show uses architectural drawings as a tool to engage viewers and get the public excited about new visions for the future. What's missing from "Burnham 2.0," though, is a new Burnham, a galvanizing figure who can serve as a nexus between the worlds of power and taste. Burnham and his allies excelled at drawing together leading architects and businessmen—the dreamers and doers. The only Chicago architect who comes close today is Stanley Tigerman, and he's devoting extra time to the city's bid for the 2016 Summer Olympics—a good cause, but one that lacks the Burnham Plan's expansive focus. Without political muscle behind them, many of these worthy ideas are likely to remain nothing more than eye-popping renderings.

THE NEW REGIONAL PLANNERS: HOW HARD WILL THEY PUSH?

There's a hint of the old business/urban planning alliance in the work of another group, Chicago Metropolis 2020, headquartered in the Inland Steel Building at Monroe and Dearborn Streets. The Chicago nonprofit was created by the same organization of business leaders, the Commercial Club of Chicago, that backed Burnham's Plan. Its leaders want to use the centennial as an impetus to get things done, like new bike and walking paths to link to the region's existing network of trails. "I don't see that this

PLAN FOR A HIGH-SPEED RAIL TERMINAL IN CHICAGO
A 21st-century example of "make no little plans," but more visionary than achievable.

is justified as a celebration if it doesn't lead to results," said Metropolis 2020 president George Ranney.

The group's color-splashed, 36-page document, "The Metropolis Plan: Choices for the Chicago Region," focuses more on comprehensive, region-wide strategies than on individual projects. But the plan has a real radical streak, urging that the region adopt an entirely new set of land-use and transportation policies. It uses advanced computer modeling to reveal how much the policies it touts will change things: "The average resident of the Chicago region would spend 155 fewer hours a year in traffic—or four work weeks.... We would spare 300 square miles of open space from development.... We would save $3.7 billion in local, water, sewer and street costs."

Yet the most important legacy of Metropolis 2020 may not be its plan, but the process it has set in motion. In 2005 Metropolis 2020 was among those successfully pushing the state legislature to create a new agency called the Chicago Metropolitan Agency for Planning (CMAP). Responsible for land-use and transportation planning in the seven-county Chicago area, CMAP is either going to be a sleeping giant that puts real muscle behind the planning aims of Metropolis 2020 or a paper tiger whose smart-growth agenda is routinely flouted by the region's suburbs.

The obscure agency is ensconced on the eighth floor of Sears Tower and headed by Executive Director Randall S. Blankenhorn, a former Illinois

Department of Transportation official. Many urban planners despise IDOT for what they regard as its tunnel-vision perspective—putting new roads through cornfields with little regard for their broader impact—but Blankenhorn is winning good reviews. "He's a complete surprise for a guy who came out of IDOT," Ranney said. "We were terrified."

CMAP's potential for clout comes from its power to rank all proposed federally funded transportation projects in the region, thus determining which are most likely to get funding and how fast. In making the rankings, the agency will take into account a wide range of land-use factors, including provision for open space, access to public transit, and affordable housing.

"The process is going to be turned on its head," Blankenhorn explained. "Past plans have started with what transportation improvements we wanted or needed, and built a regional plan around it." Now, he adds, land-use considerations will be tied to transportation proposals. Say Metra wanted to extend a commuter line to Ottawa, more than 80 miles from the Loop. CMAP would say no. Instead, Blankenhorn said, priority should be given to projects "closer to downtown, closer to the job centers of the region."

Blankenhorn has no regulatory power. He can't tell suburbs what they can—or can't—build. He is essentially trying to find a middle way between the "anything goes" policies that enabled sprawl and a restrictive "urban growth boundary," like the one in Portland, Oregon, that would rein in sprawl by limiting new development outside the boundary. "There's going to have to be suburban growth," he said. "We hope it's not as rampant as it's been in the past."

Can CMAP strike this balance? That will become clearer in 2009 as the agency unveils its comprehensive plan for the region, called "GO TO 2040." The agency will present different scenarios of the region's growth to the public this spring and summer. By the fall of 2010, the plan will go for approval to CMAP's board, which represents Chicago, Cook County, and the collar counties. During public workshops, CMAP will work with the Chicago-based Congress for the New Urbanism, a leading anti-sprawl group comprised of architects, planners, and other design professionals, to help ordinary citizens visualize what the future might look like. Their art of persuasion will be crucial. To succeed, Blankenhorn said, "we have to convince the residents."

MISTAKES AND TENSIONS

It won't be easy, at least if one controversial development—Toyota Park, the 20,000-seat stadium that is home to the Chicago Fire soccer team—

offers any indication. Opened in 2006 at 71st Street and Harlem Avenue in southwest suburban Bridgeview, the stadium is a poster child for short-sighted, car-oriented development. It sits amid a sea of 8,000 parking spaces. There are no bike racks or bus shelters. It's even named for a car company.

Though he doesn't question the stadium's location, Blankenhorn considers it one of the region's biggest recent regional planning mistakes. "There was no thought of how people could get to Toyota Park by public transportation," he said.

But Bridgeview mayor Steve Landek defends the stadium, which is now served by express buses that link it to the CTA's Orange Line. Public transit amenities, including bike racks and bus shelters, will be added, he said. Most important, in his view, the stadium changes the image of his suburb from gritty warehouses to glamorous sporting events. "This is the entrée for the southwest suburbs to say, 'We can do it too,'" he said.

Such disputes hint at the tensions that will course through the region as it celebrates the Burnham Plan centennial and prepares a new comprehensive vision that strives to live up to the great plan's standard. Should local needs predominate or regional ones? What should the region's priorities be? Are people ready to move from green gadgetry to a green way of life?

So let the conversation over the Green Region begin. Just remember: A plan isn't a blueprint. It's a vision, an aspiration. You measure its impact over decades or a century. It's guaranteed that not all of the projects that a plan proposes actually will happen. What matters more is the direction it sets and how that direction affects our quality of life. The real power of the Burnham Plan is the power of an idea: that we are forever engaged in the process of making better cities and suburbs, and that we still have the capacity to do that—in a new century, confronting new realities and imagining a new and greener future.

Chicago Tribune Magazine

POSTSCRIPT

Seizing upon the 100th anniversary of the Plan of Chicago, *state legislators and open-space advocates in late 2009 announced a series of steps designed to create a new legacy of parks and trails throughout the Chicago area, including new lakefront parkland. The steps included legislation that would transfer 100 acres of south lakefront land from the Illinois International Port District to the Chicago Park District. The lakefront property, known as Iroquois Landing, occupies the site of a former steel mill just north of Calumet Park at 95th Street. In addition, Illinois governor Pat Quinn asked the U.S. Fish and Wildlife Service to study the feasibility of establishing a national wildlife refuge in northeast McHenry County and southeastern Wisconsin. The proposed refuge, called Hack-ma-tack, could include up to 10,000 acres. "The whole idea of the centennial was to have a green legacy, just as Burnham had a green legacy," said Emily Harris, executive director of the Burnham Plan Centennial Committee.*

Shortsighted Polemics

THE IDEOLOGICAL CATFIGHTS OVER HOUSING THREATEN TO
MARGINALIZE ALL OF ARCHITECTURE

APRIL 2006

I wasn't at some do-gooder Harvard symposium when I realized that housing was back on the architectural radar screen—and generating enough heat to prompt catfights. I was at, of all places, the Isle of Capri hotel-casino in Biloxi, Mississippi, whose gaudy green and purple walls are the antithesis of Boston red brick. At a conference there last October, John Norquist—the former three-term mayor of Milwaukee, and president and CEO of the Congress for the New Urbanism—started waving the bloody shirt.

In this case the shirt didn't have real blood on it. It was a *Washington Post* story, gleaned from the Internet, about a *charrette* for the hurricane-ravaged Mississippi coastline being run by the New Urbanists, those earnest purveyors of street grids, front porches, and white picket fences. The "Mississippi Renewal Forum" their *charrette* was called. Here were the poor New Urbanists staying up all hours of the night, gulping all the coffee and Red Bull they could take, and drawing up redevelopment plans for all 11 cities and towns along the coast, from Waveland to Pascagoula, in the seemingly impossible time frame of just seven days. And what did they get in response? They got a kick in the keister from Eric Owen Moss, director of SCI-Arc (Southern California Institute of Architecture). He told the *Post's* Linda Hales that the New Urbanists' traditional town planning "would appeal to a kind of anachronistic Mississippi that yearns for the good old days of the Old South as slow and balanced and pleasing and breezy, and each person knew his or her role." Moss didn't say that Andrés Duany and Elizabeth Plater-Zyberk, the leaders of the New Urbanists, wanted to bring back the Jim Crow laws, but he might as well have.

"How does he know? What does he know?" replied an infuriated James Barksdale, former Netscape CEO and head of Mississippi's rebuilding

effort, when I asked him about Moss's volley from afar. "I thought it
was a mean-spirited thing for him to say that we all want to go back
and own slaves." Actually I thought Barksdale was being charitable when
he characterized Moss's remarks: "arrogant" would have fit the bill—or
"blindly ideological." But at least Moss was engaged enough by what

was going on in Mississippi, and the stakes were high enough that he felt compelled to say something.

For decades, reflecting the narrow formalistic worldview of architecture's late godfather Philip Johnson, housing and community-building issues have been shoved off center stage. Modernist architects were barely debating them, pretty much leaving the field to the New Urbanists. But now it's impossible to ignore housing, and not just because of the damage wrought by Hurricane Katrina along the Mississippi Gulf Coast and in New Orleans. In city after city across America, tall towers are being proposed or built, and they are not office buildings but places to live. Santiago Calatrava's planned 2,000-foot Fordham Spire on Chicago's lakefront, the most visible example of the trend, prompted this wry *Los Angeles Times* headline: "Home Is Where the Height Is."

Here's my question: Now that architects are taking shots at one another over housing, can we do better than we did in the last century, which gave us sprawl for the middle class and Cabrini-Green for the poorest of the poor? Can we close the great divide between fetishistic formalism and social responsibility? Or are we doomed to a world in which architecture's leading practitioners use their work merely to comment on social tumult rather than actually trying to do something about it?

When the seminal show *Modern Architecture: International Exhibition* opened at New York's Museum of Modern Art in 1932, the critic Lewis Mumford wrote earnestly, "The building of houses constitutes the major architectural work of any civilization. . . . It is only during the last generation that we have begun to conceive of a new domestic environment which will utilize our technical and scientific achievements for the benefit of human living." Mumford's emphasis reflected the broad-based outlook of the pioneers of modernism, who were deeply concerned with houses and housing. Exhibit A (which really was an exhibit): the 1927 Weissenhof housing colony in Stuttgart, a hillside collection of 21 buildings with white rectilinear exteriors, flat roofs, and balconies that resembled a ship's railing. These low-cost experimental designs by Ludwig Mies van der Rohe, Le Corbusier, Walter Gropius, and other leading modernists represented, according to Mies biographer Franz Schulze, "the fullest communal realization of the new art of building in concert with progressive politics."

To Johnson, on the other hand, modernism was simply a style, a phenomenon of art history, something that might reflect the human condition but wouldn't really deal with the condition of humans. His cockeyed worldview is still with us. Today the stars don't join forces to design housing for the masses. They get together to design different floors in a gimmick hotel, like the Hotel Puerta América in Madrid, where you get the fluid spaces and explosive lines of Zaha Hadid on one floor, the cool high-tech aesthetic of Lord Norman Foster on another, and so on. *Vive les starchitectes!* Just let me know when the revolution begins. Nothing could be further from the handsome sobriety of Mies's white-walled apartment house in Weissenhof or the transcendent thoughts behind it: "More important than the demand for material quality is that for spiritual quality."

All this is to say that the leading avant-garde modernists of our time, unlike their predecessors, are pretty much without a program for housing. Frank Gehry likes to call himself a "liberal do-gooder," and he does the occasional socially conscious design, but let's face it: his lefty-ness is really about progressive aesthetics, not progressive politics. And yet a world without an intelligent debate about housing is not a world you want to live in—trust me. Here in Chicago during the mid-20th century, the politics of race and class, along with bureaucratic cost-cutting, produced the ultimate perversion of Weissenhof—the endless anonymous, crime-ridden high-rises of the Chicago Housing Authority, which proved of so little lasting public value that many of them are being torn down.

But as they fall, other monsters are rising, spiritless concrete slabs heaped atop hulking parking-garage podiums. This is "plop architecture," or public housing for the urban rich. Even when the podiums get tarted up with traditional decoration, they deaden the streetscape like neutron bombs. As much as I'm excited by the prospect of Calatrava's "drill bit" corkscrewing into the Chicago sky, it's just another one-off. I'd much prefer it if someone could develop a typology that would allow lesser talents to craft downtown living quarters that are civilized if less spectacular than the Fordham Spire.

There are dangers, too, along the Gulf Coast, although I found the New Urbanists' plans for Mississippi persuasive, at least in their attempt to diagram pedestrian- and transit-oriented cities and towns. The dipped-in-aspic nostalgic vocabulary I can do without, however, especially if it proves unaffordable to all but the rich and the haute bourgeoisie. If the New Urbanists produce something in Mississippi that resembles the River Garden mixed-income housing development in New Orleans—where faux French Quarter buildings, faux shotgun houses, and faux classical revival homes form a bland suburban tableau—then the rebuilding will be a cultural catastrophe, substituting fake versions of vernacular housing as the real ones are being demolished.

Forget the rampant aestheticism and architectural blinders of the 20th century. We live in a pluralistic age, and it demands a new pragmatism. We are beyond "either/or"—we live in a world of "both/and." The issues are quality, habitability, and sustainability, not style du jour. The issue is real urbanism, not some polite, politically palatable "lite" version thereof. I'll take good New Urbanism, just like I'll take good modernism. But it's not about the starchitects and their ideologies anymore. Can't the catfighting parties on the different ends of the aesthetic spectrum just grow up and get along?

Metropolis Magazine

POSTSCRIPT

Four years after Hurricane Katrina and the Mississippi Renewal Forum, few of the New Urbanists' ideas to reduce sprawl and create more pedestrian-friendly, mixed-use communities had been implemented. The Clarion-Ledger *of Jackson, Mississippi, reported in 2009 that only one of the 11 cities and towns that took part in the forum, Pass Christian, had enacted the zoning changes recommended for it. "Others are putting the suggestions on hold or dismissing them as unrealistic, mostly because of unavailable or unaffordable insurance, a rocky economy and a resistance to change," the newspaper said.*

While aspects of the plans appeared to have had made their way onto official agendas—Biloxi, for example, was said to be planning a mixed-use development downtown—the consensus was that the Mississippi Renewal Forum had been a visionary exercise untempered by pragmatism. Former governor William Winter—an adviser to Governor Haley Barbour's Commission on Recovery, Rebuilding, and Renewal—told the Clarion-Ledger *that another forum might be necessary because the planners "failed to take into consideration some of the practical aspects of rebuilding." In Chicago, however, creative new solutions to the problem of housing already were being implemented.*

CHA Polishes Its Rough Edges

ARCHITECT DRESSES UP THE DEARBORN HOMES,
GEORGIAN STYLE, AND UPGRADES LIVING SPACES INSIDE

MAY 22, 2009

For years, public housing in America was designed according to a simple, mean-spirited creed: Don't just make it cheap. Make it look cheap. This was the shortsighted thinking, along with the misguided policy of jamming too many poor people into isolated warrens of poverty, that helped produce the now-demolished Robert Taylor Homes and the Chicago Housing Authority's other high-rise hells.

THE RENOVATED DEARBORN HOMES
Who says public housing can't be Georgian?

So it is a welcome shock to come upon the limestone decoration that adorns the once-drab brick towers of Chicago's Dearborn Homes public housing complex on South State Street. When they opened in 1950, the Dearborn Homes were the first CHA project to have elevator buildings instead of walk-ups. Now they are the first CHA project to get a classical makeover. You could pick up one of these buildings and put it down on Sheridan Road in Evanston, and no one would blink.

Backed by $28 million in federal stimulus funds, the ongoing $165.6 million Dearborn Homes renovation offers a rare bright spot amid Chicago's problem-plagued attempt to transform its notorious public housing. Here, architects are operating as design doctors, performing a combination of cosmetic and internal surgery to give new life to old buildings—and to help residents climb out of poverty.

So far, three of the Dearborn Homes' 16 buildings have been renovated and occupied. The rest will be done in phases, with the remake scheduled to be finished in 2012. The project is costing about $250,000 per apartment unit—considerably less than the $300,000 to $325,000 per unit it takes to build the housing authority's scattered-site apartments.

"It's a lot nicer than it used to be," Tawanna Williams, 32, a cosmetologist, said as she sat in front of her building at 2940 South State Street and surveyed a tension-free scene of kids playing. "It's not just Band-Aids."

The design doctor in this case is Henry Zimoch, 57, a principal at the Chicago architectural firm of HPZS and a 1975 graduate of the architecture school at the neighboring Illinois Institute of Technology. IIT is a bastion of steel-and-glass modernism, but Zimoch is no modernist ideologue. He even likes Georgian architecture, the colonial style (think Williamsburg) known for its strong symmetry and geometrical proportions.

Zimoch's approach at the Dearborn Homes was refreshingly simple: Work with the existing buildings and dress them up, Georgian style.

The buildings, six and nine stories tall, are tightly bunched amid narrow open spaces bounded by 27th and 30th Streets, Metra's Rock Island District Line, and State Street. These are the modernist "superblocks" that were supposed to provide a refuge from noisy city streets but instead isolated public housing's residents from the city around them. The original architects, Loebl, Schlossman & Bennett, designed the cross-shaped structures to encourage cross-ventilation and introduce sunlight. That was before they became vertical slums.

To most eyes, the buildings were simply brick hulks. But Zimoch knew they had good bones. And he could envision that they might be more receptive to a classical makeover than the CHA's more overtly modernist buildings, with their exposed concrete frames.

So he gave the flat-roofed structures triangle-shaped, limestone gables, topped by balls that etch a profile against the sky. Brick was removed from the corners and replaced with corner details called quoins. These limestone touches endow the once-bland buildings with a sense of texture as well as sharply defined edges. The old concrete entrance canopies were enclosed within new classically styled metal porches, which provide better shelter from the weather and a place to post each building's address.

The total cost of the adornments, Zimoch estimates, is 1 percent of the project's budget, roughly $1.7 million. In public housing's old mind-set, such an outlay would have been branded wasted money. Now, it's the ounce of prevention that's worth a pound of cure.

The CHA could have demolished the Dearborn Homes and built cheap new housing, but that simply would have replaced "vertical slums with horizontal slums," said Bill Little, the agency's executive vice president of development.

While the revamped buildings aren't going to win prizes for perfect proportions, they erase the stigma of subsidized housing and signal to residents and outsiders alike that this is a place where the norms of everyday life apply. So far, CHA officials and residents insist, it seems to be working.

"You might see a few zombies walking up and down the street, but now you only see a few of them," said Williams, who lived in the Dearborn Homes as a child and later returned. "Now, you see people walking dogs and jogging."

It would have been a cruel charade if only the exteriors of the Dearborn Homes had been revamped, but, happily, as I learned during a tour of the completed renovation at 2920 South State Street, that is not the case. The building was gutted down to its concrete frame and new plumbing, heating, and electrical systems were installed. Corridors were upgraded with walls of bright blue-and-white glazed tile. The apartments got touches of normalcy that are taken for granted in private housing—doorbells, more closet space, closet doors, modern appliances, and air-conditioning.

True, the total number of rental units will be reduced to around 660 from the original 800, due to the need to provide four-bedroom apartments and to comply with the Americans with Disabilities Act. And the rehab did not change fundamental urban planning shortcomings of the Dearborn Homes.

A mother in a ninth-floor high-rise unit cannot adequately supervise her child playing on the ground below. Streets were not reintroduced to break up the superblocks, as they have been in other public housing retrofits like Boston's Harbor Point. All the Dearborn buildings will look the same after the renovation—an upgrade, to be sure, but one that will lack the visual variety and expression of individuality of conventional American neighborhoods. At worst, Dearborn will remain a project, just a dressed-up project.

But the smartly rehabbed buildings and interiors provide reason for hope, as does the addition of private building managers, strict tenant-screening policies, and attention to the residents' social needs. Combine all those things and you have the prospect of a humane habitat—a significant shift from the bad old days when public housing was supposed to be (and look) cheap.

POSTSCRIPT

This story provoked a storm of reaction on my Cityscapes *blog, with some readers asserting that the Dearborn Homes renovation was a waste of taxpayer dollars.*

"No amount of money can ever fix this problem," said a commentator who called himself Libertarian Michael. "They DON'T WANT a chance at a good life," he said of CHA residents. The urban historian Dominic A. Pacyga of Columbia College Chicago disagreed. "I passed by these buildings just the other day . . . and I was startled at how nice they looked," he wrote. "Of course, social problems will persist, but good architecture (even a remake like this example) will lead to better communities, to a better community spirit. Thank goodness we are finally beginning to realize the importance of that for the American city."

Brick by Brick

BORN AS A HORSE STABLE, THE BRICK WEAVE HOUSE PROVIDES
THE PERFECT HOME FOR A PAIR OF URBANITE GEARHEADS

OCTOBER 2009

You know you're not in Kansas anymore when the owners of a provocatively revamped horse stable in Chicago stroll you around their quirky neighborhood. Take that yellow house across the street; legend has it that the owner's father won it in a card game. The rest of the block is a crazy quilt of turn-of-the-century worker's cottages, bastardized Italianate three-flats, and clumsily composed yuppie town houses known (not affectionately) as "Polish contractor specials."

Now this crazy quilt has a new patch: the Brick Weave House, so named by its architect, Jeanne Gang of Studio Gang Architects. Designed for advertising executives David Hernandez and Tereasa Surratt, the house is in gentrifying West Town, about two miles northwest of the muscular skyline of Chicago's Loop. The house's name comes from its most distinctive feature, a tall, two-sided, technically adventurous brick screen that shelters a walled garden and gives the owners the privacy they crave while letting honeycomb patterns of natural light pour inside. At night, the brick screen becomes a dazzling light box.

The house's interior is, in its own way, equally unconventional. There is no kitchen island, no flat-screen TV, no basement, no attic. What really sets the house apart, though, is the playful theatricality with which Gang spotlights Hernandez and Surratt's collection of cars and motorcycles. They're displayed like sculptures, on view from the dining room through a curtain-framed opening that leads directly into the garage. The detail is emblematic of how Gang embraced her clients' individuality, making art out of idiosyncrasy. Together, the exterior and interior reveal how architects are responding to new patterns of living that break from the conventions of the suburban single-family home or the yuppie town house, where the kitchen invariably flaunts granite countertops and a Sub-Zero refrigerator.

In the 1880s the Brick Weave House began its life as a wood-frame stable; over the years it grew haphazardly, slowly encrusting with brick additions, a lean-to structure, and some god-awful postwar siding. "During construction, we found large mammal bones—we assumed they were horses', not humans'," said Hernandez, 42, managing director and executive creative director of the Chicago office of Tribal DDB Worldwide.

He bought the property in 1999, attracted by its convenient, close-in location; its extra-wide lot (40 feet as opposed to the 25-foot Chicago standard); and the high-ceilinged stable space, a perfect spot to store cars and "wrench on projects." Yet the place was so ugly that when Surratt drove Hernandez home on one of their first dates, he had her drop him off a block away so she wouldn't see it.

Phase one of its transformation occurred in 2003 with a made-for-TV makeover by Nate Berkus, Oprah Winfrey's interior designer, who redid the back of the house as a sexy bachelor pad. Berkus punched a big win-

THE BRICK WEAVE HOUSE
A livable modernism, where architecture accommodates human quirks rather than ruthlessly editing them out.

dow in the back wall, splashed the floor with orange paint, and threw in Barcelona chairs and other hip furniture—enough, in other words, to look good on TV. Yet Hernandez wanted more. He pondered a restoration that would celebrate the weathered barn doors and other historic details.

But excavation revealed that too much of the original structure was gone to make authentic the rehab he had sketched on tracing paper. "It was too Disneyland," he said. "It was a facade for something that was false."

Instead, he and Surratt, 37, a creative director at Ogilvy Chicago, opted for a complete remake. On the recommendation of a friend, they hired Gang, who had won plaudits for innovative civic designs and will soon complete Aqua, an 82-story mixed-use Chicago skyscraper. Her decision to redo the stable—her first completed house—inverted the usual order of architects working their way up from houses to larger commissions. But she was attracted by the prospect of collaborating with two visual types who were passionate about design and promised not to get in her way.

"Our carrot is that we'll be the best clients you ever have. Now here's the five-dollar budget," Surratt jokingly told her. Actually, the budget was $140 a square foot, which comes out to about $450,000 for what is now a 3,200-square-foot house.

Gang's first big move subtracted an 800-square-foot chunk of the house's front, making room for the brick screen and walled garden. The screen, which consists of Norman brick with custom-made hardware in the joints, is supported by steel columns and beams that extend outward from the roof as well as horizontal trusses embedded in mortar. It is the latest in Gang's experiments with materials, making what is usually heavy and solid seem light, almost porous.

Though the result may not convince those who insist that a house's windows and doors should suggest a human face, it is not anti-urban. "It's not a wall; people come and stare through," Gang explained. The house is more social than it seems on account of its street-facing garage, which lets the couple visit with neighbors who park their cars on the street or slide up their own garage doors and tinker with their cars. Call it "gearhead urbanism."

In the tradition of Frank Lloyd Wright, the route to the front door is a path of discovery, forcing you to make turns and pass through the walled garden's soaring space. Once inside, you quickly grasp how Gang met and exceeded her clients' brief: flowing spaces suitable for big parties, integrated storage that compensates for the absence of an attic or basement, a small kitchen, and upstairs rooms that can convert to bedrooms.

To accomplish all this, Gang reversed the previous floor plan, converting the high-ceilinged stable to two floors of living space while placing the new garage on the house's flanks, where before there had been living space. The key is that the vehicle storage and the house are integrated, not separated.

From the sleekly furnished dining room, you peer straight into the garage through an opening accented by orange velvet curtains. You'll see a yellow 1968 Camaro Rally Sport or a mauve-and-black 1966 Dodge Monaco 500. "One of my first boyfriends had this car—same color," Gang said of the Dodge. The concrete floor in the dining room has tire tracks from Surratt's Ducati Monster Dark 750 motorcycle, which is occasionally invited in.

Gang lined the west side of the house's first floor with inexpensive Ikea aluminum-and-frosted-glass wardrobes, even tucking a fridge and other kitchen appliances behind them. The narrow, low-ceilinged galley kitchen, which has no upper-level cabinets (they would have been claustrophobic, the clients say) sets up for a classic architectural game of "compress and release."

Pass through it and you enter a living room that extends the full width of the house, with 20-foot ceilings and no big TV; a projector displays video on the wall instead. Wood stairs cascade down from the second floor. Concrete steps separate the living room from an adjoining library. These details create a strong sense of internal topography. And there's more spatial excitement upstairs in the master bedroom, where floor-to-ceiling glass offers views out onto the walled garden. Despite its urban confines, the place feels expansive and serene.

Even as her clients gave her free aesthetic rein, then Gang gave them something in return: a house whose architecture is at once assertive and responsive. It accommodates all aspects of their lifestyle, from their cars to their choices about deemphasizing what is celebrated in other homes to their collections of furniture and other items purchased from flea markets and yard sales. It works in part because Surratt and Hernandez display their things so well, but ultimately because Gang didn't insist on total visual control. This is a livable modernism, one that accepts—and makes a virtue of—the quirks of its clients rather than ruthlessly editing them out.

Dwell

THE BLESSINGS AND BURDENS
OF INFRASTRUCTURE

EVEN THOUGH FEDERAL DOLLARS NO LONGER FLOWED TO CITIES AS THEY DID during the Great Society programs of the 1960s, Chicago mayor Richard M. Daley found the funds to finance such exemplary public works projects as the renovation of Wacker Drive, the river-hugging boulevard originally proposed in the *Plan of Chicago*. Chicago also welcomed a sparkling new stretch of river walk and a handsome new train station beneath Millennium Park. In contrast to the one-dimensional, "shovel-ready" projects backed by President Obama's $787 billion federal stimulus package, these works of infrastructure built a new public realm as well as rebuilding roads and bridges. Yet even Daley was unable to escape the national infrastructure crisis, as evidenced by the continuing troubles—and near shutdown—of the Chicago Transit Authority.

A Grander Canyon

THE REBUILT WACKER DRIVE HAS EMERGED NOT ONLY FIXED,
BUT FINER

NOVEMBER 29, 2002

No one ever wrote a song extolling Wacker Drive as "That Great Street." And no one ever called it a Magnificent Mile. But there is no more special street in downtown Chicago, and not just because the double-deck, Beaux-Arts boulevard offers a lightning-fast shortcut between the Eisenhower Expressway and North Michigan Avenue.

Wacker stands out because it carves a curvaceous path along the Chicago River, breaking the rectilinear lockstep of the Chicago street grid. You've seen it in movies like *The Blues Brothers* or on the opening credits of WGN's evening news: a grand canyon of open space right in the city's heart—wide-open sky, pale green water, and mighty steel bridges, framed by cliffs of skyscrapers twinkling in the night.

That is why the just-completed $200 million rebuilding of Wacker Drive, which was backed by a mix of federal and state funds, may turn out to be an urban planning triumph as well as the biggest road rehab story of the year. The rebuilt Wacker has emerged not only fixed, but finer, more friendly to both drivers and pedestrians, with only a few design flaws marring an otherwise commendable combination of architecture and engineering.

In its scale and complexity, this colossal public-works project rivals the Daley administration's two great road-rebuilding efforts of the mid-1990s—moving the northbound lanes of Lake Shore Drive west of Soldier Field to create the verdant Museum Campus, and transforming State Street from an ugly bus mall to a handsome, high-quality streetscape.

But the 21-month Wacker rebuilding effort, which has entirely remade the east–west stretch of the road between Michigan Avenue and Randolph Street, is different because Wacker is a viaduct, one whose steel-reinforced concrete columns are wedged between the Chicago River to its north and the skyscrapers to its south.

The underside of this viaduct, Lower Wacker, used to be a Dickensian netherworld, habituated by the homeless. Now, cleaner, brighter, and more spacious (the city having evicted the homeless people who once camped there), it feels like the bottom of a freshly minted elevated highway—no engineering marvel, but an improved way to get from Point A to Point B.

Upper Wacker, meanwhile, looks better than it has in years. Architects have brought back a range of handsome historic features, from ornate Boulevard Electrolier streetlights to a voluptuous limestone balustrade. They also have created new elements, like classically inspired median and sidewalk planters, that harmonize perfectly with the old.

Still, a big question mark looms: Will the city will be able to carry out the as-yet-unfunded $40 million second phase of the Wacker project—a river walk that would help create a continuous waterfront promenade from Lake Michigan to Lake Street? The river walk is supposed to be lined with

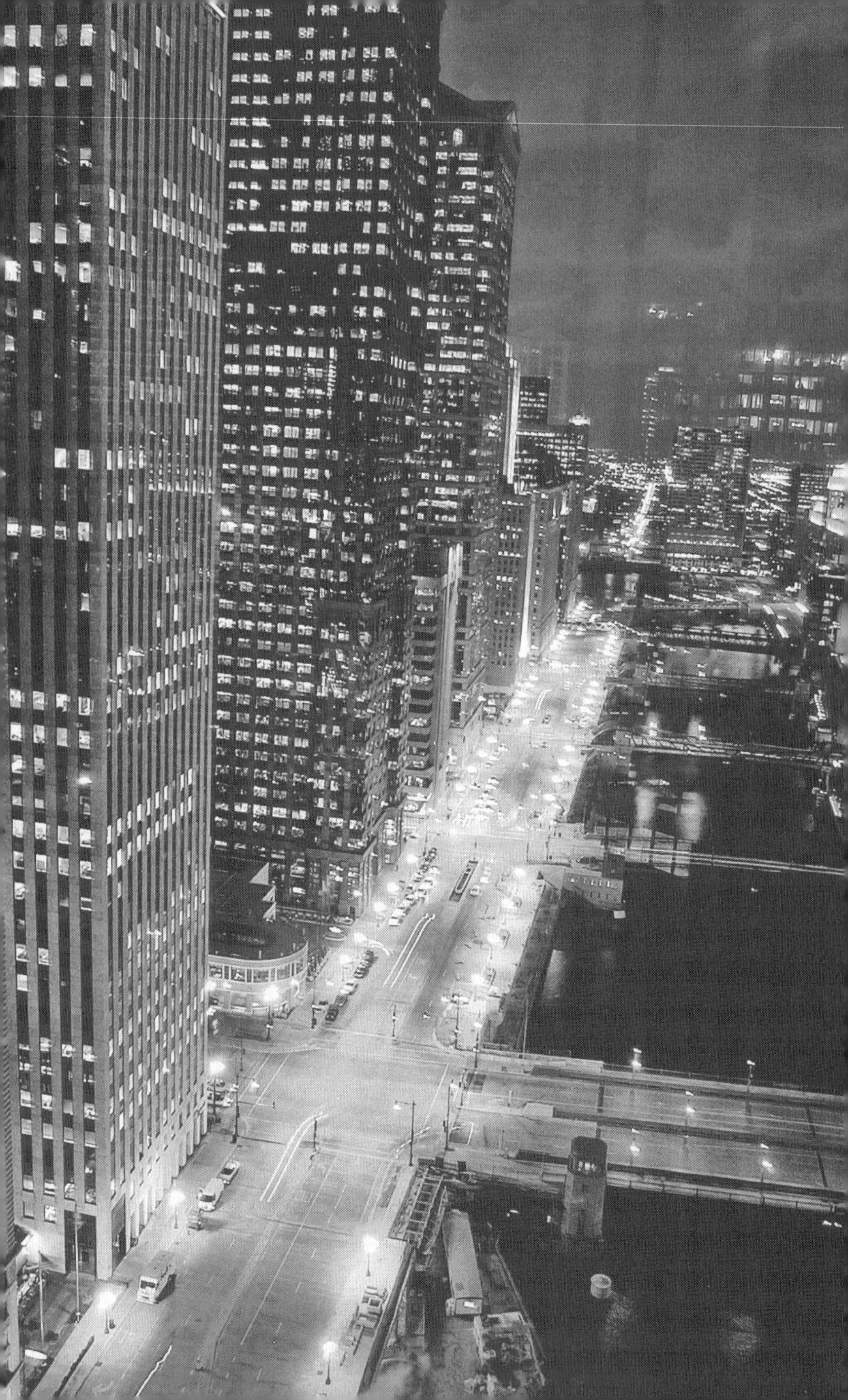

restaurants, kiosks, and other features that would draw people from Upper
Wacker down to the river's edge.

As every schoolchild in Chicago once knew, Wacker has its roots in
Daniel Burnham and Edward Bennett's 1909 *Plan of Chicago*, which
also suggested the city's almost-uninterrupted chain of lakefront parks.
Constructed in 1926, the street took its name from Charles Wacker, the
civic booster who campaigned tirelessly to realize the 1909 plan. It took
its aesthetic cues—balustrades, obelisks, and other Beaux-Arts details—
from Burnham and Bennett's desire to turn Chicago from "Hog Butcher
to the World" into "Paris on the Prairie."

For all of its traditional touches, Wacker turned out to be remarkably
forward-looking. Replacing dilapidated fish and vegetable markets along
the Chicago River, the double-deck boulevard cleverly separated cars on
the upper level from trucks on the lower level. Cars also could use the lower
level, and shortly after Wacker was extended southward to Congress Park-
way between 1949 and 1958, drivers had a terrific bypass route that enabled
them to sidestep the Loop's traffic jams and get from Michigan Avenue to
the Eisenhower Expressway (completed in 1960) in less than 10 minutes.

But decades of wear and weather took their toll, and Wacker was in such
feeble shape by the late 1990s that the lone alternative to rebuilding the
road was to permanently shut it down. Almost as bad, Wacker had become
an unsightly mishmash due to insensitive repairs (broken balusters were
replaced with concrete instead of original limestone, for example) and the
addition of contemporary elements, like modern streetlights, that were
glaringly out of place.

A DISPLAY OF COURAGE

Fortunately, Chicago got neither a shutdown nor a mindless replication of
the old Wacker. Instead, a team of architects, engineers, and officials in the
city's Department of Transportation had the courage to imagine a better
Wacker, which at once restores the original Beaux-Arts vision and offers
discrete additions that make the street's upper level more welcoming to
pedestrians and less the drag strip that Upper Wacker had become.

The job would have been merely good if the designers—DLK Civic
Design, Johnson Lasky Architects, Muller & Muller Architects, and Janet

THE RENOVATED WACKER DRIVE
An exemplary work of civic infrastructure that transcends mere "road renovation."

Attarian of the city's Bureau of Bridges—had kept the original configuration of the road and restored its historic features. But they took the project to a higher level, moving the road about 50 feet southward between Wabash and State to carve out room for a planned riverside plaza. They also added the planters, which screen pedestrians from the rush of passing cars, provide a place to rest because seats are carved into them, and delight passersby with sensuous curves that subtly recall Wacker's break from the straitlaced street grid.

There is more fine work on the lower level of Wacker's ornamental north-facing wall. The architects deftly mixed re-created features—such as arches, columns, and beautifully curving corbels—with restored elements around Wacker's curving staircases. Thousands of pieces of limestone were cut out, cataloged, and warehoused before being put back.

WHY THE CHIA PETS?

True, there are minor problems. The lower-level arches need to be filled with restaurants, as the river-walk plan suggests, so they seem vibrant instead of being black holes. And in a case of greening run amok, the architects have placed a row of urns on the balustrade, a marked departure from the original design. Though the urns complement the planters, they still look silly, like oversize Chia Pets.

But that's the only poor mark for Wacker's window dressing, which, come to think of it, isn't window dressing at all. For the street is ultimately a great urban room framed by the wall of the skyscrapers alongside it, and the additions, especially the planters, skillfully furnish that room, making it more habitable.

The changes reflect the enlightened philosophy of the city's bridge renovation and replacement program, which has wisely dispensed with the traffic engineer's aesthetic of the spiritless, purely functional span.

"I don't just have engineers showing up to do projects anymore," said the city's chief bridge builder, Deputy Transportation commissioner Stan Kaderbek, who worked with project manager Denise Casalino on Wacker. "If you can't make the environment of the city better, you shouldn't be doing it in the first place."

PRAISEWORTHY FEATURES

Any full assessment of the new Wacker also must take into account the engineering that has made the street's four-lane lower level more spacious and better lit than its infamous predecessor. The trio of engineering firms that worked on the project—Earth Tech, McDonough Associates, and Teng & Associates—deserves credit for a solid effort that does exactly what it's supposed to, accomplishing the same amount of heavy lifting with less bulk than before.

Among the upgrades: more vertical clearance, better lighting, and improved safety, due to a thick new Jersey barrier that separates the two streams of traffic.

Now that Wacker has been rebuilt with such an exemplary blend of form and function, the focus shifts to the future and whether Chicago will be able to construct the waterfront promenade that promises to transform this great Chicago street into something even greater. Only with the completion of the Chicago river walk will it be clear whether the city has decisively shifted the river's identity from old industrial waterway to new recreation mecca—less a barrier that divides downtown than a zipper that unites it.

POSTSCRIPT:

In 2005, three years after the Wacker Drive renovation project, the city of Chicago opened a new riverfront plaza made possible by the earlier shifting of Wacker about 50 feet southward between Wabash Avenue and State Street. The $4.3 million plaza, designed by Chicago architect Carol Ross Barney and her associate John Fried, included a new Chicago Vietnam Veterans Memorial and terraced lawns that proved popular with pedestrians. The gradual rebuilding process was a prime example of what I call "intelligent incrementalism," making a big plan and then implementing it step by step. That approach would bear more fruit in 2009 with the completion of the first stage of the new river walk.

Chicago's Second Waterfront

A NEW STRETCH OF RIVER WALK FURTHERS THE DREAM OF TURNING A ONCE-HARSH INDUSTRIAL ZONE INTO A PRIME PUBLIC SPACE

JUNE 28, 2009

It was lunchtime downtown and Justin Grant felt like sunning himself. But instead of heading to a tanning spa, the 23-year-old sales manager left his office building and strolled to the newest stretch of Chicago's river walk, where he stripped off his blue shirt and stretched out on a concrete bench.

"This is a great place to come," Grant said. "You can watch the boats go by."

In recent weeks scores of walkers, joggers, bicyclists, and others have discovered the just-opened river walk on the Chicago River's south bank. Stretching from east of the Michigan Avenue Bridge to State Street, the handsome, people-friendly public space marks the latest step in Mayor Richard M. Daley's ambitious drive to make the riverfront a prime public space downtown and in the city's outlying neighborhoods.

Think of it as a new lakefront. A completed river walk would offer much-needed open space for tens of thousands of office workers and downtown apartment dwellers. And it would let you do along the riverfront what you can do along most of the lakefront: walk, bike, or jog without interruption, enjoying the water along the way.

Urban planners smartly are not aiming to create a Frost Belt version of San Antonio's famous yet heavily commercialized River Walk, which is lined with shops, bars, and restaurants. They seek, instead, to complement Chicago's already-vibrant downtown with a river walk where you can find food and drink, but also "go down and touch nature," said Richard Wilson of Skidmore, Owings & Merrill, the Chicago architectural firm that is preparing a long-range plan for the river.

Chicago was born by the river and named for the wild onion plants that once thrived on its banks. But in the boom years of the 19th century, businessmen turned the river into an artery of commerce and a sewer for dumping industrial waste. The river became a forbidding trench, an *On the Waterfront* landscape of piers, bulkheads, and bollards for tying up ships. Buildings turned their backs to it.

"That was a tough place," said Tim Samuelson, the city of Chicago's cultural historian. "It was all about business."

The new river walk, on the other hand, is all about pleasure, even if it has not come cheap. Funded through the Central Loop tax-increment financing district, the Michigan-to-State stretch is expected to cost about $22 million, which works out to roughly $16,755 per foot of waterfront. That's roughly double the original estimate, an increase that the project's sponsor, the Chicago Department of Transportation (CDOT), attributes to soaring costs for fuel, steel, and construction.

Still, as designed by Chicago architect Carol Ross Barney and her firm's John Fried—the same team responsible for the pedestrian-friendly Wabash Plaza made possible by the 2002 rebuilding of Wacker Drive—the river walk combines engineering muscle and architectural élan to make a more welcoming waterfront. Indeed, it adds much-needed open space to Wabash

THE CHICAGO RIVER WALK
Turning a barrier that divides downtown into a zipper that unites it.

Plaza, just as planners from the Chicago firm of DLK Civic Design had
envisioned.

Built atop steel piles and concrete landfill, the project plugs gaps in the
existing river walk with new pathways, 17 feet wide, which slide beneath
the Michigan Avenue and Wabash Avenue Bridges. Pedestrians no longer
have to climb stairs to street level to get from one section of the river walk
to another. Now, with the new river walk joining an existing one that runs
along East Wacker Drive, there is a continuous waterfront pathway from
"That Great Street" to Lake Michigan.

The architects have nicely outfitted the river walk with simple concrete
benches and see-through stainless-steel railings that let you lean out over
the water, even if you can't quite touch it. East of Michigan Avenue, there
are boulders to sit on, evoking the marshy lowlands that preceded the
river's intense urbanization. West of Michigan, in keeping with the Beaux-
Arts splendor of Wacker Drive, the river walk is appropriately more urban
and formal. It gracefully loops around a waterfront restaurant, O'Brien's,
that has the de rigueur umbrella-topped tables.

The best stroke, however, comes in the spectacular canopies that protect river-walk pedestrians from trash falling from the bridges above. As

you pass beneath them, the canopies' stainless-steel shingles create a mirror effect, brilliantly reflecting the people beneath them, the waters of the river, even boats going by. Instead of under-bridge fear, you get under-bridge delight.

"It's like a linear 'Bean,'" said Andrew Gleeson, a senior architect at the Chicago firm of Murphy/Jahn, as he ate lunch along the new river walk. He was referring, of course, to the *Cloud Gate* sculpture, also known as "The Bean," in Millennium Park.

While this stretch of river walk has faults, including some areas with too much concrete, it nonetheless sets a high standard for the next burst of development. The city will soon advertise a request for proposals for the State-to-Lake Street portion of the river walk, according to Michelle Woods, the CDOT project manager who oversaw the first portion. And Skidmore, Owings & Merrill is preparing to present to the Chicago Plan Commission a long-range "framework plan" for the 1.3-mile-long trunk of the river between Lake Street and Lake Michigan.

The plan, still in draft form, calls for creating four "identity districts" along the river, explained Wilson, Skidmore's urban planning practice leader. Among the districts would be a new chunk of green space at the confluence of the river's North and South Branches. It would extend 50 feet into the water and feature a restaurant or some other "destination amenity."

That vision, perhaps too commercial, is a vast leap from what you see now if you peer down from the bend in Wacker Drive toward the river's edge: a lifeless dock, strewn with trash, where one recent morning a homeless man rested on a sleeping bag.

The city is wisely concentrating on the south bank of the river because it controls the land there. The north bank, in contrast, is primarily in the hands of private owners, as is most of Chicago's other riverfront land. Because of the recession, that land is unlikely to be developed for years, meaning that urban planners' visions of fishermen and strollers on river walks along the river's North and South Branches, far from downtown, also won't be realized anytime soon.

Still, a pause offers time to think and plan. And as the lakefront reveals, it can take decades, if not generations, to transform a city's mindset and map.

One might have reacted with cynicism in 1909 when, in the *Plan of Chicago*, Daniel Burnham urged Chicago's leaders to transform their chopped-up assortment of lakefront parks into a sparkling and continuous chain of greenswards and beaches. Yet for the last 100 years, completing that vision has been Chicago's grand civic project. For the next 100 years, in the downtown and beyond, the city has its work cut out for it: turning the riverfront into an equally great public space.

New Randolph Street Station Works within Its Limits

RENOVATED TRANSIT HUB A BRIGHT SPOT IN DAILY COMMUTE

JANUARY 23, 2005

Mourning the 1960s demolition of New York City's Pennsylvania Station and its soaring Beaux-Arts spaces while simultaneously deploring the cramped, low-ceilinged terminal that replaced it, the architectural historian Vincent Scully once remarked that a traveler coming through the old station entered the city like a god. Through the new one, he famously observed, "one scuttles in . . . like a rat."

That putdown applied equally well to Metra's old Randolph Street Station, an underground terminal located south of the Prudential Building and east of the Cultural Center on Michigan Avenue. The strictly utilitarian station had no heat, no air-conditioning, and no natural light. When it rained hard, water seeped through the joints of upper Randolph Street overhead and poured into the station. Commuters actually walked through the underground space with their umbrellas up. The unflattering adjectives used to describe the station were all *D*-words—dark, dingy, dank, depressing.

But now, after an intelligently conceived, precisely executed renovation designed by Skidmore, Owings & Merrill of Chicago, the Randolph Street Station has been transformed into a bright, open, and visually dynamic gateway for thousands of Metra Electric and South Shore Line commuters. With its shimmering, wave-shaped ceilings and ticket counters that evoke the sleek, streamlined Zephyr trains of the 1930s, the project is a classic example of architectural inversion, making the underground seem as light and airy as a puffy white cloud.

GLITZ NOT IMPORTANT

No one, it's plain, is going to rank this handsome but spatially modest station on a par with great train sheds of Europe or the luminous, mostly underground station that Zurich-based architect and engineer Santiago Calatrava has designed for the World Trade Center in New York. Yet that was never part of the brief for this $23 million job, which has opened after

THE NEW RANDOLPH STREET STATION
Making the underground seem as light and airy as a puffy white cloud.

years of delays caused by emergency repairs to upper Randolph and the endless rejiggering of Millennium Park, which sits above tracks just south of the station.

A grand architectural statement was out of the question because the Y-shaped, 30,000-square-foot station is sandwiched between sloping upper Randolph Street above it and commuter railroad tracks below it. What the architects and their team did instead was to accept and even embrace those constraints in a design that brings a dash of ceremony to the drudgery of commuting. The result is an object lesson in how to wring visual excitement out of an extremely tight space.

Skidmore, Owings & Merrill designed the project with Teng & Associates, the engineer and architect-of-record, and Metra's chief project manager Richard Duffield, an old railroad hand. Faced with the prospect of a cave-like interior, SOM design partner Peter Ellis toyed with the idea of punching skylights into upper Randolph but abandoned it after learning that there was so little leftover space in the road that the skylights would have to be minuscule.

Instead, he and his colleagues asked themselves a challenging question: How could they make this the lightest and most visually arresting underground space in Chicago? No easy thing, that. The city, after all, boasts such subterranean gems as Helmut Jahn's tunnel between the two concourses of the United Terminal at O'Hare International Airport. There, a rainbow of colors washes the curving side walls, and the neon sculpture above the moving walkway is a visual knockout.

Even if the Randolph Street Station doesn't get to United's level, it's still very good because of its highly visible architectural finishes and some not-so-visible engineering moves that have made the station noticeably more spacious and comfortable.

One of the best design elements is the wave-shaped ceiling, which takes advantage of the ever-changing ceiling heights caused by the slope of upper Randolph. Made of perforated stainless steel with a satin finish, these custom-designed pieces form arches that give the station spatial pop, even though they are decorative rather than structural and the lowest of them are just 7½ feet above the floor.

Equally attractive are the blue-and-white terrazzo floors, in which thin white lines resemble railroad tracks traced across a field of sky blue. The track patterns seem like pure decoration, but, in reality, they serve as signs, articulating pathways to the train platforms. Especially at rush hour, when the tightly quartered station still seems a bit crowded, that helps to move commuters through the station quickly.

There is more handsome railroad imagery in the sleek ticket booths, which evoke the corrugated stainless-steel bodies of Metra passenger cars and the Zephyr trains of yore. Yet the booths seem anything but nostalgic because they are equipped with bands of sophisticated LED lights that alert commuters when an attendant is available. While all this is well handled, the station's success is every bit as much the result of Teng's essential but unglamorous engineering moves.

SPANNING METRA TRACKS

The key move extended the concourse eastward on new structural framing that spans the Metra Electric tracks. That made room for back-of-house heating and cooling equipment. The ticket booth area was shifted 50 feet to the east, freeing up space for a new seating area, which can accommodate 65 people. Its openness makes the entire station appear more spacious. In addition, the newly extended concourse allows South

Shore passengers to get to and from their trains within an enclosed space rather than passing over a bridge enclosed in chain link and open to the elements, as they once did.

Much remains to be done at the Randolph Street Station. Metra is evaluating proposals from developers who will lease the shops that line the underground pathway leading into the station from Michigan and Randolph. And passengers are letting Metra officials know they would like to see a clock in the station and larger displays of train arrival and department information.

Even so, what has been accomplished to date is impressive. The sensuous, curvilinear geometry of the station celebrates the motion of trains, endowing what had been an utterly banal space with the romance of travel and the energy of modern life. Nothing could be more different from the pallid postmodernism of the renovations done to Union Station in the early 1990s. And nothing could be a more welcome change from the old rat hole that once sat beneath upper Randolph.

POSTSCRIPT

In 2006 a newsstand and other shops opened at the Randolph Street Station, finally bringing rail commuters the amenities they craved. By then, in recognition of the popular appeal of the park above it, the terminal had been renamed Millennium Station. It was formally dedicated in 2007.

The Way We Move—and Live

AMERICA'S INFRASTRUCTURE CRISIS ARRIVES ON
CHICAGO'S DOORSTEP

SEPTEMBER 16, 2007

A short-term bailout has put off a Chicago-area transit "doomsday" for now, but this much is clear: The national infrastructure crisis—the one that became so glaringly evident in New Orleans, with its floods and failed levees, and in Minneapolis, where an interstate highway bridge crumbled into the Mississippi River—sits menacingly on the doorstep of "The City That Works."

It has been easy to brush off or even ignore this crisis because Mayor Richard M. Daley has cunningly plotted ways to fix roads and bridges,

THE CHICAGO TRANSIT AUTHORITY'S DIVISION STREET STATION
When transit arteries suffer, so does the body politic.

plant thousands of trees, and generally make his city shine despite a federal spigot that no longer pours out money like it used to.

But that was not so easy last week, not with the scourge of planned CTA service cuts and fare increases ready to lash hundreds of thousands of riders in the city and its suburbs, which also depend on the agency's bus and rail service. The short-term $24 million funding advance engineered by Governor Rod Blagojevich and accepted by the Regional Transportation Authority may only put off the pain in the short run.

With its potential to disrupt daily routines and psyches, the CTA's predicament reveals how nearly every aspect of modern life is interlaced with anonymous networks of transportation, water, communication, and power—and how shortsighted politicians from Washington on down have let those networks fall apart. The CTA blames a $110 million state funding shortfall for the transit mess.

The crisis is training a harsh spotlight on the vast array of public works—airports, bridges, dams, flood-control tunnels, railroads, roads, transit, and wastewater treatment plants—that we regularly use but rarely pause to consider. "For most of us," as the Chicago-based designer Bruce Mau once wrote, infrastructure "is invisible. Until it fails."

Woe to the politician who throws his weight behind a multibillion-dollar infrastructure project that no one can see but that drives up property taxes.

Little wonder, then, that when the American Society of Civil Engineers issued a national infrastructure report card in 2005, the grades were not exactly "Head of the Class" material: nothing higher than a C+ and an overall average of D. Through 2010, the report card projected, the nation's total infrastructure investment needs are $1.6 trillion. And that's just to maintain existing infrastructure.

A case in point: the CTA's beleaguered Blue Line, which includes a 17.5-mile leg from the Loop to O'Hare International Airport. That leg once was a modern marvel, combining truly rapid transit with attractive, even architecturally impressive, stations by such top design talent as Helmut Jahn and Skidmore, Owings & Merrill's Myron Goldsmith. In 1984, when the Loop–O'Hare stretch was completed, the trip from downtown's skyscrapers to the airport's terminals took just 35 minutes.

Yet one day last week, under ideal conditions—the sun was shining, the morning rush was almost over, and the trains were practically devoid of people—Blue Line run no. 209 made the journey in 53 minutes, the end of the trip a painfully slow, herky-jerky ride over defective tracks leading to O'Hare.

As the Blue Line's ups and downs suggest, infrastructure is not an act of God. For better and for worse, people design it, execute it, pay for it, and maintain it (or don't). Ever since the Minnesota bridge collapse, the airwaves and editorial pages have been full of debate about America's aging infrastructure and whether the federal gas tax should be raised to fix it. But to frame the debate that way, as though it were simply about technical problems and how to correct them, ignores infrastructure's far-broader impact on the way we live.

A bridge, for example, isn't just something we drive across. As the handsome, neoclassical Roosevelt Road Bridge that links Chicago's Near West Side to the Museum Campus reveals, we might also value a bridge for how it looks, whether we can walk or bike across it, how it helps or harms the neighborhoods on either side of it, and how it affects real estate values. Ideally, as this span shows, a bridge isn't just an artery. It's connective tissue. It doesn't do just one thing. It gives the public a multi-dimensional bang for its buck.

To take aesthetic issues out of the public policy equation, observed Gregory Dreicer—curator of the exhibition *Me, Myself and Infrastructure* at the Chicago Architecture Foundation—is itself an aesthetic choice, one that wrongly assumes that engineers are objective technocrats who can single-handedly solve society's problems.

Americans learned the fallacy of that view in the 1950s and 1960s, Dreicer said, when engineers rammed highways through the delicate fabric of vibrant city neighborhoods, essentially destroying them. In bridges, as in buildings, one size should not fit all.

Still, customization does not necessarily come cheap. When Chicago's Department of Transportation began a model bridge renovation and replacement program in the mid-1990s, the thinking was that spans like the one at Roosevelt Road would cost anywhere from 10 to 20 percent more than standard designs pulled out of an engineer's manual. However, the tab for a simple modernist bridge, free of classical slipcovering or visual pyrotechnics, will be considerably less.

"It is possible to make things look better without spending any extra money," said structural engineer and bridge designer R. Shankar Nair, a senior vice president and principal at Teng, a Chicago-based architecture, engineering, and development firm. "It might even save money, too."

Now, confronting New Orleans after Katrina, Minneapolis after the bridge collapse, and a Chicago that has temporarily stepped back from the brink of a mass-transit "doomsday," Americans have no excuse for overlooking infrastructure. The question is whether they look at it with blinders or through lenses that recognize that our environment shapes our destiny.

POSTSCRIPT

Chicago's transit problems worsened, even though the Chicago Transit Authority achieved a major reduction in the number of slow zones on the Blue Line between O'Hare International Airport and downtown Chicago by early 2009. Elsewhere on the CTA's 224-mile, 8-line rail network, as the Chicago Tribune *reported, more trains were again forced to operate at lower speeds because of an increase in potentially unsafe conditions. Later in the year, as Chicago made its unsuccessful bid to host the 2016 Summer Olympic Games, the CTA's subpar conditions were widely viewed as a liability. The Games were awarded to Rio de Janeiro, which promised to build new subway lines and create a new bus system as part of a $14 billion Olympic overhaul. The CTA instituted a new round of service cuts in February 2010.*

HIGH HOPES AND

SOBERING REALITIES

THE INAUGURATION OF BARACK OBAMA RAISED HOPES THAT THE NATION WOULD finally address such fundamental problems as its faltering mass transportation systems and that architectural discourse would shift from its relentless focus on stand-alone icons to a new emphasis on connective tissue and the public realm. As the passage and implementation of the controversial stimulus plan—the $787 billion American Recovery and Reinvestment Act of 2009—revealed, change had indeed occurred, but it was merely a first step.

Good-Bye, Icons; Hello, Infrastructure

OBAMA INAUGURATES A NEW ERA OF ARCHITECTURE

JANUARY 25, 2009

The age of the architectural icon—that extravagant, exuberant, "wow"-inducing building on a pedestal—is dead, or more precisely, in its death throes. And what will replace it? President Barack Obama, who once dreamed of being an architect, had something to say about that in his inaugural address: the age of infrastructure.

Rarely do events so boldly bracket the death of one design era and the dawning of another as they have in recent days. On January 14, the

BARACK OBAMA'S INAUGURATION
When America ceased to be in "infrastructural denial."

developer of a proposed kilometer-high skyscraper in the Persian Gulf playground of Dubai announced he was shelving the project, the mixed-use Nakheel Tower, which would have been as tall as three John Hancock Centers stacked atop one another.

Then, six days later, Obama issued his blueprint for recovery: The nation "will act—not only to create new jobs, but to lay a new foundation for growth," he said. "We will build the roads and bridges, the electric grids and digital lines that feed our commerce and bind us together."

With the Nakheel Tower, the Chicago Spire, and other would-be icons stopped dead in their tracks, and with the new president shining a spotlight on anonymous but essential public works, it's clear that the deepening recession has brought us to something more than just a pause. It's looking more like a pivot point. Or at least it could be if Obama delivers on his promise to reshape the contours of our metropolitan areas as well as revive the economy.

"In a funny way, the recession has been good for making these mega-projects stop," said Pauline Saliga, executive director of the Chicago-based Society of Architectural Historians. "It's giving us a little breathing room, a little time to reassess where we're going with all of this."

The icon age was born in 1997 with the smash opening of Frank Gehry's Guggenheim Museum in Bilbao, Spain. The titanium-clad museum, with its dazzling collage of shapes, spawned a new "build it, and they will come" mentality: hire a star architect, or "starchitect," give him or her free aesthetic rein, and watch the tourists or the buyers arrive.

Museums did it. Colleges and universities did it. Condominium developers did it. Indeed, whole countries, such as China and Dubai, did it to change their images or put themselves on the map. A global band of starchitects—Gehry, Rem Koolhaas, Zaha Hadid, Daniel Libeskind, and Santiago Calatrava among them—seemed to be designing all of the world's signature buildings. And, in truth, a lot of what they designed was breathtaking.

It's hard to imagine Chicago without Millennium Park, which brought new life to a once-moribund corner of Grant Park with Gehry's festive music pavilion and such interactive sculptures as Anish Kapoor's *Cloud Gate*. Similarly, Milwaukee would seem incomplete without the Calatrava-designed addition to its art museum, where a mechanically operated sunshade spreads over the main gathering hall like a bird's wings. The same goes for Beijing and the Bird's Nest stadium that was the centerpiece of the 2008 Summer Olympic Games.

Yet icons divorced from infrastructure are nothing more than empty set pieces, objects sliced out of the fabric of everyday life.

When the levees of New Orleans broke in 2005, Hurricane Katrina laid bare a breakdown of infrastructure and social bonds—a toxic mix of private luxury and public squalor. Even as McMansions swelled the average size of the American single-family home, the nation's commitment to the public realm was shrinking. That was evident not only in New Orleans' flooded Lower Ninth Ward, but also in crumbling roads and bridges, as well as schools with outdated and overcrowded classrooms.

If nothing else, the economic constraints of the new era are likely to induce a new aesthetic austerity. After art deco and its fabulous riot of zig-zagging, multicolored ornament, the few buildings that were constructed in the 1930s were noticeably simpler than their Jazz Age predecessors. Sober doesn't have to be dull, though. Just look at the restrained, art moderne glory of New York's Rockefeller Center.

But the real issues transcend style. They are about whether the new infrastructure will help usher in a new set of urban growth patterns—dense neighborhoods where you can walk to the corner store—or whether new roads and bridges will simply reinforce exurban sprawl. On that, there is no consensus, as is made clear by the brewing controversy over the U.S. House Appropriations Committee draft of the multi-billion-dollar stimulus bill and how much it will devote to rail and transit systems versus highways and bridges.

However the debate is settled, it is significant that it is occurring at all. Nothing like this happened during the eight years of the Bush administration. In recent days, at least, articles about infrastructure have temporarily supplanted the usual fare of starchitect-designed museums and skyscrapers on architecture websites. Architects scrambling for work say they are looking to the public sector. That's where the money is, after all.

A new age is at hand, though the old one isn't completely over. The end of the building boom will deliver a mixed-use skyscraper called the Burj Dubai, which, at a jaw-dropping height of more than 2,600 feet, seems sure to remain the world's tallest building for a while now that the rival Nakheel Tower has been put on hold.

Though such behemoths will dominate the headlines, the conversation already is shifting away from the "wow" buildings that have dominated architecture for the last dozen years. What matters now is whether Obama's infrastructure investments can transform the American landscape as well as sow the seeds of economic recovery. Icon architecture is no longer the issue du jour. It's sustainability—and survival.

Back to Basics

OBAMA'S INFRASTRUCTURE PLAN WON'T MATCH THE
GREAT NEW DEAL PUBLIC WORKS, BUT IT MOVES AMERICA
IN THE RIGHT DIRECTION

SPRING 2009

In the heady days after Barack Obama's election, many of the nation's architecture critics, myself included, had visions of *grands projets* dancing in our heads. We evoked memories of Franklin D. Roosevelt's Works Progress Administration (WPA) and dreamed of new bridges, power plants, and other infrastructure that would uplift the nation's tattered public realm. A WPA mural–style illustration for *New York* magazine, picturing Obama alongside muscle-bound construction workers and one of those structurally outlandish, frightfully expensive Santiago Calatrava bridges, succinctly captured these hopes.

Today that grandiose vision already looks like a mirage.

Calatrava bridges? Fuggedaboutit. The stimulus package, which will cost $787 billion and aims to save or create as many as 3.5 million jobs, is focusing instead on back-to-basics stuff like repairing highways and bridges, making federal buildings more energy efficient, and weatherizing modest-income homes. In other words, we're going to be seeing more humble bridge-deck repairs than knock-your-eyes-out bridges.

All the same, I don't mind the plan's emphasis on the architecture of pragmatism rather than the architecture of spectacle. Nor am I especially troubled by what some critics are calling its lack of a coherent strategic vision. To me, that shortcoming is less important than dealing with the obvious bigger issue of putting unemployed construction workers and architects back to work, along with this less obvious one: in the wake of the economic meltdown and the credit crunch, we've entered a new time.

The age of self-indulgent icons is over. The age of society-serving infrastructure has begun. Across the land there are examples of the sort of creativity that architects—and the architects of public policy—can bring to these seemingly humdrum projects.

Fred Bernstein skillfully laid out such an approach in a 2005 *New York Times* story cleverly headlined "In My Backyard, Please: The Infrastructure

A BRIDGE ON THE SOUTH SIDE OF CHICAGO
The work of rebuilding a nation began with unglamorous projects like this, not a new Works Progress Administration.

Beautiful Movement." In it he detailed how highly regarded designers like Steven Holl were turning unsexy commissions like water-filtration plants into award-winning aesthetic gems.

Holl's plant on the edge of New Haven is a long, pipe-shaped sculpture covered in stainless-steel shingles that is said to recall the sculpture of Anish Kapoor. It teaches a significant lesson: Big infrastructure buildings have to be beautiful and offer amenities like green roofs and public parks. Otherwise, because of the inevitable NIMBY factor, they'll never get built.

Here's another idea I can pass along based on my experience of covering Mayor Richard M. Daley in Chicago for nearly 20 years. City-building is a long-term process, not a one-shot deal, and it begins with basic steps that chart a path toward bigger ones. Nation-building may work the same way. The point is to get going—now. Obama can tweak his infrastructure initiative in 2010.

When Daley first came into office, architects joked that he had "City Beautiful Instincts," as though he were some sort of latter-day Cro-Magnon dragging his knuckles on the ground. But Daley wisely persisted with simple infrastructure improvements that his constituents, the voters, could see—building more than 80 miles of landscaped medians, planting more than 500,000 trees, and the like. Block by block, the city changed—not all of it, to be sure, but significant chunks. Only after he got the basics down did Daley embark upon Millennium Park and his other *grands projets*.

The other thing worth remembering about Daley's public works is that they tend to draw people together, unlike those of his father, Mayor Richard J. Daley, for whom expressways and public housing projects sometimes served as tools to keep poor blacks and white ethnics apart. Millennium Park offers a rare piece of such common ground in a region that remains balkanized along the lines of race and class. Obama picked up on this theme in his inauguration speech, hailing the power of infrastructure to "bind us together."

It was disheartening, then, that Congress ultimately struck from the recovery bill a provision that would have directed $200 million toward rehabbing the crumbling National Mall. Yet the bigger picture holds reason for tempered optimism, especially because the final legislation provides a healthy $8 billion for mass transit. That could accelerate the drive for high-speed rail networks and other green ways of getting around.

From water-treatment plants to fixing up federal buildings, the myriad projects in the legislation represent a first step toward rectifying the shameful lack of attention the nation has paid to its public realm. Obama is moving things in the right direction: away from splashy architecture and back to basics. Only by tending the garden of our shared spaces can we truly make democracy flower.

Oculus

POSTSCRIPT

One year after Obama signed the stimulus package into law, this much was clear: while the measure had put America on the right track, the journey was going to be bumpy.

Originally, the new president aimed to create public works on a grand scale, embracing traditional infrastructure projects, like fixing roads and bridges, as well as new projects, such as extending broadband service to rural communities. But as written by congressional Democrats and accepted by Obama, the stimulus package funded a grab bag of tax cuts, jobless benefits, and other measures. Public works were simply one piece of the legislation and by no means the biggest one.

Infrastructure spending in the first year of the stimulus was largely devoted to quick fixes, like repairing roads. If Illinois was any guide, state departments of transportation were spreading asphalt and concrete like so much peanut butter. Such measures were remedial rather than transformative, repairing old frameworks rather than creating new ones. But they were justifiable on two grounds: they began to address the nation's infrastructure backlog, and they put people to work quickly. To critics who charged that the stimulus was failing to make a long-term impact on the economy or the landscape, the Obama administration had a ready reply: Wait. The second year of the stimulus, administration officials argued, would pack more punch than the first, as investments in infrastructure, energy-efficiency upgrades, and other areas kicked in.

Our broader story, then, ends inconclusively, but tellingly. We began with ruins, and we end with ruins. The first set of ruins, at the World Trade Center, could be blamed on terrorist fanatics. The second set of ruins, evident in America's vast array of crumbling bridges, rail lines, and levees, was a failure of our own making—the result not of violence but of negligence. Private splendor and public squalor were two sides of same coin, starkly reflecting which values had currency in post-millennium America and which did not. "Our architecture," the great Chicago architect Louis Sullivan once said, "reflects us, as truly as a mirror." Never has that observation been more true than in the tumultuous age of terror and wonder.

ACKNOWLEDGMENTS

A BOOK ABOUT ARCHITECTURE, LIKE ARCHITECTURE ITSELF, REFLECTS THE WORK
of many hands. In assembling this collection of columns, and in writing the
columns themselves, I have been assisted by many people who contributed
their time, creativity, and ideas.

At the University of Chicago Press, I want to single out the work of my
editor, Mary E. Laur, who helped shape the framework of the book and
improved innumerable aspects of it with her sound judgments and keen
insights. I also wish to thank the Press's director, Garrett Kiely, for his
support of the project; editor Paul Schellinger for his comments on the
manuscript; editorial assistant Kira L. Bennett for her assiduous work on
photo permissions; senior manuscript editor Erin DeWitt for her sharp
copyediting; graphic designer Isaac Tobin for his elegant layout; and pro-
motions director Mark Heineke for his energetic efforts.

At the *Chicago Tribune*, I am particularly grateful to news administration editor Randy Weissman, who generously facilitated the reuse of
Tribune columns and photographs. In addition, I want to recognize the
following for their contributions: editor Gerould Kern, managing editor Jane Hirt, deputy managing editor Peter Kendall, first deputy metro
editor Mark Jacob, associate managing editor for entertainment Geoff
Brown, entertainment editor Scott Powers, sports editor Tim Bannon,
and literary editor Elizabeth Taylor. Also deserving thanks are assistant
entertainment editor Carmel Carrillo, features copy chief Bill O'Connell,
editing and presentation desk editor Nancy Watkins, features copy editor

Stephanie Reynolds, and researcher Leilia Arnheim. I also would like to acknowledge these former *Tribune* editors and reporters: Ann Marie Lipinski, James Warren, James O'Shea, Jeff Lyon, Patrick T. Reardon, and Charles Leroux.

The work of many *Tribune* photographers graces these pages. Thank you, especially, to E. Jason Wambsgans, Chris Walker, Nancy Stone, and Zbigniew Bzdak, as well as former staff photographers Bob Fila and Kuni Takahashi. Photo editors Andrew Johnston, Meg Theno, and Maggie Walker—along with graphics supervisor Margaret Garrity and photo archivist Mary Wilson—helped me transfer photos from the *Tribune* to the University of Chicago Press.

The editors of several architecture and design magazines have made their mark on this volume. Thank you to Robert Ivy, Suzanne Stephens, and Clifford Pearson of *Architectural Record*; Nadav Malin, Jane Kolleeny, and Joann Gonchar of *GreenSource*; Martin Pedersen of *Metropolis*; Michele Posner and Aaron Britt of *Dwell*; Kathrin Day Lassila and Mark Branch of the *Yale Alumni Magazine*; and Kristen Richards of *Oculus*. I also wish to thank my colleagues and friends in the field of architectural criticism— most notably, Paul Goldberger of the *New Yorker*, Ada Louise Huxtable of the *Wall Street Journal*, John King of the *San Francisco Chronicle*, and Inga Saffron of the *Philadelphia Inquirer*.

My good friends Joel Kaplan, Gary Marx, and Pete Nelson have been a constant source of support and good humor as this project unfolded. So have my parents, Arthur and Virginia Kamin; my mother-in-law, Barbara G. Mahany; and my sister and brother-in-law, Brooke and Richard Rapaport. The biggest thanks go to my wife, *Tribune* writer Barbara Ann Mahany, my brightest star, and to our sons, Will and Teddy, who selflessly allowed their dad the precious time to pursue this project. It was a joy to write this book. But it is a greater joy to again have the time to linger over simple pleasures, from long conversations at the dinner table to walks along the sparkling waters of Lake Michigan.

ILLUSTRATION CREDITS

Photos are by *Chicago Tribune* staff photographers unless otherwise noted.

THE URBAN DRAMA

World Trade Center, p. 4, U.S. Navy photo by Chief Photographer's
Mate Eric J. Tilford
New Orleans Bywater district, p. 8, Chris Walker
Chicago's Federal Plaza, p. 13, Bob Fila
Chicago's Daley Plaza, p. 16, Bob Fila
Treasury Department Building, p. 19, E. Jason Wambsgans
Pennsylvania Avenue, p. 21, E. Jason Wambsgans
Washington Monument, p. 24, E. Jason Wambsgans
Newark Liberty International Airport, p. 27, E. Jason Wambsgans
O'Hare International Airport, p. 30, E. Jason Wambsgans
Libeskind plan for ground zero, p. 33, courtesy of Studio Daniel Libe-
skind
Freedom Tower, p. 39, courtesy of Skidmore, Owings & Merrill LLP
Crown Fountain, p. 44, Kuni Takahashi
Cloud Gate, p. 47, E. Jason Wambsgans
Pritzker Pavilion, p. 51, Charles Osgood

Grand Plaza, p. 58, Zbigniew Bzdak
Museum Park Towers, p. 63, Zbigniew Bzdak
Washington Mutual branch bank, p. 68, David Klobucar
McDonald's, p. 72, Phil Velasquez
Avenue East, p. 76, Phil Velasquez
The Bernardin, p. 79, Antonio Perez
The Contemporaine, p. 83, courtesy of Will Kamin
Serta International Center, p. 86, courtesy of Andrew Metter
Aqua, p. 91, Michael Tercha
Aqua, p. 92, Michael Tercha
Plan for Trump Tower, p. 98, Skidmore Owings & Merrill rendering
Fordham Spire plan, p. 102, Fordham Company
Chicago Spire plan, p. 107, courtesy of Shelbourne Development/Santiago Calatrava
Supertall engineering graphic, p. 111, Phil Gelb and Max Rust
Trump Tower from the Chicago River, p. 117, E. Jason Wambsgans
Trump Tower from Wabash Avenue, p. 119, E. Jason Wambsgans
Burj Khalifa, p. 124, Kuni Takahashi

Milwaukee Art Museum exterior, p. 132, Nancy Stone
Milwaukee Art Museum interior, p. 136, Nancy Stone
Walt Disney Concert Hall exterior, p. 138, Al Seib. Los Angeles Times photos, © 2003. Reprinted with permission
Walt Disney Concert Hall interior, p. 141, Anacleto Rapping. Los Angles Times photos, © 2003. Reprinted with permission
Denver Art Museum, exterior of Frederic C. Hamilton Building, p. 143, © Denver Art Museum 2006. All Rights Reserved
Denver Art Museum, interior gallery detail of Frederic C. Hamilton Building, p. 144, © Denver Art Museum 2006. All Rights Reserved
Spertus Institute exterior, p. 147, Chris Walker
Spertus Institute interior, p. 150, Chris Walker
Bloch Building exterior, p. 155, Jeff Nightingale, courtesy of The Nelson-Atkins Museum of Art
Bloch Building interior, p. 158, courtesy of Roland Halbe
Modern Wing of the Art Institute exterior, p. 161, Chris Walker
Modern Wing of the Art Institute interior, p. 162, E. Jason Wambsgans
Nichols Bridgeway, p. 165, Michael Tercha

McCormick Tribune Campus Center at IIT, p. 170, courtesy of Illinois Institute of Technology

State Street Village at IIT, p. 174, courtesy of Illinois Institute of Technology

Campus Recreation Center at University of Cincinnati, p. 179, courtesy of Lisa Ventre, University of Cincinnati

THE CHANGING FACES OF PRESERVATION AND CONSERVATION

Maxwell Street, p. 186, E. Jason Wambsgans

Facades on Wabash Avenue, p. 188, E. Jason Wambsgans

Old Cook County Hospital, p. 193, Zbigniew Bzdak

Soldier Field, p. 196, Chris Walker

Art & Architecture Building at Yale, p. 201, courtesy of Michael Marsland, Yale University

"Test Cell" at IIT, p. 207, Zbigniew Bzdak

Seth Peterson Cottage, p. 210, Toni Stroud

Crown Hall, p. 212, David Klobucar

Shaw Technology and Learning Center, p. 214, William DeShazer

Green roof on Chicago's City Hall, p. 217, Chris Walker

Yannell House, p. 222, Chris Walker

Grand Rapids Art Museum, p. 226, courtesy of Grand Rapids Art Museum

A NEW ERA AND NEW CHALLENGES

Sculpture in downtown Naperville, p. 234, Terrence Antonio James

High-speed rail terminal plan, p. 237, courtesy of David Lillie, Michael Cady, Elba Gil, and Andrés Montaña

Mississippi Renewal Forum, p. 241, Nicole LaCour Young

Dearborn Homes, p. 245, Phil Velasquez

Brick Weave House, p. 249, courtesy of Steve Hall—Hedrich Blessing

Wacker Drive, p. 254, Terrence Antonio James

Chicago river walk, p. 259, Bill Hogan

Randolph Street Station, p. 262, E. Jason Wambsgans

Division Street Station, p. 265, Phil Velasquez

Obama inauguration, p. 269, Nancy Stone

Pershing Road bridge, p. 272, Scott Strazzante

INDEX